"The SLT principles outlined in this way I think, plan and act as a leader. L helped me in successfully creating and change across a range of schools and cc

*Noel Rawlii*

*Collₑgₑ, ₑᵤₑₑₙₛₗₐₙₐ, ₐᵤₛₜᵣₐₗᵢₐ*

"*Improving Schools Using Systems Leadership* has the potential to become a pivotal compendium within the global literature on Systems Leadership. Concepts and foundations are introduced and applied to schooling and the work of the principal, concluding with the pertinent question, what does this mean for schools? This book is a must read for educators of our future generation of leaders."

*Paul Lynch, James Cook University,*
*Queensland, Australia*

# Improving Schools Using Systems Leadership

It is easy to underestimate the impact that school organisation has on the behaviour, effectiveness, engagement and creativity of the teachers, staff and students who work within it. It also has a marked effect on the well-being of staff members, and how families and the community relate to the school. Attempts to improve school organisation are often short-term "initiatives" that only cover only one or two aspects of what it takes to organise a school effectively.

*Improving Schools Using Systems Leadership*, in contrast, provides those involved in the design and delivery of educational services with a coherent and easy-to-follow framework to help run an effective organisation. Based on theory, real data on education improvements at school and regional level, and case studies, this book demonstrates how Systems Leadership can be used to improve school organisation. It integrates models of leadership, teamwork, capability, structure and systems to help make them more effective in improving the learning outcomes of students and also sustain this improvement over time.

This book explains how Systems Leadership can and has been applied in schools to bring clarity to the purpose, structure and systems within a school and have a major impact on its success. As such, it is an essential text for school leaders and managers looking for practical tools to help improve the working lives of the people within their organisation, and hence their effectiveness.

**Ian Macdonald** is a Chartered Psychologist and founder and director of Macdonald Associates, an international organisational consultancy. He is also an Honorary Fellow at Brunel University, teaches at Surrey Business School and works with NHS Wales. He continues to consult to a wide range of organisations around the world.

**Clive Dixon** has been a teacher, principal and executive director of schools and was the Regional Director of Education and Training in Far North Queensland from 2007 to 2013. Clive currently works as a consultant, coaching school leaders using Systems Leadership in schools.

**Tony Tiplady** is an experienced educator, trainer, Indigenous youth specialist, mining operations manager, organisation effectiveness coach, Systems Leadership coach, consultant and practitioner.

# Improving Schools Using Systems Leadership

## Turning Intention into Reality

IAN MACDONALD,
CLIVE DIXON AND
TONY TIPLADY

 Routledge
Taylor & Francis Group

LONDON AND NEW YORK

First published 2020
by Routledge
2 Park Square, Milton Park, Abingdon, Oxon OX14 4RN

and by Routledge
52 Vanderbilt Avenue, New York, NY 10017

*Routledge is an imprint of the Taylor & Francis Group, an informa business*

© 2020 Ian Macdonald, Clive Dixon and Tony Tiplady

The right of Ian Macdonald, Clive Dixon and Tony Tiplady to be
identified as authors of this work has been asserted by them in
accordance with sections 77 and 78 of the Copyright, Designs and
Patents Act 1988.

All rights reserved. No part of this book may be reprinted or
reproduced or utilised in any form or by any electronic, mechanical,
or other means, now known or hereafter invented, including
photocopying and recording, or in any information storage or
retrieval system, without permission in writing from the publishers.

*Trademark notice*: Product or corporate names may be trademarks
or registered trademarks, and are used only for identification and
explanation without intent to infringe.

*British Library Cataloguing-in-Publication Data*
A catalogue record for this book is available from the British Library

*Library of Congress Cataloging-in-Publication Data*
Names: Macdonald, Ian, 1950 October 23- author. | Dixon, Clive,
    1956- author. | Tiplady, Tony, author.
Title: Improving schools using systems leadership : turning intention
    into reality / Ian Macdonald, Clive Dixon and Tony Tiplady.
Description: Abingdon, Oxon ; New York, NY : Routledge, 2019. |
    Includes bibliographical references and index.
Identifiers: LCCN 2019004644| ISBN 9781138556140 (hardback) |
    ISBN 9781138556119 (pbk.) | ISBN 9781315149868 (ebook)
Subjects: LCSH: Educational leadership. | School management and
    organization.
Classification: LCC LB2806 .M19 2019 | DDC 371.2—dc23
LC record available at https://lccn.loc.gov/2019004644

ISBN: 978-1-138-55614-0 (hbk)
ISBN: 978-1-138-55611-9 (pbk)
ISBN: 978-1-315-14986-8 (ebk)

Typeset in Stone Serif
by Swales & Willis Ltd, Exeter, Devon, UK

MIX
Paper from
responsible sources
FSC
www.fsc.org    FSC™ C013985

Printed in the United Kingdom
by Henry Ling Limited

*This book is dedicated to the improvement of educational opportunities for all.*

# Contents

# Acknowledgements

The authors – Ian, Clive and Tony – acknowledge the many people who contributed to the writing of this book. From those who willingly entered into time-consuming, mind-draining conversation on the who, what, where, when and why of the whole enterprise, to those who rescued three forlorn writers with a timely injection of spirit or a paragraph of thoughts, we thank you all.

The authors are indebted to the people working in schools in Far North Queensland for their continuing application and development of Systems Leadership in schools and their willingness to share their experience with their colleagues and us. We can think of no better purpose for using Systems Leadership than improving the educational opportunities of young people across the diverse communities of Far North Queensland. This is what drove us to write this book and keeps us inspired year after year. Working with Aboriginal and Torres Strait Islander people in their communities and schools is both a privilege and provides some of our most rewarding experiences.

In Australia, doing the work and then writing about it really challenges our mythologies of leadership and mateship, especially our reluctance to be seen to stand out from the crowd. So, many thanks to principals Ken Maclean, Judy Ketchell, Mark Allen, Tony Whybird and Bruce Houghton, who have provided case studies of the outstanding work of their schools. Each one is worth a book of its own.

Richard Huelin, who was an assistant regional director in the Far North region, added his perspective and knowledge to our discussions and assisted greatly in the preparation of data and the development of the graphs. Richard led the teaching and learning agenda with principals in the region and according to John Fleming is the best he had encountered.

Tony and Clive have never met Deborah Ussher, but we do not need to rely on Ian's word that she exists, because there just has to be a wonderful person working in his office in London; she makes everything happen, as it should. She is the glue that binds this book. Thanks to Deborah for all her help in organising our work. We would also like to thank Daphne Tiplady, who worked tirelessly to prepare the manuscript for publication. We are indebted to her for patience with the work and us.

Each of us is lucky to have extended families, including children and grandchildren. Love and thanks to our partners in life's great adventure – Gwyn, Linda and Cheryl – who often found themselves coming second to the various meetings, days writing, travel, never-to-be-disturbed piles of paper and grumpy moods it took three old *amigos* to write a book. *Gracias a nuestras hermosas esposas.*

# Introduction

## Context

When we think about the effectiveness of education we primarily think about teachers and the way that they teach. While this of course is of significant importance we may underestimate the impact that school organisation has on the behaviour of teachers, staff and students, and their well-being. Our experience is that the way that we set up and run an organisation definitely does have a significant effect on behaviour and the effectiveness, engagement and creativity of teachers and indeed all the staff in the organisation. It also affects the way that families and the community view and relate to the school. Student achievement is also influenced by the quality of the leadership, the structure and the systems that either enable or hinder productive and creative work.

There are many different ideas, often fragmented, about how to lead, design and set up organisations. They are often short-term "initiatives", subject to fads or flavours of the month. Such ideas often come and go or only cover one aspect. They may assume that the answer is in one or two activities, such as "leadership", "collaboration", "empowerment", "creativity", "innovation" and so on. Such approaches can be well intentioned but can be vague as to the "how" and certainly unclear as to what behaviour change is expected or what new systems and structures need to be implemented to underpin any change. As a result there can be significant variation in approach and results but without a clear understanding of what actually works well and why.

Systems Leadership is a comprehensive and coherent framework, which provides concepts, models and tools for school leaders and managers in education to use in their work to improve the working lives of people and hence the effectiveness of their organisation. It actually provides a predictive model as to what works well according the context. In short, it gives you the benefit of foresight (Macdonald, Burke and Stewart 2018).

## Purpose

The purpose of this book is to demonstrate how Systems Leadership can be used to make schools more effective in improving the learning outcomes of students.

## Overview of the book's contents

The book is presented in three parts. Part I outlines the concepts, models and tools of Systems Leadership with particular reference to their application in schools and in the educational units that provide support and services to schools. School leaders will have opportunities to reflect on their own leadership experiences, their engagement in leadership development and their current theory and practice of educational leadership.

Systems Leadership is a coherent theory and is practical in nature; it provides the how as well as the what. This means it is possible to apply the concepts, models and tools in everyday work while simultaneously developing a greater understanding of the theory. A synergy of theory and practice is difficult to find in the typical leadership course, program, workshop or conference, which offers either an interesting theory to consider or a grab bag of strategies, purported to solve your problems.

Part II outlines how Systems Leadership was implemented in the Far North region of the Queensland Department of Education and Training from 2008 until 2013. The improvement agenda was developed through five key priorities and although these will be included in the discussion, the focus of this book is the planned implementation of the concepts, models and tools of Systems Leadership in schools and work units across rural, remote and urban areas and in various contexts.

In Part III we look at results. This includes data from across the region and case studies of tried and proven examples that illustrate how Systems Leadership can be used in schools of different size, location and complexity. The case studies illustrate how a consistent application of the concepts, tools and models can lead to improved effectiveness. The examples have been developed by school leaders working in a range of settings and should assist the reader to reflect on their experiences. Discussion of various systems implemented in schools can generate a more informed understanding of the common operational needs of schools, the work required of various roles and the part played by central and regional offices in relation to school effectiveness.

The authors filled three key roles in the implementation of Systems Leadership in the Far North region. Throughout this book they will be addressed by their role title. Wherever possible the authors acknowledge the many others who made significant contributions in the region at that time.

The external consultant, Dr Ian Macdonald, although based in the UK, has extensive experience working in Australia and has a long-term association with Far North Queensland, having worked at Napranum on the western coast of Cape York Peninsula during the 1980s and with the management of Comalco (now Rio Tinto), which operated a mine in Weipa and utilised Systems Leadership. Ian has worked with a wide range of organisations throughout the world and is engaged in education at a number of levels. His significant contribution to the work in Far North Queensland was underpinned by a personal commitment to the purpose.

Tony Tiplady was recruited into Far North Queensland to the position of Manager, Organisational Effectiveness. He had experience in education and training in remote areas and had used Systems Leadership in Napranum (where he and Ian first worked together from 1986) and as a manager working for Comalco in western Cape York. His role in Far North Queensland included planning the implementation in the region and supporting regional managers and principals to do the work. He was heavily involved in training and coordinated the work of the external consultant with principals and regional officers.

The Regional Director, Clive Dixon, identified the need for a coherent organisational approach and had the authority to initiate the work and to allocate resources to ensure it was completed. He had been the principal of nine schools throughout Queensland; three of these were located in the Far North region. Clive had worked in various roles in the region, in the central office, and as an Executive Director had supervised schools in remote areas. He has always been driven by a desire to understand what leads to improvement for students not just in the classroom but in the entire environment of the school and community, and therefore by a need to understand what drives productive, constructive and creative behaviour.

This is not just a story of inputs, celebrating the glory of implementation. The work undertaken in the region resulted in clearly defined outputs and improved outcomes for students in a range of indicators including state-wide benchmarks and the National Literacy and Numeracy Assessment Program (NAPLAN). In this book the authors illustrate how Systems Leadership can be used to improve the effectiveness of schools to achieve better outcomes for students.

Because of what he saw as a lack of a coherent approach to organisation, and the lack of a deep understanding of what actually worked and why it worked, Clive introduced and implemented Systems Leadership as a regional priority in schools and work units in the Far North region of the Department of Education and Training from 2010 until 2013 (when he retired). Preparation for implementation preceded 2010. It was integral to the work undertaken in the region and underpinned the improved performance achieved during that time. Of the many factors which impact on the success of a consultancy, the experience in Systems Leadership and other priorities indicated that the greatest value came from consultants whose work was based in theory and also provided practices, models and tools to do the work. He continues to work with schools in a consultancy, advisory and coaching role.

Systems Leadership provides this link between theory and practice and the book *Systems Leadership: Creating Positive Organisations* written by Ian Macdonald, Catherine Burke and Karl Stewart (2018) acted as a manual during training and as a reference when people were busy doing the work. A copy of the book was purchased for every regional manager and principal as a symbolic step in committing to this work.

In assessing the potential of an initiative to meet the identified needs of the organisation, a critical issue is whether the principals, managers and executives have the capability required to lead the implementation and sustain the work. The Working Together courses (explained in Chapter 14 of this book), which had been developed through Systems Leadership to give people practical experience in using the concepts, tools and models, were readily available and over time were tailored to meet the specific needs of individuals and teams. At the time of writing more than 400 school leaders and other key staff have been trained through these courses. Resources had been made available to the region to develop the capability of school leaders and some funding was directed towards this training.

In the Far North region there were more than ninety schools, with campuses based on more than 120 different sites, including remote communities on Cape York and islands in the Torres Strait. While not all schools adopted Systems Leadership extensively, the implementation impacted on all schools and had a lasting effect on the culture of the region. Despite the changes of regional leaders, many principals continue to apply the work and it is also used in a small number of schools in other areas of Queensland, particularly by principals who have previously worked in the far north. Work has now also begun in the UK, involving schools in England.

More widely, practitioners of Systems Leadership work in various organisations from small businesses to major corporations, from private enterprises to not-for-profit organisations, from government departments to community groups. They work in countries across the world and are members of the Systems Leadership Development Association. The purpose of the association is to support practitioners in the effective development and application of Systems Leadership. Under this umbrella organisation, principals in the far north of Queensland have voluntarily established their own Systems Leadership Association (SLA) to support school leaders in applying Systems Leadership in schools.

In education sectors and schools it is common for initiatives to come and go depending on trends in educational thinking, the interests of leaders and the decisions of governments. Systems Leadership was implemented in the far north at a time when regional directors had the authority to take local circumstances into account and implement different strategies within the parameters of departmental policy to achieve designated outcomes. If this level of authority is removed, the work of the regions can become transactional and is reduced to implementing the plans of central directorates and responding to issues as they arise.

In the authors' experience, the most successful outcomes are achieved when the purpose is articulated clearly and the work required to achieve this is mapped and assigned to roles. It is unhelpful if restructuring is perceived as a competition for authority between school and region, district and region, or region and central office.

The authors are particularly interested in the application of Systems Leadership in the context of school education for Aboriginal students and Torres Strait Islander students. Commonly referred to by educators as "Indigenous education", the education of these students often lacks clear purpose and is rife with mythologies that underpin a range of failed strategies and practices. Despite this being a national focus through Closing the Gap, a strategy established in 2008 by state and federal governments to improve the lives of Aboriginal and Torres Strait Islander people, the outcomes of these students have shown little improvement. Doing more of the same is not the answer. Our work shows that Systems Leadership can and does contribute to closing that gap without a huge extra injection of funds or specialist resources.

Using Systems Leadership in various contexts has proven that the values continua (see Chapter 5) is at the heart of understanding an organisation. It can be applied across the broad spectrum of cultures, including those of Indigenous people. Although this will be covered in more detail throughout the book, it is important to note the holistic nature of Systems Leadership and how it contrasts starkly with the piecemeal strategies, which are proffered to fix problems in organisations and in society in general, but at best provide a chimera of short-term relief. Systems Leadership can be applied in any context and while this book focuses on schools in a region, we believe that it would bring similar, positive results when implemented in an individual school or across a whole school system anywhere.

# 1 *From headmaster to school leader*

This chapter discusses the changing nature of leadership in schools. Although it relies heavily on the Australian context, the reader will note similarities with trends and practices in other countries, particularly through the developed world.

The professionalisation of school teaching in the second half of the twentieth century impacted on the work of school leaders and the developing field of educational leadership. The headmaster in the 1960s was literally the head master or head teacher. With few limited resources, the headmaster demonstrated the most effective pedagogy to teachers, provided them with the lessons they should teach, showed them how they should assess and ensured that this happened by observing lessons and testing students.

The headmaster had a high degree of authority over how the school operated. The boundaries of the school were closed, with community and parents having limited involvement in decision making. While some might look back at these times through rose-coloured glasses, the good old days were only as good as the capability and intentions of the people in those roles.

The arrival of the "principal" in the 1970s was a sign of changing expectations. In Australia it was an indication that the influence of the British education system was declining, and educators were paying more attention to trends in education in the United States and other nations. In Western countries the work of teachers was becoming increasingly professionalised and the teachers who previously were trained in teachers' colleges now enrolled in universities to complete four-year degrees in education. Moving from training in teaching methods to a broader tertiary education reflected the significant change in the nature of teacher education and the role of teachers.

Different ways of thinking about classroom organisation and the role of the student in learning emerged. It was a time of exploration, when the desks were unscrewed from the floor and new buildings and furniture and a wider variety of resources were delivered to schools to facilitate new pedagogies. The role of professional development became more important in developing teachers' skills to meet these new expectations. This formed the basis of a mythology that professional development is provided by experts and occurs out of school hours and at a location outside of the school.

In the 1970s and 1980s the direction of a school depended largely on the preferences of the principal, and school performance depended on the capability of the principal and individual teachers. Apart from the visit of a supervisor in the form of a school inspector or superintendent there was no objective means of determining the performance level of students or the improvement in student learning over time. Growing teacher professionalism encouraged teachers to take more responsibility for their work and be less dependent on school leaders. Teachers began to develop their own units of work from common syllabi and there was a growing recognition of the needs of individual students.

In these circumstances pedagogy in any classroom depended on the preferences of the teacher. There was little consistency in pedagogy from one school to the next and there was no guarantee of consistency from one class to the next, even in the same school. A child's success depended largely on whether he or she was allocated to a class with a capable teacher. In the Far North region this situation was referred to euphemistically as "creating your own adventure".

During the 1980s and 1990s principals were required to be less directly involved in teaching and learning. The idea of the self-managing school with the promise of greater local autonomy also meant increased reporting requirements. Paradoxically the additional autonomy which, it was argued, would allow school communities to make better decisions and be more responsive to local needs came with additional work and more compliance measures. Different versions of the "self-managing school" emerged in jurisdictions across the developed world.

The annual visit by a principal supervisor in the 1960s to review and report on every aspect of school operations was replaced with a host of accountabilities and reports to various sources outside of the school. The derivation of the word "reform" – that is, *forming again* – proved to be true. Stability was replaced with a cycle of reform and restructuring which seemed to the people who worked in schools to cause ongoing disruption for little gain.

School leadership in the 1990s was embodied in the "administration team". More middle managers were funded in schools to deal with the growing complexity, and studies in leadership and management expanded. Working in teams and engaging in collaboration were easily accommodated in the lexicon of educators because these concepts aligned to their mythologies associated with classroom management and pedagogy. A stronger focus on student outcomes caused significant dissonance because it challenged mythologies of teachers and principals who cherished privacy of practice.

In the role of a professional "manager", principals were likely to be trained in program management. Annual action plans and strategic plans for a longer term were developed in set formats and key performance indicators were developed to measure and report progress. In response to community expectations and the corporatisation of education departments, new systems were introduced to replace the "in house" approaches to health and safety, child protection, governance, assessment, planning and reporting.

Principals were required to work more broadly in the community and to engage with other agencies for the benefit of their students. Schools provided opportunities for parents and caregivers to be more involved in their children's education, and in most systems across the world, parents played an increasing role in school governance through school and district councils that approved or endorsed the decisions made by the professional educators.

In some countries, teaching is a highly unionised profession and teachers' unions have a high degree of influence over education policy and how it is implemented. The purpose of unions is to provide better conditions and remuneration for their members. They argue that what is good for teachers must be good for students; for example, additional funding should be used to reduce class sizes so that teachers can provide more individual attention to students. While this argument seemed logical, it may have related more to the working conditions of teachers than concerns about student outcomes.

In *Visible Learning: A Synthesis of Over 800 Meta-Analyses Relating to Achievement* (2009) John Hattie concludes that class size has a minimal effect on student learning outcomes. The resources from this high-cost strategy could have been better used on strategies that cost less and result in a high-effect size. However, if a strategy requires teachers to change their practice, then teachers' unions may resist them.

From the 2000s the work in schools was impacted significantly by technology. Testing programs allowed the achievement of every student in a particular year level to be compared with other students across a nation and internationally. Intranets and specialised systems provided databases with point-in-time information on students, staff members and most aspects of school operations. Faster, more widespread communication meant reduced response times, greater oversight of operations, increased scrutiny by the media and exposure to intrusive social media. The boundaries were broken down and the privacy of schools and classrooms disappeared.

Developments in information and communication technology challenge traditional teacher-directed pedagogy and as a subject in its own right, Information and Communication Technology competes for a place in an over-crowded curriculum. Principals and teachers are faced with more complex technical aspects in their work, and demands to interact and work with a wider range of stakeholders require sophisticated social processing. A school may be one of the few remaining not-for-profit institutions that engages with a significant cross-section of people in a community.

An occupational health, safety and well-being survey conducted annually since 2011 by the Institute for Positive Psychology and Education Faculty of Education and Arts at the Australian Catholic University reported that in regard to Australian principals:

The two greatest sources of stress that have remained consistently high over the length of the survey have been

I.   Sheer Quantity of Work, and
II.  Lack of Time to Focus on Teaching and Learning.

(Riley 2017)

The issue of well-being is covered in more detail in Chapter 2 of this text and further discussion of the expectations of teachers and principals is included in Chapter 13.

Significantly, there are no commonly agreed or coherent organisational theories or models that apply across the whole field of educational leadership. Developing school leader capability is described as "professional development" and more recently "professional learning". In general, school leaders learn through experience and a succession of activities provided through conferences, workshops, systemic training, programs, courses and work-related projects.

In many countries, professional standards set out what principals and other school leaders are expected to know, understand and do to achieve proficiency in their work. These are intended to guide reflection on current practice and enable users to develop their leadership knowledge and skills through their day-to-day practice. The methodology for this approach is often expressed in terms of reflection, inquiry and collaboration.

In an article titled "A Brief History: The Impact of Systems Thinking on the Organization of Schools", Siegrist et al. (2013) trace the development of our understanding of organisations and how this relates to schools. The authors emphasise the difference between treating an organisation as a machine rather than properly recognising the complexity of social systems.

This aligns with the views of Macdonald, Burke and Stewart (2018), who emphasise the importance of a social process in bringing about change. Siegrist et al. argue that the process of working from the parts of the role to develop the competencies expected of principals and teachers is inadequate because it does not take into account how those parts interact. Siegrist et al. go on to say:

> Principal competencies are all products of analysis. By observing out-standing principals and breaking down their behaviours, it is assumed that exemplary practices can be identified, taught, and replicated by others. Of course, this is not true, but it sounds rational. Herein exists the deceit of the current analytical mental model.

Systems Leadership always starts with identifying the work that is required to achieve the purpose of the organisation. Organisations operate in a context and work is performed in a context. Systems Leadership is valued by principals because it helps them to understand this context and consequently their role and provides them with the tools and models to do the work to improve their school. A significant benefit is a common language based on the common understandings developed through using Systems Leadership. Team members can achieve clarity in understanding the work they need to do and how they can work together to achieve their purpose.

## McKinsey: the world's best-performing schools

In September 2007 McKinsey & Company published "How the World's Best-performing School Systems Come Out on Top". It reported research into twenty-five school systems, including the ten best-performing school systems in the world.

> The experience of these top three school systems suggest that three things matter most:
>
> 1.  Getting the right people to become teachers; and
> 2.  Developing them into effective instructors; and
> 3.  Ensuring that the system is able to deliver the best possible instruction for every child.

Although these may seem obvious, they were not as evident in practice and certainly not easily put into practice.

The McKinsey report described the performance of school systems in stages of poor to fair, fair to good, good to great and great to excellent. Challenging the notions that one school is the same as the next or that every school should independently determine its own approach, the research argues that to improve performance, there are strategies which should be used at all stages of performance, and there are also different interventions required at each stage.

> Our research suggests that six interventions are common to all performance stages across the entire improvement journey: building the instructional skills of teachers and management skills of principals, assessing students, improving data systems, facilitating improvement through the introduction of policy documents and education laws, revising standards and curriculum, and ensuring an appropriate reward and remuneration structure for teachers and principals.

Plans to improve school performance fail when the strategies do not match the developmental stage of the school. Not all schools are at the same stage of development and to improve they need to do different work. If a school system is working from poor to fair then the emphasis should be on structured, systematic approaches to get the basics right. If a school system is working from great to excellent performance, then the emphasis is on teachers and school leaders collaborating and creating opportunities for innovation.

This is consistent with our proposition that organisational structures and systems impact on the behaviour of staff, students and community members. However in contrast to this approach the current situation is that change is expected to occur quickly with limited understanding of how it affects the people who work in schools. Everyone working in schools is busy but not necessarily effective and the next change comes before the last one is completed, causing fatigue, disassociation and counterproductive systems and behaviours. Principals are consumed by the churn of busy work at the expense of the productive work of their role. Social boundaries have broken down to the extent that the day-to-day issues which beset our society find their way into these special places called schools where our children go to learn.

While the public conversation is about teacher quality, there is rarely a shared understanding of what "teacher quality" means. We should clarify the work teachers and principals need to do in a school to ensure student outcomes continue to improve. Teaching should be developed as a system, which incorporates the most effective pedagogies and provides the scope for teachers to apply their judgement, capability and creativity to maximise student learning. While governments promote "autonomy" (a poorly defined concept, often used as a matter of convenience) as the answer to improving school performance, the emphasis should be on developing systems to allow people in schools to do the work required.

Despite the various programs, policies and changes in Australia, achievement standards of students in international testing programs have declined and limited improvement made in the National Assessment Program of Literacy and Numeracy (NAPLAN) and in closing the gap between Indigenous and non-Indigenous students.

The release of results of the NAPLAN each year is followed by predictable commentary. The reporting authority typically recommends that the good news stories of improvement in isolated schools should be examined, so that other schools can do similar things and also improve. State governments manipulate the narrative and point to incremental improvements or more impressive results in specific areas. Academics from faculties of education in universities downplay the importance of the NAPLAN as "point in time" information and warn parents that there is too much emphasis on testing, causing anxiety in students. Teachers' unions agree there is too much emphasis on testing, and proclaim that it increases the stress levels of teachers and the solution to poor performance is increased funding. The representatives of governments argue about funding levels, where the responsibility for funding lies and the proportion of funding appropriate for private and public schools.

In our view these arguments ignore the real issues and provide no way forward to improve student outcomes. The regular media blitz shows no real understanding of the drivers for all students to achieve their potential. Inadvertently, this misunderstanding actually reinforces assumptions that children from poor backgrounds are not capable of doing as well as other students. This poor analysis would lead us to believe that the brilliance of an individual school, teacher or principal will save the day.

Selecting "good news stories" as examples of what every school should do is not a precise or effective enough response. Funding is important and needs to go to the schools and students that need it the most, but more important is using funding to do the right things and not spending more money on the same things that produced this unsatisfactory result in the first place.

Schools are busier and more complex. Teachers and school leaders are challenged by increasing needs of students, parents and the local community while at the same time responding to the demands of governments, various departments, private providers, unions, media, associations, pressure groups and statutory bodies. The people who work in schools are wary of increasing expectations and a cycle of change, which creates overload, results in little improvement and is barely implemented before the next solution is being proposed.

In the media, the public discussion of school education focuses on broad themes of funding models, national curriculum, improving teacher quality and increasing school autonomy. While these are important, none in itself is the answer and none addresses the core issue of how schools should organise and manage their work to be most effective. Our impoverished thinking on school education has resulted in a dependence on ill-defined notions of "best practice" and allowed the development of an unhelpful dichotomy where on one hand a school is considered to be the same as the next, while on the other it is argued schools are different and should make their own decisions to meet the needs of students.

Our view is that a deeper understanding of how schools and school systems are organised is what is required. This includes an understanding of how the elements of systems interact and are affected by the behaviour of those in or interacting with these systems. This is why Systems Leadership was chosen as a way of understanding and dealing with these complexities in order to improve the outcomes of all of our students.

# PART 1

# *Understanding the concepts and tools of Systems Leadership*

# 2 Understanding the impact of organisation on well-being

When we think about schools and education in general we naturally think first about teachers. We think about the teacher in the classroom, the quality of the teaching and perhaps the nature of the training that the teacher has received. On reflection we might also think about the cost of education: whether schools have sufficient money, whether people are paid appropriately and, especially in countries where the state is the main funder, whether the taxpayer is getting value for money.

There are less obvious but equally important issues: What is the purpose of education? What is the purpose of the school? What is the purpose of the many administrative systems operating within the education system as a whole and within schools? Another issue that we may not pay as much attention to is: How is the school set up and run? In particular, are those arrangements more or less likely to achieve the purpose?

We are probably not surprised to hear many teachers, when considering whether they enjoy their work, make comments such as, "I really like the children but I am just overwhelmed by the paperwork and all the other requirements and changes in policy that we have to implement." A teacher might also say, "I really enjoy teaching but I'm not enjoying working at the school, there is no real leadership, there are staff cliques, people don't support one another, I'm looking for another job." In fact, whether a teacher stays in the profession may be more influenced by the way the work is organised and the way they are led than anything else.

Over the past few years there has been growing recognition of the cost to staff and students of increased expectations with regard to work and outcomes. This recognition has taken the form of the examining of well-being at work. There have been many publications in this area both in education and in the public sector in general (Kern et al. 2015, Watson 2006). Many approaches have been recommended, including mindfulness for both staff and students, and much more attention is now being paid to mental health. Staff and students have suffered stress and anxiety, with many teachers leaving the profession or students disengaging from school. Students have been struggling to find ways to cope and succeed in the face of this pressure. While these approaches can be very helpful in coping with the immediate situation, we believe that Systems Leadership can help to address some of the root causes that are to be found in the way that schools and colleges are organised. As we argue in this book one problem is that there is not a shared, agreed view, theory or model to underpin good organisation. As such there is not a shared language and therefore a shared meaning of terms, even those as basic as "work", "leadership" or "culture". There can be a lack of clarity around people's roles, tasks and authority and poorly designed systems that hinder rather than enable work. The result is considerable wasted effort and time in a context where time is perhaps the most precious resource. Everyone is busy but not everyone is as efficient or effective as they could be. This in turn leads to frustration and conflict, which further drains energy and effort from productive and creative work. Our experience, explained in this book, demonstrates that considerable time and effort can be saved by good organisational arrangements as well as high-quality leadership. This releases the teachers' capability to concentrate on the work that really matters in school; that is the education of students and is the reason that most people came into the profession. We do not want staff, students, parents and the local community to be trying to achieve their purpose despite the system; rather, the system should be enabling them to achieve the purpose. Poor organisation undermines well-being, drains energy and leads to burnout. The use of Systems Leadership can help to reduce these pressures so that staff and students can not only be more effective but also enjoy going to school (RSA, n.d.; UK Dept of Education, 2015; Waters and White, 2015; Weinberg and Doyle, 2017).

In the UK we have also been working with the charity Eikon, which specialises in this area, is fundamentally concerned with improving well-being and recognises that root causes of well-being lie in the way the school is set up and run.

It is interesting to note that, although many books are written about work and organisations it is rare to find a clear definition. The word "work" is used often and in many different ways. The *Oxford English Dictionary* refers to *expenditure of effort, striving, exertion of force in overcoming resistance, tasks to be undertaken, achievement, employment, earning money* and *to have influence or effect,* to mention only a few. So, when the teacher says she is "going to work today" this could mean many different things, including the location of the school, physical effort, mental exertion and so on.

The definition of *work* in the physical sciences is, of course, very clear (work = force x distance). We are concerned with a different form of work. Despite the many social meanings of the term "work", we have found it useful to define *human work* as follows.

---

**Box 2.1   Definition of *work***

Work: turning intention into reality.

---

Many people have great intentions, which are easy to talk about and put into mission or vision statements or strategic papers, but without work they remain just dreams and aspirations. Work is the process by which an idea generated by a person becomes evident in the external world and open to recognition. While this undoubtedly requires effort, it is not simply the expenditure of effort. This definition we use is closely related to Jaques' definition, and can be seen as such by reference to his explanation in his book *A General Theory of Bureaucracy* (1976: 100, 113), in which he says:

> The term work refers to activity, to behaviour, to that human activity in which people exercise discretion, make decisions and act so as to transform the external physical and social world accord with some predetermined goal in order to fulfil some need.

In short, turning intention into reality (Jaques 1976: 101).

We are concerned here with that human definition of work and in particular the different ways that people turn intention into reality and the different roles that they have in contributing to the overall purpose.

Work is essential to our psychological well-being as it is the means by which we demonstrate that we can be productive and make a difference in the world.

As Macdonald (1990) wrote, "The whole process allows the person to identify themselves as an active agent in the world." Work is sometimes seen as a burden, especially if we do not feel that our intentions have been taken into account. In such circumstances we are little more than an object, or just a convenient means to help somebody else achieve their intention.

This is why it is so important for a leader to engage with team members so that all of the team genuinely share the purpose (intention). They, therefore, identify with the purpose and have the opportunity to gain recognition for their contribution to the result.

To put it very simply, *if* in performing work

1.  We are prevented from realising our intentions (either by others or ourselves), and/or
2.  We do not get recognition for our contribution to the process and result, then
3.  We will not only be alienated from our work but our identity will suffer.

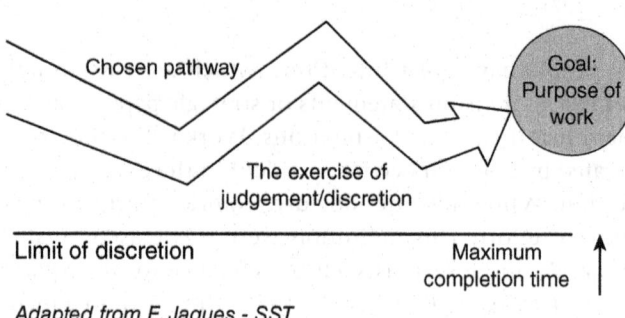

**Work** is the exercise of discretion in making decisions
in order to achieve a productive purpose.

*Adapted from E. Jaques - SST*

**Figure 2.1**    A representation of "Work"

This definition, "turning intention into reality", clearly extends beyond the realm of employment work. We see very young children "working" extremely hard, applying intense concentration and effort, experiencing immense frustration and joyful success, processes we continue throughout our lives if we are to enjoy a positive identity. We sometimes call this "play", and it certainly contains experimentation but is often very serious, as anyone who interrupts such activity will know.

If we think about work in schools, we have activity that is directed towards achieving a goal that can be specified in advance. Such goals may be fairly simple and visible, such as cleaning a classroom, or they may be more abstract and complex, such as implementing a new curriculum throughout a large school. Whatever the activity, it will always be bounded by constraints or limits. These can be variously described in terms of the laws of society (written and unwritten), policies of the organisation, the specific authority of the role and, more particularly, the resources available (material, money, people and time).

We can see that this purposeful activity involves turning intention into reality. We can now look at a useful way in which this can be done.

## Task clarification and assignment

If the purpose is to be achieved, then work has to be done. Many different contributions are made by people in different roles. Work is usually done in the form of tasks that can vary in terms of complexity and length of time and effort required. In the school context where time is so precious, we have seen considerable amounts of time and effort wasted because of a lack of clarity. Someone completes a piece of work only to find that it is not what was wanted. Sometimes the misunderstanding may be slight but at other times may be such that the person feels unappreciated or devalued. We have often heard the phrase "I wish that you had told me that in the first place!" Now, we can never completely remove ambiguity – indeed, creativity can flow from ambiguity. However, in most day-to-day work a lack of clarity is not creative but actually results in a muddle and poor results. The ambiguity should be resolved between the parties concerned in the clarification of the task, not in its enactment. People should not have to second-guess what is wanted and then suffer the consequences when one or another gets it wrong.

Throughout our work we have encouraged the use of a task model that has improved working practices and costs nothing to implement (see the case studies later and Chapter 10 on teamwork).

This model introduces a simple discipline that requires the following elements to be clarified before a task is enacted. Note that this clarification is all about what is to be achieved, not how it is to be achieved. This leaves the discretion as to the how to the task doer, along with the relevant discretion and decision-making described in the definition of *work* above. Being clear about what is wanted is neither overbearing nor authoritarian. This clarification is a process that involves the two or more people involved.

The work of the leader, or the task assigner, is to lead the process and then in the end decide upon the elements described below. The team member, or task doer, makes suggestions, proposals and comments that contribute to the process. The purpose of the process is that there is a resultant shared view of the work and so both parties leave with the same view of the task to be done.

The elements of a task are described below.

## CONTEXT (C)

The context for the task essentially describes the environment and the relative importance of what is being done. Setting the context should provide information as to whether the environment is positive or negative. For example, we may be looking at a proposed meeting between a teacher and a community group. How positive or negative is the group likely to be? How important is this meeting given the current situation? If a new system is being implemented, how is it likely to be viewed? Has there been any preparation or training? We do not want a situation to occur where the task doer says after the event, "I wish you had told me beforehand just how critical that meeting/system was."

## PURPOSE (P)

Here we need to be precise as to why we are doing this activity. The purpose should be able to be explained in a single sentence without the use of the conjunction "and". For example, the meeting might be one where a teacher will receive feedback that involves criticism of his or her performance. Is the purpose to improve the performance? If we think about a staff meeting the purpose may be less obvious. Is the purpose to share information, to report progress, to do some work?

Many staff go into meetings or discussions without knowing or having a shared view of what the purpose is. As a result, there will inevitably be different views as to how successful the meeting was.

## QUANTITY (Q)

The purpose eventually needs to be expressed in terms of outcomes. For example, a head of department might be asked to suggest improvements with regard to the curriculum or teaching methods. How many recommendations are needed? If this is a written document, how long should it be? Again, being imprecise about the quantity can lead to disappointment because there is not enough, or a waste of effort because the quantity is not actually needed.

## QUALITY (Q)

Quantity is not enough; we also need to be clear about the quality of the output. Should the recommendations contain references or examples from other schools? Should they involve inputs from other staff members, students and families? Do we want a written report or simply some notes or dot points? Do we need a presentation? Using what method? Sometimes it is difficult to determine the quality quickly, and indeed discussions between the task assigner and the task doer lead to a clarification of the quality, which had not previously been thought through.

## RESOURCES (R)

This element clarifies the resources that the task doer is authorised or is expected to use. How much money can she or he spend? Are there other staff available to help? What materials can be used? We do not want people over- or under-using resources because they are not clear with regard to the limits. Again, it is surprising how often people are not clear about the resources available to them.

## TIME (T)

Finally, we need to be clear about when the task needs to be completed. One of the worst examples is when somebody is asked to do something "as soon as possible". Does this mean that he or she drops everything else, or does it mean as soon as the person can, given all the other things they have to do at the moment? Using such phrases is unfair and lazy. Of course, there may be a precise single point in time. There may be a range; for example, "sometime next week". However, there is always a maximum completion time and it needs to be clear whether completing a task before that time is advantageous or not.

Thus, these elements need to be clarified between the task assigner and the task doer. This allows the task to be done using discretion as to the "how".

This model of CPQQRT has played a significant role in reducing wasted effort by clarifying a shared expectation before the task is carried out. Depending upon the task there may be a need for considerable discussion, or indeed very little. Usually the more complex the task the longer the discussion to clarify the elements. This is not an authorisation process whereby one person on their own determines these elements, but rather a means of clarification. However, it is the leader who makes the final determination. The return on investment of this model is very high as it costs nothing to implement but can reduce confusion and wasted effort. Often it is useful to write down these elements so that both parties can refer to them but that is not always the case, as some tasks are relatively short and simple, and perhaps where there is already a mutual understanding there is therefore no need to make a written record.

Returning to the model of work we can see that tasking as described does not interfere with the "how". The creation of a pathway or method of achieving the goal is the challenge, and these challenges can be more or less difficult or complex (see Chapter 3).

*Creating this pathway is, thus, unique to the individual; it is like a signature and part of our identity. To a casual observer it may appear to be the same for either a number of individuals performing the same task or an individual repeating an activity, but close observation will always reveal some difference, even if very small.*

Herein lies the opportunity for improvement. Human beings have a natural drive to improve methods. Think of an occasion when you have attempted a task for the first time. It is almost impossible to prevent reflection on how to do it better next time. Often, in the way that we organise work or design and implement systems in organisations, we inhibit this process or even actively try to prevent it. Nonetheless, most people will at least think about improvement even if they cannot act on those ideas.

Thus, in summary, when tasks are assigned, the leader assigning them should be clear about the context of the work; for example, the policy of the school, the capabilities of the children in the class, the importance of this work at this time. The purpose must also be clear: to improve the behaviour of a particular child so that they can participate in the class. The quality requirements of the output (goal) as well as the quantity requirements must also be clear; for example, to prevent one child's behaviour from being disruptive. In addition, the person performing the task needs to know what resources are available and what limits are operating. Last but not least, the time to completion must be clear.

Whatever the complexity, all these activities require work. They are all about turning intention into reality and they all require the person to work out the best way (the how) of achieving the goal. All these types of work, in their own way, can be satisfying and creative.

The affirmation or our contribution to the process and outcome of work, especially when positive, recognises that we exist and that the output of our thinking has genuine worth; it encourages us to use and develop our capabilities. This is why recognition of work is so important. It is very significant for the leader to accurately recognise the different contributions of team members.

We use the term "recognition" because it is a neutral term and does not presuppose a successful outcome, unlike "reward". It is essential to understand why a process failed to produce the desired result, and this needs to be recognised in order to improve the process we use in the future. Recognition or apparent failure does not necessarily imply the negative aspect of blame, as the person may have done everything she or he could or was supposed to do. Without proper recognition there can be very little learning.

## The domains of work

Systems Leadership includes a model that describes work in any organisation or role in three domains. They are the Technical Domain, the Commercial Domain and the Social Domain.

We have found this model very useful in understanding educational services and running schools.

The Technical Domain includes all the specialist, professional expertise that is relevant to the organisation and the roles within it. In education the primary Technical Domain is teaching, including pedagogy underpinned by

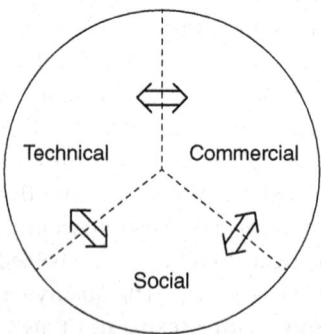

**Figure 2.2**    A model that describes work in any organisation or role in three domains

theories and models of practice. This primary Technical Domain is linked to the purpose of the organisation. Of course, if we look at education as a whole there are other professions and specialisms that have their own technical domains, such as accounting, health, nutrition, statistics and others that provide support and service in the delivery of education.

The Commercial Domain includes everything that is concerned with cost, in the form of expenditure and revenue in terms of the sources of income that will meet the costs. This domain is present in all organisations – private, public and not-for-profit – as all organisations incur costs and need revenue. The Commercial Domain is not just about whether an organisation actually makes a profit or not. The domain is obviously highly significant in the education sector. The cost of salaries, equipment and capital items is rightly a major concern in the delivery of educational services, whether in the private or public sector.

The Social Domain includes all the arrangements and the organisation of people that are needed in order to get the work done. Thus, it includes the way the organisation is structured in terms of roles, reporting relationships and authority. It includes all the systems that are required to get the work done, not just in the people area but right across the organisation. It also includes all the social processes that are needed so that people work effectively to the best of their ability. In short, the Social Domain covers all the aspects that we might call the culture of the organisation. It is essentially all the ways that people relate to each other in their working relationships.

We distinguish these domains because they involve different types of work, but they are all necessary for the success of the organisation. They all interact and must be integrated by the leadership if the organisation is going to achieve its purpose. They all are equally important. It is not very helpful to have excellent teachers if there is not enough money to pay them. It is not very helpful to have plenty of money and potentially good teachers if the organisation's arrangements prevent them from being effective.

## HOW THIS MODEL IS USED

We have found this model especially useful in providing clarity. It is interesting to note that if someone applied for a job as a teacher it would certainly not be sufficient for them to say, "I think I would make a good teacher because I seem to get on with children. I even have children of my own. So please can I have a job?" The response would be: "Well, what qualifications do you have? What training have you had and have you worked as a teacher anywhere?" We would want to know the nature of the qualifications and training in detail. Furthermore, once the teacher is in the role he or she will be expected to operate to a curriculum, use a pedagogy and have objectives and lesson plans, and not simply to occupy the children for several hours a day. There are clear expectations. The Technical Domain is usually based on tested practice and professional principles.

Looking at the Commercial Domain, if when applying for a job – any job – in education a person asked what the salary might be, it would not be acceptable if the answer was: "Well, let's not be too pedantic about that, I'm sure you'll find it is sufficient." We would want a precise answer. Similarly, a head teacher or principal really does need to know how much revenue they are likely to receive if they are to be confident of meeting the costs that are necessary to run the school. It is recognised that uncertainty in these areas and lack of precision makes work much more difficult to plan and complete.

However, when we come to the Social Domain such precision suddenly seems to be less important, or even pedantic. We appoint people to significant leadership roles managing many staff and commanding significant budgets without the standardised training with reference to accepted and shared underlying theories that we would expect in the other two domains. We do not generally apply the same rigour. Although there are some training courses they are often much less precise in terminology. They may well include exhortations with regard to what may be the latest fashionable idea: "collaboration", "empowerment", "leadership" or "innovation" (or even a combination such as "collaborative empowerment" or "innovative leadership").

However, are these based upon shared definitions or a coherent theory that links all of the social processes together? Do they provide an understanding of structure, systems and leadership based upon theories of capability that are all integrated? This is what Systems Leadership offers, and if introduced into the Social Domain provides what some people call "joined-up thinking" and prevents what other people refer to as "silos". It provides an understanding of why people behave as they do in response to organisational arrangements, and more importantly how to encourage productive behaviour, building a positive organisation where people want to give of their best.

We propose that precision in terminology and a shared understanding of language in the Social Domain is as critical for the effective functioning of schools as precision in the other two domains. We argue that terms such as "leadership", "teamwork", "culture" and even terms such as "manager" or "supervisor" need to be understood if people are to work together in a constructive and productive way. The lack of shared meaning, definitions and language in this area leads to confusion, a waste of effort and even conflict. If we make words mean whatever we want them to mean, then we are stuck in Wonderland with Alice.

Take a moment and write down your own definition of the following terms: "teamwork", "culture", "leadership", "structure", "authority", "manager", "supervisor", "system", "collaboration" and "innovation". Would your definitions be the same as your colleagues? It is not unusual at this point for us to meet the response that we are being pedantic or restrictive, stultifying creativity. However, this does not seem to have stultified creativity in other disciplines, such as physics, biology, medicine, psychology and so on, where clarity around meaning, definitions and processes has led to enormous advances and improvements in the delivery of associated services.

We are not arguing for rigidity or dogma simply for discipline and clarity. Further such definitions are not set in stone; they are working definitions and principles that need to be tested further. Being clear may paradoxically encourage questioning and testing. It is lack of clarity that fosters the use of power and intimidation.

Another use of the STC model is in the design of roles. When thinking about any role it is useful to consider the nature and volume or work in each of those domains. Depending upon the particular role the proportion and nature of work in each domain will vary. For example, we would expect a classroom teacher to have a higher proportion of their work in the Technical Domain and although there will be elements of their work concerned with the Commercial Domain, teachers individually rarely have significant budgets. Similarly, the amount of time teachers spend in meetings and/or operating systems should be minimised, although some of that work, particularly discussions with colleagues, will be an essential component of the role. Compare this with the role of the head teacher or principal. She or he will have a significant part of their work in the Commercial Domain; many large schools have significant budgets running into millions. Also, they will have a critical part of their work in the Social Domain in terms of leadership, the creation of a productive culture and the design or modification of whole school systems. We found this model a useful tool in designing roles and in the sharing and understanding of the critical work of each role.

We also mentioned the importance of clarity of purpose. We argue that any organisation, including or even especially a school, needs to be clear about its purpose both as an organisation and in terms of the roles within that organisation. Everyone in the school should be clear how their work is contributing to the overall purpose. Any activity that is not contributing to that purpose should be questioned, and if it cannot be linked to the purpose should be eliminated. Whenever we look at organisations we find a large number of activities which take time, effort and resources but that are not linked to the purpose of the organisation. Furthermore, we have introduced a simple discipline that helps the people think about purpose. We ask people if they can state the purpose of the organisation and the purpose of their role in a single sentence without the conjunction "and". This has led to many very interesting discussions and questions that help clarify the work at both an organisational and individual level. We find that simple and clear purpose statements are much more helpful to people than many so-called mission or vision statements that often tend to be abstract and non-specific in terms of behaviour. In our work we found that this question also applies to the design of systems (see Chapter 7). Discussions around purpose tend to be a lot more grounded and practical than some of the vaguer discussions around vision or mission statements.

## The Three Questions at Work

This in turn is linked to another simple tool that is part of Systems Leadership, which is the Three Questions at Work.

We have found that when an organisation is working well and being effective in achieving its purpose, the people in the organisation are able to answer three simple questions.

1.  The first is: What am I meant to do?

    *This question clearly refers to the work of my role and the extent to which I am clear about the expectations of me, how I am meant to achieve them and how this work fits in with others and contributes to the purpose of the organisation.*

2.  The second is: How well am I doing?

    *This question refers to the extent as to how I receive feedback and information as to whether I am actually achieving those expectations. This does not simply refer to comments or information from my manager or supervisor but also feedback from colleagues, parents and other stakeholders. How does such feedback match my own experiences and judgement?*

3.  The third question is: What is my future?

    *This question clearly refers to my career and my ambitions (which do not necessarily include promotion). It also refers to information as to how the school or larger organisation is performing and what future it has.*

Using these questions, we can see how clear people are about their work, current and future, and predict that if people cannot answer such questions, or if there is significant ambiguity with regard to answering those questions, they will not be satisfied in their role and will become distracted or disengage from their work over time. We can also see that if we create an organisation where people can answer such questions, we need to design appropriate systems and structures that enable such clarity (see Chapter 7).

## Conclusion

Our basic proposition is that lack of clarity, rigour and precision in the Social Domain leads to confusion and wasted effort. This confusion reinforces the culture of busyness rather than effectiveness. Some people might counter this by saying that we can never be precise. They may say that there is always ambiguity. Of course there is! However, there is no need to add to that unnecessarily. Also, we have found that people who like to keep things vague or unclear often do so to maintain their own power. They can then move the goal posts when they like, re-define terms as they wish and take advantage of the confusion. It is much more difficult to operate on the basis of power when there is clarity. Working in any school where there is lack of clarity with regard to roles, expectations, authority and leadership causes distress, increases stress and contributes to a lack of creativity and enjoyment in the workplace. If we consider how much time and energy is needed to teach young people, any distraction or impediment can discourage even the most dedicated teacher or staff member. Our experience is that relatively less time and effort has historically been put into improving work in this Social Domain. However, because of the dedication and commitment of most staff, education continues despite the organisation and systems rather than because of them. Many staff, including teachers, leave a school or the profession entirely because of poor organisation and leadership. We cannot afford to waste time or lose talent. We found that improving clarity in the Social Domain led not only to improved satisfaction of staff but even more importantly to improved outcomes for students.

The failure to be clear about work adds to the stress. Staff have enough pressure to meet ever increasing expectations without having to second-guess what that work is. Well-being is undermined when staff spend hours in meeting with no clear purpose, poor context and vague outcomes. None of this is necessary.

# 3 Organising work: understanding complexity

Clearly, some work is more difficult than other work. Some tasks take more time to complete than others. The pathway needed to achieve the goal may be more or less difficult or complex; it may involve more or fewer abstract variables, in other words, elements that cannot be seen or touched. For example, designing a remuneration system is more complex than arranging desks.

Whatever the complexity, all these activities require work. They are all about turning intention into reality and they all require the person to work out the best way (the how) of achieving the goal. All of these types of work, in their own way, can be satisfying and creative.

Large organisations are characterised by layers or levels of structure. We refer in general terms to shop floor workers, operators, etc. We talk about supervisors and first-line managers, then middle managers, executives, managing directors, vice-presidents, presidents, chief operating officers and chief executive officers. In the civil and public service and the armed services there are ranks and grades forming a quite deliberate hierarchy. Even in smaller organisations there are managers and reporting structures. People over the years have criticised or attacked hierarchy but it is surprisingly robust and can be traced back through history (Jaques 1976; 1990). Notable writers such as Weber (1922); Blau and Scott (1962); Burns and Stalker (1966); Dawkins (1976); Lane and Tripe (2006); Mintzberg (1979); Morgan (1986); Simon (1962); Whyte, Wilson and Wilson (1969); and many others have all described and analysed this organisational feature.

These hierarchies are not simply levels of authority or an "outdated command and control" framework. This over-simplistic critique misses the point that such structures should actually be a hierarchy of the complexity of work. The authority flows from this complexity, not the other way around. If people in roles "higher up" in an organisation are not doing work of higher complexity they are not adding value and should not have the associated authority.

Tasks of similar complexity can be bundled together to form a role that can be placed at an appropriate level in the organisation (level of work). Many organisations do this in a muddled way because they do not have a clear means of differentiating between levels of management, salary grades, complexity of tasks and mental processing ability.

Being clear about the complexity of work required at each level allows each level upwards to reflect a qualitatively more complex and abstract way of perceiving and acting in the world of work. More importantly, we have a specific rationale for the generally vague term of "adding value". Each level, potentially, adds value to the work of the level below by setting it in a broader, more complex context.

This is what employees intuitively refer to when they comment as to whether the person in their manager's role actually is experienced as a real manager or just adding to the bureaucracy. Most critically, in terms of power and authority, if the manager does add value, it is more likely that the team members will accept the manager's authority. This is in contrast to the power exercised by the more senior, higher-graded colleague who adds no value through his or her work and is resented when he or she tries to assign or review work.

We refer to these levels of work as qualitatively different types of complexity of tasks requiring qualitatively different types of mental processing ability. How to describe and recognise them is, however, not in itself simple.

There is ample evidence of qualitative differences in the way that people order their worlds and go about their work. The book *Levels of Abstraction in Logic and Human Action* (Jaques, Gibson and Isaac 1978) describes a range of theories of discontinuity and compares them. It goes on to compare a further range of theories including Bennett (1956–1966) on mathematics, Bloom and Krathwohl (1956) on education and Kohlberg (1971) on moral development. Further theories that are even more well known, such as those of Piaget (1971) and associated researchers, have hypothesised and experimentally demonstrated such discontinuities in the way people perceive and act in their worlds. Stamp (in subsequent work; 1978) clearly describes similarities between the discontinuities found in her own work and that of Jaques, Macdonald and others.

While these are general descriptors, there is a need for those trying to design and run real organisations, including schools, to have more precise, behavioural descriptors.

Below we describe these differences in general terms. Later, in Chapter 13, we discuss in more detail how this applies in education.

# Level I: Complexity I (R1)

---

**Box 3.1    Level I: Hands on**

Hands on – completing concrete procedural tasks.

---

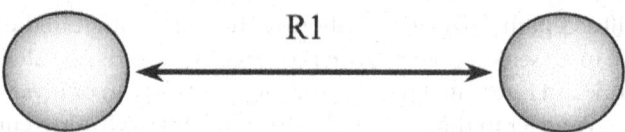

Typical tasks might be completing forms, cleaning a room, servicing a vehicle, entering data. The completion of tasks at this level does not take longer than three months.

At Level I there is direct action on immediately available material, customers or clients. There is a clear understanding of the work to be done, the procedural steps to be followed and how they are linked. Direct physical feedback indicates whether the work is being performed correctly. The work is often immensely skilful, with significant use of practical judgement, discretion and adjustment by touch and feel or trial and error if previously known solutions or learned trouble-shooting methods do not work. A known pathway is followed until an obstacle is encountered and then practical judgement is used to overcome the problem or assistance is called for.

Relationship one is direct. The person and their work are rarely separated. This also gives rise to the reality that people doing this type of work do not take their work home. At the end of the day or shift the person goes home and can leave their work until their next shift. This is typically the type of work of a teacher aide or clerical assistant.

## Level II: Complexity II (R2)

> **Box 3.2    Level II: Diagnosis**
>
> Monitoring and diagnosis of operational processes.

2

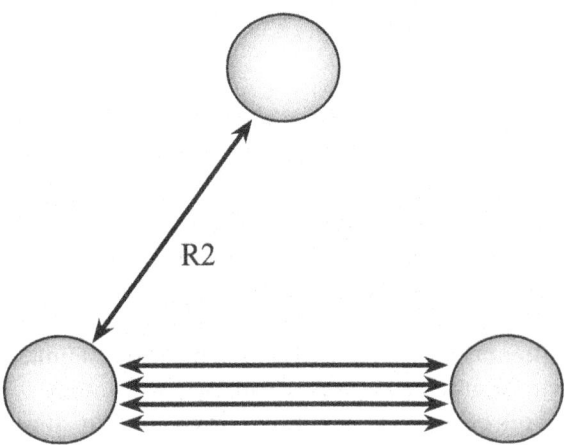

At Level II, the key work is diagnosis. This is done using established, known systems and processes. Significant data is collected in the form of suggestions from those operating the process and from the flow of directly observable events. Improvements and modifying actions may be taken on the basis of this information. Diagnostic patterns may be learned through training and education; for example, in engineering, social work, teaching or nursing. Indicators of learned patterns (algorithms and systems) are sought to recognise significant data and so identify the specific pattern that is operating in this instance in order to formulate alternative methods of performing tasks, to decide whether the diagnosis is correct or that the case is from another pattern.

There is still direct access to the area of work and often physical contact with the work.

Here the person can now reflect (R2) on the work (R1). They can think about it away from the activity. They can mentally compare ways of approaching it. This is the first level of real planning and the first level of professional work associated with teachers, social workers, nurses, solicitors and others. Such work examples include designing individual care or teaching plans for individuals, or comparing and identifying different ways of servicing vehicles. This is usually the appropriate level of work for a classroom teacher.

# Level III: Complexity III (R3)

---

**Box 3.3    Level III: Systems**

Discerns trends to refine existing systems and develop new systems within a single knowledge field.

---

Work of Level III complexity requires the ability to recognise the connections between data from a flow of real events within a single field, or discipline, and to discern the linkages between them. Trends are analysed and systems are proposed.

Because the work of hypothesis generation and testing remains within one field or discipline, Level III capability will not in itself recognise the impact of the proposed system on a different system in another field. Also, information that arises from what is not there (negative information) is not recognised as significant. This inability to comprehend the simultaneous effect of planned activity in other fields causes many system failures.

Work of Level III complexity can create high-efficiency productive systems or optimise existing systems through the application, for example, of rigorous cost analysis, work method development and risk analysis. Level III complexity

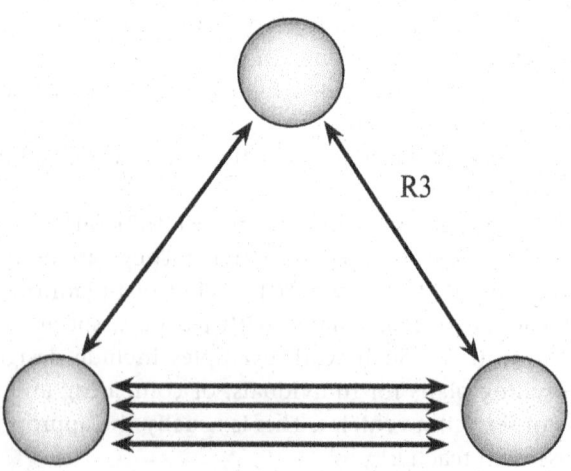

work is well suited for the leadership of a department of up to 300 people in a typical enterprise, recognising that geographic spread, technology variation and work type all have a bearing on the number of people and resources being managed. It is also well suited for highly specialised stand-alone roles requiring great depth of knowledge in a particular discipline.

Here the triangle is completed. The person here is able to consider the difference between a special cause or one-off and a systemic cause. That is, the system itself is at fault or needs improving. This level is suited to lean manufacturing, analysis and interpretation of actual data, benchmarking and comparison. However, it does not go into the abstract world of imagining what is not there or does not currently exist. It is the world of best practice or, rather, common practice and is the bread and butter of many large management consultancies.

The work of a principal of a small school or head of department of a large school could well be appropriate to Level III.

# Level IV: Complexity IV (R4)

---

**Box 3.4    Level IV: Integration**

Integrating and managing the interactions between a number of systems.

---

At Level IV there is a need to imagine and construct relationships between systems that are working in parallel and simultaneously. This demands a quality of thinking that crosses and integrates a number of fields or disciplines (if this and that, then the other) in order to see the risks, benefits, costs and potential delays. A key feature is that this integration may well involve a sacrifice in the effectiveness or efficiency, or both, of the functioning of one or more of the systems or processes so that the work is more productive. The language is often of trade-offs and conflicts. Thus, being able to identify and predict conflicts means that some or all of the systems can be modified or adapted. Alternatives are seen as both/and rather than either/or.

This is often referred to as the first strategic level, where an organisation's policies have to be understood, articulated, expressed and promoted in the design and operation of an integrated set of systems. However, things may not be as they appear. Production rates may be up but the facility may still be in trouble. Negative information is significant and made use of. Design and monitoring of a range of systems at this level has to be done without being able to observe the entire physical area of work.

Level IV is also the first level where resources must be sacrificed in order to achieve priority objectives. In business this is typically money or time. In the

4

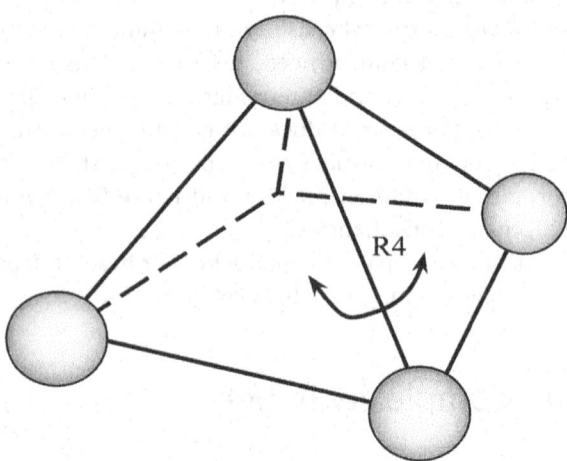

military it is far more difficult, as a commanding officer must send men and women into a situation where they are likely to be killed in order that the overall battle may be won. Officers who have been in this situation have described the incredible pain of doing so. (At Level III, leaders will try to save lives and resources even when this leads to a poorer overall outcome.)

Imagine now a pyramid. The R4 complexity means that the person must imagine how one system impacts or might impact on another from a different field. A person may be imagining what the social implications are of a technical change. This is the first real level of systems design since most organisations have systems interacting with each other. We might think of this as system design that appreciates and allows for the effect of first-order consequences. This may well be appropriate for the work of a principal of a large school or college.

## Level V: Complexity V (R5)

**Box 3.5    Level V: Whole system**

Shaping and managing an organisation within its environment – maintaining the organisation's systems and processes so that it is self-sustaining within that environment.

# 5

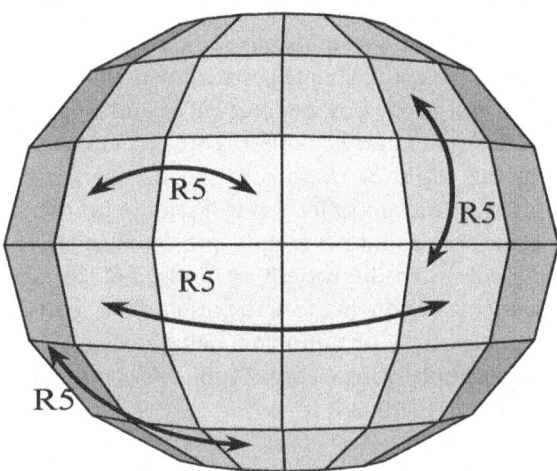

At this level, entire theories and not just principles are used to link multiple knowledge fields or disciplines. As a result of understanding and predicting the environment, the organisation is modified to address and minimise any potential negative impact (social, political or economic) from the environment; for example, by deciding what work the organisation should be doing in five years' time. This complexity of work also includes managing the effects that a change of direction will have by redesigning the systems of the organisation and the capability it has to meet the new conditions, while ensuring the organisation is still achieving its purpose. An organisation will not only be able to construct the relationships between systems, but the second- and third-order consequences of those relationships will also be foreseen. This includes understanding what impacts changes in one part have on another part of the organisation. Management by example and the use of symbols are crucial tools.

Work at this level is associated with boundary conditions and the interactions between the environment and the entity/entire organisation. The objective of leadership at this level is to have the organisation maintain a productive contact with its environment – economic, social, cultural, technical, legislative, natural – as this boundary changes. In this instance the entity is not a physical location like a school but an abstract entity like an education service or perhaps a multi-academy trust.

The work will involve complex organisational projects such as major information management systems and new technological or people systems. The data on which the work is based is both abstract and concrete, observable and unobservable, with a need to recognise remote, second- or third-order consequences and multiple linkages between cause and effect. Negative information, the absence or non-availability of specific data – that is, what is not there – becomes much more important and is used extensively.

At Level V the pyramids have formed a sphere with all the apexes at the centre. We have a complete system. At this level the work involves understanding and predicting consequences and impacts of change in any one part of the system on *any* other. Thus, R5 encompasses the system. We are now in the world of second-order consequences. It is interesting to hear how often politicians or leaders will refer to unintended consequences. They may claim "we could never have predicted this". They dismiss criticism by saying "only with the benefit of hindsight". In fact, our view is that such unintended consequences are the result of poor analysis, over-simplification of a Complexity IV or V problem being reduced to Complexity III or below, a classic example being George W. Bush's comment "Mission accomplished" regarding Iraq in 2003.

# Level VI: Complexity VI (R6)

---

**Box 3.6    Level VI: Shaping the future**

Shaping the organisation of the future – creating the ethic on a national and international basis that allows entities to function and manages the relationships between entities of a significantly different character.

---

The work at this level demands direct appreciation of and interaction with the external social, political, technical and economic environments in order to influence and mitigate any possible negative impacts on the organisation/businesses or promote changes that will be to its advantage. Essential to this is constructing an overall framework in which the relationships between fundamentally different types of organisations can be understood and managed. This may involve managing the relationships between two organisations built on very different organisational assumptions, principles and purposes, such as the relationships between a commercial company and government or a mining company and an Indigenous community. It also involves the ability to form relationships by understanding sometimes very different perspectives and how they might be addressed productively. Managing this framework of relationships enables you to construct policies that influence and, if done well, enhance the organisation's reputation, often internationally. Level VI requires the ability to build mutually beneficial relationships between people from organisations with possible competing purposes. It requires the ability to construct mental models that are entirely new. It often is characterised by the ability not only to handle but to live with, even enjoy, paradox.

Compliance with the legal framework is insufficient at this level; ethical frameworks for behaviour need to be created through the development and application of policies and systems, which will make the organisation acceptable within its environment over the long term. Such actions may well be seen as an unnecessary burden in the present. The organisation does not simply comply with local laws, such as those involving child labour or safety but sets its own (higher) standards. Long-term goals are set and policies and corporate systems are shaped and audited to achieve them. If this work is not done well, organisations are constantly exposed to unexpected, major, destabilising problems, which distract attention and drain energy from the business. If done well, this work will add significant national and international value to a brand or reputation over time.

The work at this level is often seen as political and involves building constructive external relationships with relevant leaders and opinion-formers. Within the organisation, leadership will be demonstrated primarily by symbolism and observable example.

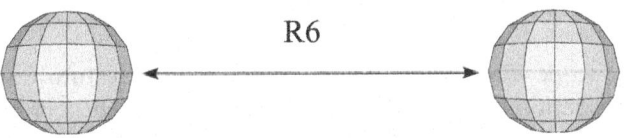

R6 looks very much like R1. However, instead of the poles being a person and their work, the poles at Level VI are made up of Level V entities.

We also describe levels work of higher complexity; they are described elsewhere (2nd edition) as the levels described so far cover the work we have examined in our writing of this book.

If businesses, government agencies and non-profit organisations are to meet their goals and survive, they must have people within their organisations who can work at the levels required to achieve their goals in their respective environments. The quality of work carried out at all levels of the organisation will determine the quality of results obtained. Thus, as human beings we should delight in all levels of work. We all have something to contribute to the whole.

In the previous chapter we discussed the domains of work: Social, Technical and Commercial.

Here we explore another categorisation of work that can apply in all domains: Operation/Service/Improvement.

# Operation work

This is all the activity that delivers the core work of the organisation and directly relates to its purpose. In education, particularly in schools, this is the work of teaching. It involves the delivery of the curriculum and everything that relates to the core work of the school in achieving its purpose.

# Service work

Of course, that work cannot go on unless there are services provided. Teachers need to be paid, school buildings need to be maintained, grounds need to be kept, suppliers and need to be paid and the organisation needs administrative services in order to function.

These two elements of Operation and Service work are fairly obvious and if this work is not done it becomes obvious very quickly. If the staff providing this work are absent the impact is immediate and it needs to be addressed. Children need a teacher in the classroom, and the receptionist or administrative assistant will be missed very quickly.

# Improvement work

This work while less obvious is critical for the future well-being of the organisation. This is the work that analyses the current situation and suggests improvements. This may include improvements in the design and implementation of systems. This work requires reflection, analysis and the ability to make proposals. Organisations, like schools, that are under time and cost pressure can often sacrifice this work because it is not immediately obvious when it is not done, or when it is not done properly. However, as we know, the context changes, demands change, and unless there are ongoing improvements to the structure and systems the organisation will inevitably drift into inefficiency and decline. Finding the time or, rather, making time for this sort of work is difficult. We recommend that it is clearly built in to the work of the role. Where possible it is useful to actually have full-time or almost full-time roles in an organisation dedicated to this work. One common mistake is to build this work into key operational roles. It is very difficult for someone in a critical leadership role with significant numbers of people in direct reporting roles to make the time to do this work properly, even if they are capable of such work. As the saying goes, "The urgent is likely to drive out the important." Thus, in organisations that are time-poor, this Improvement work is neglected, and inefficient systems continue to run which in turn drive unproductive behaviours and take up more time. This vicious circle adds to the pressure and stress increases while well-being decreases.

In the most successful applications of Systems Leadership work this Improvement work has been done, especially with regard to the design or redesign of systems, and this investment of time has been repaid not only in terms of improvements in efficiency and well-being but more importantly in the improvement of student outcomes.

However, it does take courage and capability to do this work. Firefighting and dealing with crises and emergencies can seem a lot more obvious and spectacular than the sometimes less glamorous work of improving the way the school is set up and run. Also, not everyone is actually capable of doing this work effectively, as we will discuss below.

## Conclusion

Work is different in kind. Some tasks are qualitatively more complex than others. If we understand these differences we can design roles more effectively, describe the work more clearly and put the right people into those roles. Furthermore, we can distinguish between the demands of Operation work and Service work and deliberately make room for the Improvement (or support) work that is necessary to keep the systems and structures up to date and relevant.

# 4 Our capability to work and the consequences of a poor match

## Role and person

Under normal conditions, all work roles have minimum mental processing requirements, if the work of the role is to be performed successfully. However, individuals who fill those roles may or may not have an ability to match those minimum requirements. There are people in roles with requirements that exceed their mental processing abilities; others are in roles that require less than their full mental processing abilities. Significant research has been done in this area (see, for example, Csikezentmihalyi's work on "flow"; 1997).

## Elements of individual capability

We have explained that all organisations require work to be done. That work differs in kind: from designing a new product, to developing a long-term plan, to stacking shelves, teaching children or maintaining equipment. Some of this work requires significant leadership work with people; other work requires more technical knowledge and skill. It is fairly obvious that not everyone can carry out all of the tasks equally successfully. This is not just a question of volume of work but the nature of the work itself. People's skills and ability differ. A positive organisation is one where each person's skills and ability match the work they are required to do. In order to consider assigning work appropriately so this matching can be achieved, it is necessary to have a concept of human capability.

We have found it remarkable that many organisations do not have a shared concept of human capability. They will talk of experience, education, training, interpersonal skills and competencies, but do not have an overall, coherent articulation of capability. There may not be agreement about what elements of capability can be influenced or learned, and how this might be done, apart from having people attend training courses. One hears comments to the effect that "so-and-so is quite bright", but there is often no real consideration of what this might mean in terms of observable behaviour at work.

Unless we have a view that every person can perform any nominated work if they have the interest and training to do so, we do need an understanding of human capability, how it may vary from person to person and how it may, and may not, be changed. In this chapter we will explain our concept of human capability and then raise some questions of comparison and why we have not incorporated some of the more popular concepts of human capability.

When selecting a person for a role or considering a person for a particular project or task, the following elements are critical. We will define and discuss each in turn. All of these elements should be examined when making the selection, although some are more open to influence than others (see Box 4.1). The object is to identify the attributes an individual needs to bring to the task so he or she is able to perform it effectively and efficiently. Each of these is then defined.

---

**Box 4.1    Elements of individual capability**

- Knowledge
- Technical skills
- Social process skills
- Mental processing ability
- Application – desire, energy and drive applied to work.

---

## KNOWLEDGE

Knowledge here consists of two categories: the first comprises knowing part (or all) of an accepted body of knowledge, and the second is knowledge that has been self-generated, often described as "experience".

Knowing all or part of a body of knowledge is what we refer to as scientific meaning. It is concerned with knowledge of currently-agreed-upon definitions, theories or facts; for example, nuclear physics, the periodic table, algebra, calculus and/or other scientific disciplines. In the arts there are also bodies of knowledge covering facts: Who wrote *Great Expectations* and who are the main characters? And knowledge about opinions: Do you know Christopher Hill's analysis of the English Civil War? Essentially this element is about what we learn in schools, colleges and universities and from our own research. Employers and educationalists may differ as to what is important to learn but it is about learning subjects from an established curriculum. We make assumptions about the knowledge an individual has in specific disciplines from the shorthand of qualifications, even though there are debates about the value of degrees from certain universities or institutions.

Another type of knowledge is self-generated – heuristics. Thus, a person may have knowledge gained as a result of their experience of people with mental illness, living in a large family or travelling internationally. The point about this self-generated knowledge is that it may not be organised into disciplines or accepted structures. It is more difficult to test but can be elicited by careful questioning and listening.

All roles and all tasks require some prior knowledge and it is important to be clear about what is required and to what extent the person being considered for the work has such knowledge.

## TECHNICAL SKILLS

> This element refers to a proficiency in the use of knowledge. It includes learned routines that reduce the complexity of work required to complete a task.

It has been recognised that having a skill makes a task easier. It essentially reduces the complexity of a task because you do not have to think through or work out the process to carry out the work. This emphasises the difference between knowledge and skill. I may have a significant amount of knowledge about the internal combustion engine, but can I change a piston? I may know all the letters on a keyboard, but can I type?

The need for skill and the difference between knowledge and skill is most apparent when we learn a new skill: driving, playing tennis, skiing or touch-typing. At first it is very difficult to steer, change gear and keep an eye on the road at the same time. Gradually the processes become less conscious until it is internalised and second nature. This allows us to concentrate on what is really important. In the case of driving, not having to think about steering, braking or changing gear allows us to concentrate on the road, other traffic and pedestrians. This is most apparent when we suddenly have to consciously re-engage with the process because of an unexpected event such as a sudden flat tyre or cracked windscreen.

In effect, technical skills once acquired do not require much cortical brain activity. This effectively allows more room for the cortical activity to be applied to real and current problem solving (see "Mental processing ability" below). The more pressing the immediate problem, the more important the embedding of the skill. A fire fighter does not want to be working out how breathing apparatus works while in a burning building. A combat soldier does not want to try and remember how to load a rifle in the middle of a battle.

We recognise that certain skills appear to be learned or acquired more easily by some people than others. We recognise that some people have what is usually referred to as a natural aptitude. Others appear to have no aptitude at all: they are all fingers and thumbs or, more technically, they suffer from dyspraxia. We do not intend to discuss this in depth here as our experience is that technical skills in organisations can be taught to most people if they are sufficiently interested.

Whatever the work, as we have said about knowledge, it is critical to identify what skills are required and make an assessment as to whether and to what extent a person has, or could quickly acquire, the skills required to perform the work successfully.

## SOCIAL PROCESS SKILLS

Work is an activity with a essential social element. Our survival requires social cohesion. Values are embedded deeply in the process of all human relationships. Recognition of the central significance of social process is evident throughout this book. Understanding and managing social process is critical (see Box 4.2).

---

**Box 4.2   Definition of *social process skills***

Social process skills are those skills that give the ability to observe social behaviour, comprehend the embedded social information and respond in a way that influences subsequent behaviour productively.

---

This element is at the heart of leadership. Too often in organisations we have seen leadership roles given to people who are very technically skilled and/ or intellectually very able but who have poor social process skills. The result is usually damaging, if not disastrous, and at times tragic if the person involved is lost as to why he or she is failing as a leader. Poor leadership also damages the people subject to it.

By *social process skills* we do not mean the ability to be nice or get on with people. Social process skill is required for handling confrontations, disciplinary issues or poor performance. In many voluntary organisations people equate good relations and social process with being friendly or not upsetting people, whereas we are referring to the ability to get work done. This misunderstanding is evident in education, where difficult conversations may be avoided and poor performance denied. It is interesting that teachers know the importance of taking on difficult behaviour with children but the leadership in schools may avoid confronting such behaviours by staff members.

As discussed throughout this book, relationships with people are not soft science. This area can be highly complex and sensitive. Brute force, oppression or intimidation will fail over time and it will not release capability. If we are not to objectify people, we must understand how they see the world. We must understand their mythologies and how they view themselves, each other and us. In addition, we must work out ways of influencing relationships so that they are directed to a productive purpose, not simply to building the harmony of the group. In short, if we put too much emphasis on output and thereby ignore social process, that output will not be sustained over time. If we put too much emphasis on social processes designed to generate person-to-person harmony, we will degrade our ability to achieve the output required.

This highlights a fundamental difference between work relationships and friendships. Work relationships exist to produce goods or services that are valued by others. Friendships exist for the sake of the relationship. A friendship does not have to be productive or even particularly valued by others outside the friendship. Friends can just be with one other. Confusing these different types of relationship will lead to problems. It is not necessary for people at work to be friends as long as they behave towards each other positively according to the values continua (see the next chapter). It is not necessary for friends to engage in highly productive work. This does not mean that work colleagues cannot be friends, or that friends cannot be actively engaged in making or doing things, merely that the social processes are different. You may have experience of, or know of, friends who have embarked on a business venture or turned a hobby into a business who have become disillusioned. You may have experience of, or know of, colleagues who believe they have been let down by people at work: "I thought you were my friend – why did you apply for that job?"

The authors have long been wary of companies that promote a lot of social events, bonding, inviting spouses and partners to events and talking about work being like a family. It is not that these are inherently bad, but they can cause confusion and cynicism when the invitation is really a requirement and the social, bonding event is really a covert assessment centre. Also, families are not always harmonious or constructive!

In this book, by *social process* we are referring to a person's ability to establish good, productive working relationships both directly and indirectly through teamwork and delegation. It requires an interest in and genuine regard for people, an appreciation of people not as production units but as creative and curious individuals who have their own unique way of seeing and being in the world.

This element, that for many years we have termed "social process skills", has some similarities with the more recent term "emotional intelligence" (Goleman 1996). While we have detailed differences and concerns with that concept, we do agree that this element has been underestimated by many organisations as an essential part of successful working relationships.

## MENTAL PROCESSING ABILITY

Perhaps the least familiar of the elements that make up our formulation of human capability is mental processing ability (often referred to as MPA). We begin with Elliott Jaques' definition of cognitive processes: "the mental processes by which a person takes information; picks it over; plays with it; analyses it; puts it together; reorganises it; judges and reasons with it; and makes conclusions, plans and decisions, and takes action" (1989: 33). These mental processes are the way an individual organises his or her thinking when working (attempting to turn intention into reality).

The richness and diversity of the world that each person creates is indicative of the complexity of the mental process that a person can apply to make sense out of their experience of the world. Because our environment is constantly changing, this effort to make sense of it is a continuous process. It requires constant work – turning intention into reality.

From our own experience we know that people are more able or less able to comprehend the information available to them in a given situation and its relevance to the work at hand, and to formulate cause-and-effect relationships between events they experience in the world. People show differences in their ability to generate and test hypotheses about relationships and to predict the outcome of a course of action. All of us have differing abilities to do work.

Each of us perceives the world in our own way. Some people will see the world as it presents itself in front of them; they are most comfortable with what they can directly see and even touch. They like direct links between the action they take and the result they get. Their solution will deal with what is immediately present. Other people will see that the results they want cannot be achieved directly, and that many different systems and outside influences will have to be changed if there is to be a successful outcome. The difference is in the way different individuals take in and organise information, how broadly they see the interrelationships of what is going on, and how much they can encompass in their formulation of their world.

For example, there is a vehicle with a broken gearbox. To one person that is the problem and it can be fixed today. Another person realises that while the damaged gearbox can be replaced today and the vehicle put back in action, he or she appreciates that driver behaviour may have been part of the cause and considers how it might be rectified. A third mechanic considers that the original design of the gearbox could have a part to play and thinks through how this might be corrected. Finally, a fourth person might question the use of vehicles for this type of transport and proposes an alternative. All of these views are valid and helpful. We need to ask: What is the work required by whom?

We argue that these different ways of seeing the world are divided into distinct groupings, rather than MPA being seen as a gradual, continuous line along which the whole population is spread. People have different types of MPA that are directly related to the levels of work discussed previously in Chapter 3. Each approach to the world and problem solving is discrete, so someone with Type II MPA will see a problem and its potential solutions in a completely different way from someone with Type IV MPA. The person with Type II MPA will simply not see the problem with the same range of variables, relationships and consequences. These differing approaches are neither right nor wrong, but their appropriateness depends upon the context and the inherent complexity of the particular task to be accomplished.

## APPLICATION

> **Box 4.3     Definition of *application***
>
> Application: the effort and energy that a person puts into applying the other elements of capability to their work.

People may be very able in terms of mental processing, and very skilled in managing social processes. They may have great general knowledge and technical skill, but unless they actually apply it in the workplace it is of only latent value. Practising managers value this attribute of application for its obvious practical relevance.

When one of the authors (Ian Macdonald) worked for the British Civil Service Selection Board, this element was divided into "drive" and "determination". Kolbe (1991) refers to it as "conation", a term we like, which is defined as the desire to perform an action. Essentially this is the element that affects not whether a problem can be solved (by someone) but whether it will be solved. A person with high application has the drive to see a task through to completion, providing they have the MPA and skills to resolve the inherent complexity of the task.

# So why not include experience, competencies or personality/temperament?

Many models of capability include experience as an element; we do not. Rather, we incorporate what is usually meant by experience in our concepts of knowledge (especially self-generated knowledge) and technical and social process skills. We deliberately do not use it as a separate element because we have found it often leads to a trap. This trap is to ask for experience which translates to years or time doing something, rather than what has been learned from doing it. For example, "Oh good, she has three years' experience in teaching in remote schools." But what has she actually learned?

Concentrating on knowledge leads to specific questions directed towards the extent and specific content of the experience.

We do not use the extremely popular term "competency". This is for two reasons. First, at a more general level, "competency" is not sufficiently specific. Competency fits well when unpacking other elements. For example, in technical skills, we need to ask in what process should a person be competent for this role? We regard competencies as related more to specific skills in the technical, commercial and social areas. The second reason for avoiding "competency" is that it is poor at discriminating different levels of work and complexity. For example, is a person competent in terms of leadership? Does this mean at any level of work?

With regard to personality or temperament, we see this as a possible negative distraction. We argue that the work of a role can be filled and successfully achieved by people with very different personalities. Only at the extremes, virtual mental illness or psychopathy, does personality have a significant bearing. We can fall into traps of assuming that sales people should be extroverts, and that leaders should be charismatic.

We have seen Myers–Briggs type indicators used creatively to better understand team dynamics and individual differences in working style, but we are very wary of associating any specific personality type with a role type.

# Nature or nurture

When discussing any human attribute, there is usually a debate about what is inherited, constitutional, innate, learned, acquired and so on. Many people have devoted a great deal of time and effort to such questions over millennia, and they cannot be resolved here in a few paragraphs. When it comes to the issue of leadership of an organisation, providing the opportunity for people to improve their capability requires us to address the nature/nurture debate because it is important to determine where it is worth expending the resources.

## MENTAL PROCESSING ABILITY

Despite these caveats, we cannot ignore the reality of the differences between people as demonstrated in their performance of work, especially with regard to MPA. We see the way in which a person makes sense of the world (making order of the complexity of the chaos) as essentially fixed by the time a person reaches early adulthood. We have not seen successful examples of adults learning entirely new mental processes and being able to solve original problems of a type that previously they were unable to resolve. We accept absolutely that people can learn techniques and methods that enhance their current abilities or help realise potential. In other words, their capability to carry out work through time can increase, while their MPA remains constant.

## TECHNICAL SKILLS

We have seen plenty of evidence for the acquisition of skills, even late in life. While some people appear to have more aptitude than others (hand/eye coordination, for example, or balance or dexterity), most skills are teachable to the level of organisational requirement. Some aspects of very fine craftwork or sporting prowess may be more difficult to learn and are either due to aptitude or life-long learning. For the purposes of this book and the range of activities covered by most organisations, from our observation it is possible to teach the technical, mechanical and other skills required to work effectively to the great majority of people.

## SOCIAL PROCESS SKILLS

Again, we believe these can be taught. We do not subscribe to the simple "born leader" theory. It is inevitable that early experiences and opportunities can strongly affect this area. A person brought up and encouraged to engage in social processes is more likely to be adept and skilful than someone brought up either in a more isolated milieu or someone who has been encouraged to develop relationships with objects rather than people.

It is interesting to note here the general, but not exclusive, nature of socialisation for boys and girls. While this has been changing in recent decades, girls are still more often encouraged to engage in social process (talking, discussing, analysing relationships) and playing social games (including dolls rather than soldiers). Boys are likely to be socialised into interest in mechanics or technical or electronic games.

The analogy for social process would be more like learning a language. If it happens early in life, it is easy and natural and the facility is both acquired and used with apparently little effort. Learning a language later in life is not only physically more difficult; it requires more determination, effort and desire. It is not, however, impossible. It can also be likened to musical ability. Some people have an "ear" for music. They can hear a piece of music and then just play it on an instrument. Such people are rare, as indeed are people who are truly, totally tone deaf. Most of us fall somewhere in-between. We do have musical ability and it can be enhanced by training and practice.

## KNOWLEDGE

Clearly, knowledge can be more readily and easily acquired than skills and can be expanded throughout life. It is, by definition, learned. Even self-generated knowledge acquisition continues. People, however apparently fixed in their ways, will not be able to prevent learning even if it is uncomfortable. However, the rate of learning and hence the amount that can be learned will vary and will also vary from person to person. This rate of learning, or building the knowledge base, will depend to an extent upon the knowledge already held about a subject and the interest and attention paid during the opportunity to learn. However, one very important determinant of learning rate that is often not appreciated is a person's MPA. A person who can order high levels of complexity, construe and understand complex patterns and derive the relationships that exist between the variables in play will build and acquire knowledge at a faster rate than another person who is unable to do this but may be presented with the same opportunity to learn. This ability to build knowledge rapidly from the experience of the chaos is sometimes described as learning from first principles.

Thus, while we all continue to acquire knowledge, the rate at which we do so, its inherent intricacy and our subsequent use of it to perform work are dependent upon our MPA.

## APPLICATION

In accord with Kolbe's concept of conation, we recognise that some people appear to have more energy, drive and determination than others. Whether this is innate or strongly influenced by early experience, we do not know. What we do know is that application in the workplace is very strongly influenced by the context. This includes, in order of influence:

- The quality (that is, behaviour) of the person's immediate leader, including how well, or poorly, the leader clarifies expectations and gives feedback
- The structure and systems of the organisation: Is the work of the role clear? Does it have proper authority? Are the work systems helpful in achieving goals or are they layered in red tape? Are the resources necessary for the work readily available?
- The general quality of relationships; this includes other leaders, the manager-once- removed and work colleagues
- Symbols: the quality of the equipment, plant, housekeeping and the attention to safe practice

So, while some people do give up before others, and few of us have the drive and determination of the explorer Ernest Shackleton, for example, this element, for most people, is strongly influenced by their environment. In Gallup and other work surveys there is a consistent message that the main reason for people leaving an organisation (for negative reasons) is poor leadership in the form of the person's immediate manager.

One of the authors (Macdonald 1990; Macdonald and Couchman 1980) observed and documented significant changes in behaviour, especially in "application", when the context changed for people with learning difficulties.

## Consequences of our capability model

We have seen many instances of people developing their overall capability. Teachers have learned how to be better leaders by improving their social process skills. We have seen people acquire more knowledge and technical skills. Professional development can contribute to improvements in all these areas. However, we have not seen people learn how to acquire higher levels of MPA. It is a fairly common aspiration that people should use their capability to the full. In doing so, people experience high levels of work satisfaction and engagement. Csikszentmihalyi's discussion of being "in flow" connects well with the concept of well-being.

However, if we understand the nature of MPA we can see that people can be promoted or appointed into positions where the work is beyond their MPA. This situation usually has one of two outcomes. First, the person may reduce the complexity of the work and simply engage in work that they are capable of. The higher-level work that is essential to the work of the role is simply not done. So, for example, a principal of a school may not be capable of carrying out work of Type III complexity. This will mean that all problems are seen and treated as individual cases and the underlying systemic causes are either not understood or addressed. The systems design or redesign work is not done, or is done very poorly. If the person does not have the MPA to do this work, no amount of training or support will rectify the situation.

The other outcome associated with the lack of MPA is where the person does actually recognise that the work is not being done and experiences severe stress, works ever harder and puts in more hours but continues to fail to achieve the intended work of the role.

This results in an enormous cost not only to the individuals concerned but also to the school and educational system as a whole.

## Caveats

While we can describe and discuss capability, this is not very useful unless the work has been clarified. We always start with the work that is required to achieve the purpose of the organisation. The alternative is to reshape and redesign roles to fit the individual. In time, the work of the organisation is determined by the needs and abilities of the staff, not the work. This may be an expedient response but leads to failure to achieve the purpose, and high cost to individuals and the organisation as a whole.

# 5 *What do we mean by "culture"? The universal values model*

In earlier chapters we mentioned how, within the Social Domain, there are not shared definitions of commonly used terms. A classic example of this is the term "culture". We often hear that there is "a problem with the school's culture", or "the culture needs changing" or it is "a cultural problem", or that "we need to build a better culture". However, what exactly is meant in each case is not always clear and certainly there is not always a shared view of what needs to be done. As is often the case, we stay in the general and find it too difficult to be specific. Again as mentioned earlier we do not even have a shared definition of what we mean by (human) work.

Systems Leadership defines work as "turning intention into reality". It is always easier to state an intention than the much more difficult task of creating the reality. Creating the reality requires a clear understanding of what needs to be achieved and a clear idea of the processes and systems required to achieve it. This is exactly what professional knowledge is intended to do: help us turn an intention, such as educating a child, into a reality. A profession – for example, teaching – sets out a goal and articulates the way or ways to achieve that goal. Professional knowledge explains that particular methods, processes and systems are the means to achieve particular outcomes. This is true in medicine, psychology, teaching, nursing, architecture, engineering and all the major professions. The articulation of a body of knowledge based on shared definitions has taken us from the world of magic and mystery to one where we can test our approaches and improve our practices. Some of course like the world of mystery and magic; it sounds more poetic and romantic, but actually it is maintained because therein lies power. As long as the "secrets of success" are kept exactly as secrets, power can remain with the few, and perhaps more importantly such "secrets and mysteries" are not amenable to argument or testing. The "profession" remains in the hands of an exclusive elite.

The alternative to this mystical elitism is not a purely dull, rational, bureaucratic or rigid world. It is rather a world where people are challenged to think up new ways of doing things, be truly creative and have the courage to put those ideas to the test.

So, in order to be effective, we do need some clear definitions including what we mean by "culture". For some people "culture" refers to ethnicity or nationality or food or the arts. When we talk about an organisational culture we are usually referring to acceptable or unacceptable behaviour.

But how do such cultures come into being? How do rules or norms become accepted or rejected? Unless we understand how to answer these questions it is difficult to create the culture that we might want to build. The culture of a school should not be a mystery or magic, or we are putting the education of our children at risk.

At the core of culture is behaviour, and behaviour that creates or destroys social cohesion. In this chapter we will look at some key concepts and tools that help to explain the nature of culture. In the next chapter we will look at the tools of leadership that help to create a culture.

While behaviour is an essential part of culture, our proposition is that human culture is based upon values. We have probably all heard people explaining other people's behaviour with the phrase, "Well, they have different values." Such a statement drives social differentiation and creates a world of "them and us". It is divisive and immediately implies one set of values is better than another . . . which of course is always *our* set of values!

The authors and Systems Leadership propose a fundamentally different view and one that is quite radical as it starts with a proposition that "all people and all social groups actually share the same set of universal values". This is true whether we are talking about families; social communities; organisations, including schools; and any group where people must come together in order to achieve a purpose. If we think about our history as a species, then it is quite difficult to understand how we have survived at all. After all, from the earliest times we have been surrounded by creatures that are faster, stronger and bigger than us. We suggest that our survival is due to our ability to form socially cohesive groups that could work together to achieve a mutually beneficial purpose. In simple terms we as human beings can out-organise the competition. Our social cohesion is the key; we are at heart social beings who need each other to survive and achieve anything.

Our proposition is that if we are to form socially cohesive groups then we must behave towards each other in ways that demonstrate to our potential group members that we are trustworthy, honest, fair, courageous, loving and respectful. If we demonstrate behaviour that indicates that we are untrustworthy, dishonest, unfair, cowardly, unloving or disrespectful we will destroy the social cohesion of the group. In fact, demonstrating behaviour that is negative regarding any one of those values will threaten social cohesion and our

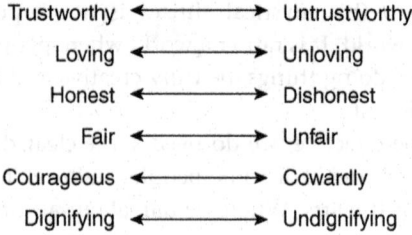

**Figure 5.1**     Values continua

continued membership of the group. (For a fuller explanation of the origin of this model, please see Macdonald, Burke and Stewart 2018).

The values listed in Figure 5.1 are not a matter of choice, they are not company values, they are not school values, but they are a set by which we all judge behaviour all the time, whether we are aware of that or not. When one of the authors (Macdonald) presented the values continua as part of a presentation to an organisation in Oman he was thanked for including "Islamic values" in the presentation! The same author also presented it to a First Nations Community in Ontario, Canada; they asked him how he had found out about their "grandfather principles" that had been handed down orally from the earliest times! They resonate with people, and helped establish relationships in our work in Queensland and especially the Torres Straits, where people said it was compatible and complementary to their YUMI culture (see in detail the Tagai case study in Chapter 16).

Although we argue that all human groups share the same set of universal values, this does not mean that we all interpret behaviour in the same way. Let us consider some behaviour that might be seen differently through different lenses. In all the schools that the authors attended in their childhood, corporal (although thankfully not capital) punishment was an accepted part of school life. Parents did not usually complain about the existence of corporal punishment, but merely whether the behaviour of the child was sufficient to justify it. This is certainly now no longer acceptable in schools in most if not all Western countries. One recent example from a UK school highlighted the difference when a parent (from another country) admitted to a teacher that he beat his children at home with a cane. He found it difficult to understand that not only was this not acceptable in the school but was not acceptable at home either. After all, he said, that was how he was brought up.

We could consider a range of moral questions around behaviour; questions as to whether it is ever loving to smack a child, whether it is ever courageous to walk away from an insult, whether it is fair to give one child a reward and not another, whether it is ever respectful to ignore somebody, whether it is ever justified to tell a lie, or what behaviour would undermine other people's trust in us. Different people have different views about the specific behaviour that demonstrates positive or negative values.

Some would quite definitely say that it is courageous to walk away from an insult, while others might see this as an act of cowardice.

So, while we share the same values we do not always share the same opinions as to what behaviour demonstrates those values.

This is no different in a school than in wider society. So where do these different views about the behaviour come from? They are essentially heuristic; that is, we gradually absorb them through our experiences as we grow up. We are not necessarily conscious of this process but we are watching and listening all the time. We learn from the moment we are born, from our families, from our friends, from school, from the media, from all sources that we come into contact with. Some lessons are taught directly, especially from parents and teachers, and some more implicitly from literature, media and general observation. This process effectively forms a lens through which we see the world, the lens through which we rate and judge behaviour whether we want to or not. We learn that certain groups of people are to be trusted and others not so. Think for a moment of the reputation of doctors, politicians, second-hand car sales people, lawyers, managers, real estate agents, indeed almost any social group you can think of. People will have their views as to where they stand on the values continua, or rather, more correctly, how they rate their assumed behaviour on the values continua.

These lenses are not fixed for all time; indeed, they are changing, if not constantly then gradually as we observe the world and have our views reinforced or challenged. Further, why we rate certain behaviour as positive or negative may be quite difficult to explain because these lenses have been implicitly formed heuristically over time. We are not conscious of this process most of the time and indeed if we were it would take all of our attention.

## Mythologies

Our views are formed through direct and indirect experience. They are summaries of our experience based on a blend of emotion and reason. As people we are neither wholly rational nor wholly emotional. Our views are formed through a combination of logic and feeling. We justify views on the basis of stories and explanations that are a mixture of both. The term in fairly common usage at the moment, "narrative", is similar to what we are calling "mythologies". Our mythologies are the ways and stories that we draw on to explain and justify our ratings of behaviour on the values continua. They are our beliefs and assumptions about what is acceptable and unacceptable and why that is the case. Understanding people's mythologies is critical to understanding behaviour in organisations. If you have had really poor experiences in school as a child, it may well have formed mythologies about teachers that are difficult to put aside even though times have changed. Clearly some mythologies are more deeply embedded than others and experiences that have caused strong feelings either negatively or positively may be very difficult to challenge. Although we use the term "mythology" we do not use it in the sense that such mythologies are untrue. The real meaning of a mythology is a story that is told as if it is true. It is a combination of *mythos* and *logos*, the emotion and reason explained above. The purpose of mythologies (and all classic stories) is to teach people, especially young people, what is acceptable and unacceptable behaviour and often what is heroic and admirable. The mythologies bind the culture.

In case we think mythologies are only in the past, think of the popular, classic stories of today, often told through film and literature. Think about *Harry Potter*, *The Lord of The Rings*, *Star Wars* and similar stories that have at their heart the struggle between good and evil and tell us clearly whose behaviour we should emulate and what is courageous or cowardly, fair or unfair, trustworthy or untrustworthy and so on.

## Culture

One thing that is certain is that when we meet people with whom we share mythologies, and therefore we rate behaviour the same way on the values continua, we are mightily attracted to such people. In our experience the attraction to people who share our mythological lens is generally stronger than other variables such as race, gender or ethnicity.

Thus, our definition of a culture is simply: A group of people who share mythologies.

A key characteristic of a culture is that the members feel safe and comfortable with each other and tend to reinforce each other's mythologies. Challenging mythologies is a dangerous practice since it threatens social cohesion. This is also true in virtual cultures, which are now very strong on social media where people continually relate to people with the same views or lens, constantly reinforcing each other's views and usually also denigrating views that are not consistent with their mythologies. For example, we can see that in political terms, not just in social media but in the divisions in society and political movements exemplified by the 2016 US Presidential election and the Brexit vote in the UK.

## Conclusion

The culture is both that which binds people together and the source of potential division and conflict when it becomes "them and us". In this chapter we have put forward a model and concepts that are intended to help think more clearly about what we mean by *culture* and *behaviour*. We have found these models help people to understand why people behave as they do. By using the values continua and by trying to understand mythologies we can begin to consider why someone thought it was "fair" or "loving" to do what they did. When we are at a loss to explain behaviour, we can fall back on to the simple explanations of "MBS", that is Mad, Bad or Stupid. These easy explanations allow us to dismiss the behaviour, whereas our approach is to genuinely try to understand why someone is behaving as they are. Without this deeper understanding we have little hope of influencing or changing that behaviour, and then our only recourse is power or physical force, approaches that have been somewhat overused in the world to date.

This chapter has explained the model. The next chapter looks at how this is put into practice.

# 6 *The tools of leadership: building a culture*

In the previous chapter we discussed culture, what it means and how cultures are formed. There is clearly a difference between describing a culture and deliberately building one. Systems Leadership identifies that building culture is at the heart of the work of the leader. The situation in many schools where we have worked was that the desired culture had not been specifically articulated and many school leaders had little or no training in understanding organisational behaviour or organisational design. Of course there were many general statements about the "what", but far fewer about the "how". Further, there was no shared understanding of the definition of a culture and certainly no shared underlying model about how to create one. This was one of the main reasons why the regional director chose Systems Leadership as a model to help those in leadership roles better define what it was that they wanted and then how to create it. Again, as will be described later, staff in the region, including 113 principals and 217 other personnel, went through training in Systems Leadership (between 2010 and 2013) specifically to help them to design the structures and systems that would enable them to build their cultures.

For many years and in many organisations Systems Leadership has been used to help people create a socially cohesive productive culture (Macdonald, Burke and Stewart 2018). The purpose of the culture is to achieve the purpose of the organisation rather than building an organisation simply to sustain itself.

This chapter describes the tools of leadership needed to create that productive culture.

This model and the tools described within it have been used in many different countries and many different types of organisations across all sectors since the 1990s. While the core model remains the same and grounded in Systems Leadership, its application needs to be contextualised to the specific situation taking into account local conditions. The model and tools apply equally in the education sector as in other sectors. The principles are generic while the application is specific. The basic model is set out in Figure 6.1 and then explained in terms of how a principal/head teacher or indeed any leader might use it.

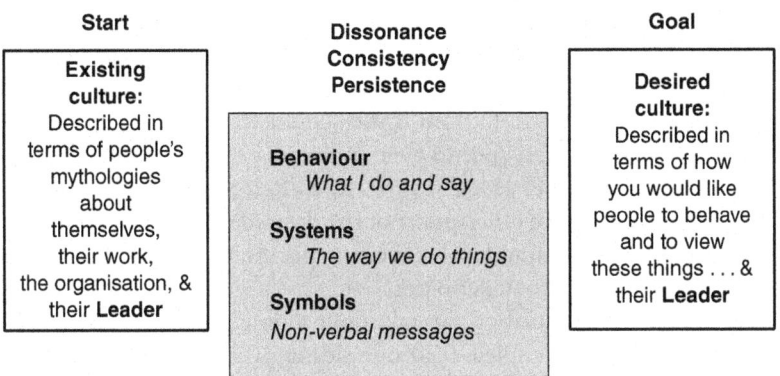

**Figure 6.1**    Tools of leadership

Essentially the model is based upon a gap analysis. That is, it describes where we would like to be, compares that with where we are now and then looks at how we can actually get there.

The way that we use this model with principals (or indeed any leader) is to first look at what we are trying to achieve; that is, our goal or the desired culture. Now, this might sound a little like a vision statement and indeed in some ways it is. However, it requires very specific descriptions of what we would actually see and what we would hear if the culture we desire was actually in place. It is both practical and realistic. So, if we take the example of a school, we would not want a general description such as "a place where people trust each other" or " a place where people are productive". We want a description of what that actually looks like. So the question we ask is a very practical one, such as: "If I were to visit your school and it was functioning as the desired culture, what would I actually see?" Let us start at the entrance: "Would it be clearly signposted?" "How would I be received at reception?" "What do the grounds look like?" "How are the students behaving?" "How are the teachers behaving?" "What does it sound like?" "Does this differ according to the time of day?" "How are the teachers teaching, how are the teachers supporting each other and interacting and how does the leadership behave towards the teachers, students and other staff?" We also need to look through the lens of other stakeholders; for example, parents, local community members, visitors and so on. The next questions we ask are, "What are the mythologies about the school and how are they expressed by different stakeholders?" "What do students say about the school, and how do they rate the behaviour of teachers and support staff on the values continua?" "How do parents rate the behaviour of students and staff?" Of course there are many other questions that could be asked but the characteristic is that they are direct and observable. As can be seen from this process, the resulting description of the desired culture is not the usual couple of paragraphs or even one page of a mission statement, but a detailed description of how all stakeholders would behave and the mythologies they would hold if the school was working to the desired culture. Of course we can go into even more detail and it is up to the school principal and his or her leadership team to determine the extent of that detail with regard to the description of the desired culture. The point is that any such description should not leave out specific behavioural components or any one of the major stakeholders.

This process of articulation can take quite a time and our experience is that it is not necessary to complete it in one sitting. It is better to make the draft statements and revisit them. All this needs to be done in the context of the articulation of the purpose of the school. Again this purpose statement should be made with the Systems Leadership discipline of being expressed in a single sentence including a measure, without the conjunction "and". Although this is quite a time-consuming process it tends to stimulate significant discussion and creativity and innovation as to what the desired culture ought to be. It is creative because of its detail. It does not take long for a leadership team to come up with only some general statements, such as: "We want a school where everyone works well together." It is much more difficult, but also much more useful, to describe what that actually looks like in practice and in behavioural terms. This is also necessary because if we only stay at the general level we might have as many different pictures in our heads as there are heads with regard to what that looks like.

Having described the desired culture in significant detail, this description can then be shared with other staff members and stakeholders, depending upon the discretion of the principal, for their input, comments or questions.

We can now move on to the second step, which is to consider how the current culture is actually operating and compare it to the desired culture. Now, in some areas the existing culture and the desired culture may be very close. We do not assume that the desired culture is always some ideal state far from where we are now. However, there certainly may be areas where the gap is quite considerable. It may be that these are the areas that need most work. Working with the leadership team, we can now build up a detailed picture and not just stay with general statements, however laudable they might be.

The third step brings in the three tools of leadership. They are the tools of behaviour, systems and symbols. (We will discuss the importance of all three in more detail in chapters 7 and 8).

## Behaviour

By this we literally mean the way that people behave in the school (or organisation). This includes the way people talk to each other or do not talk to each other, and the way that people support each other or do not support each other. We do not use general terms such as "collaboration" or "empowerment", as such terms can again mean different things to different people. What we want are actual examples of behaviour that would be described as collaborative, or descriptions of behaviour that could be described as empowering. Precisely because people are creative and innovative, until we share what we mean by these terms it is difficult to gain real agreement or alignment. Somebody might think they are collaborating while another might not agree. In one school the principal was criticised for not collaborating because she did not put her decisions to a vote of her leadership team. Some other team members thought that collaboration meant that they should go along with her decisions. Others thought that collaboration was concerned with the way that classroom teachers interacted and was not particularly aimed at the senior leadership team. A well-intentioned initiative had simply caused confusion.

## Systems

By this we do not just mean either IT systems or the large systems impacting on the whole school. We mean all of the systems and processes and procedures that operate in the school. We refer to all the ways that people are expected to carry out their work. This includes the organisational structure, which is a system of distributing authority; the pedagogy; the administrative systems; the disciplinary systems; school applications and enrolment; attendance; relationships with families and communities; indeed, all the "ways of doing things", both those that are documented and those that are generally understood through practice. Systems are supposed to enable and encourage effective working and the achievement of purpose. However, anyone who has worked in any organisation, including schools, knows that there are many systems that actually hinder productive work and make working life less enjoyable than it could be, as well as less productive. The impact of systems, in our view, is underestimated both positively and negatively, as is the complexity of work required to design productive systems. We will discuss this further in the next chapter. However, systems are one of the key components of the Social Domain. As we discussed earlier, having these organisational arrangements poorly designed and poorly functioning can have a huge impact on student outcomes and staff well-being as well as the school's reputation.

## Symbols

By this we mean all the non-verbal messages that are transmitted in an organisation. Schools have very significant symbols; for example, many if not all

schools have a badge, logo and uniform. These are very important in convey-
ing messages both within and outside the school as to the state of the school.
Think about the situation where school uniform standards are not particularly
monitored or upheld. What does it say if there is a massive variation in student
presentation? How does this look to people in school and the community?
We take note of how much pride there is in being a member of the school
and wearing the school badge. Think how symbolic housekeeping is when you
enter the school grounds. For example, what conclusions do you draw if the
playground or school grounds do or do not have litter on them?

In schools signage is often highly symbolic; for example, with regard to
who is allowed to go where. Is it easy to find your way around? Consider the
way that classrooms are arranged, what is on the walls, what is on displays,
what does the entrance in reception area look like, and so on. These are all
highly symbolic and send messages to all stakeholders as to the state of the
school at any time.

We are using this model to consider the current state of behaviour systems and symbols and consider whether the behaviour, systems and symbols
are encouraging and helping to build the desired culture, or are they indeed
undermining or contradicting the desired culture and leading it in a different
direction? Again, this is the core work of leadership; to consider all of these
issues and then to work out the plan of action based around systems, symbols and behaviour as to what needs to change and in what order. No two
schools will have exactly the same desired culture. Neither will any two schools
have the same action plan as to what systems, symbols and behaviour need to
change if the desired culture is to be created, but all schools can use these tools
and then build that desired culture.

You may also have noticed on the model three other words between
the existing culture and the desired culture. These are *consistency*, *persistence*
and *dissonance*. They are all also important in building the desired culture. If
changes are to be introduced – for example, a specific requirement to change
behaviour – then there needs to be a consistency in application. Variation in
application will not only cause confusion but also often encourage cynicism
and a lowering of trust in the leadership.

Similarly there needs to be persistence over time. Many teachers have
experienced changes in the form of so-called "initiatives" or "policies/
priorities" that do not last or have been superseded. Even where there is considerable enthusiasm to begin with, that enthusiasm peters out like a firework
and they are left to await the next display, again with increased cynicism or
simply weariness.

Finally, we use the term "dissonance" because in Systems Leadership we
argue that the dissonant experience is needed if change in behaviour is to occur.

It is a fundamental human need that we need to feel safe and to feel safe
we need a predictable environment. Basically we are very quick learners. It does

not take us long, when we first start working at school, to understand the rules, the norms and the mythologies that sustain the current culture. Such lessons are not all contained in the induction process. We learn them by observation, and from coaching and advice from helpful and sometimes not so helpful colleagues. We soon "learn the ropes" and build up certain expectations that help to shape mythologies about the school and the people in it. We come to expect both positive and negative behaviour; we encounter both positive and negative systems and symbols.

Taking a particular example, say that we have come not to expect any feedback from our head of department. Then it is a dissonant experience if that head of department starts to give us feedback. At first, we may just consider this as an exception, a one-off, and we will usually come up with some explanation, such as they are in an unusually good mood, or perhaps it is their birthday. However, if this behaviour persists we will have to revisit expectations and in the language of the previous chapter reformat our lenses and create new mythologies to explain the new situation.

We have noted that it usually takes three data points or experiences of something different to convince us that something has really changed. The first experience can be explained away as an exception, the second experience as a coincidence, but a third experience indicates to us that a systemic change has happened. This applies also in ordinary life. We can predict that if you take children somewhere three times in a row – for example, going to the cinema three Wednesdays in a row, having fish and chips three Fridays in a row or going swimming three Saturdays in a row – you can be sure that if anyone asks them after the third time what they do on certain days, they will say, "We always go to the cinema on Wednesdays, we always have fish and chips on Fridays and we always go swimming on Saturdays." This also works the other way round; if you do not do something three times in a row they will say, "We never go swimming on Saturday any more."

## Conclusion

In this chapter we have taken the specific definition of culture and described it as the leader's work to create a positive and productive culture. We have explained how it is important to be very specific about what it is we want to create, so that can be shared, discussed and worked on and there can be an alignment rather than a wide range of interpretations of what that desired culture actually looks like in practice. We have looked at how it is important to include all stakeholders in our considerations and then to examine the systems, symbols and behaviour likely to create a culture and identify the systems, symbols and behaviour currently creating barriers to building the desired culture. In doing this work we need to apply persistence and consistency and create dissonance if change is to occur. It is not easy work. It is easy to stay at the general level but that is one of the problems we see when people operate in the Social Domain. The Social Domain requires shared definitions, models, tools and discipline if productive cultures are going to be created and maintained. This is the work of leadership. Leadership is not just about supervising others but examining the complexities within working relationships and designing the organisation so as to build the culture that delivers the best education possible for the students.

# 7 *Systems and structure*

In the last chapter we looked at the tools of leadership and how they can be used to create a productive culture that achieves the purpose of the organisation. This chapter and the following one look in more depth at some of those tools.

One of the themes of this book is the importance of language. The way that we use words and the confusion that arises when we use the same word to mean different things can have a very detrimental effect, especially when we do not realise it is happening. As we have said, even terms such as "culture", "manager" or "leader" can mean different things to different people.

When we think about an organisation such as a school what do we actually mean by "organisation"? Clearly the use of the term "organisation" implies some sort of order, some sort of predictability and reliability, and that at its heart there is some purposeful activity that can be seen, experienced and reviewed. But how much order is appropriate? What is good organisation? We offered some simple questions earlier that indicate whether an organisation is working well or not – the three questions are: "What am I meant to be doing?" "How well am I doing?" "What is my future?" But what else helps us design a good organisation and what rules or principles should we use? In many professions – for example, medicine or engineering – there are well-established shared definitions of principles, theories and models that we can largely rely on and although they are constantly being updated there is a fundamental body of knowledge that is sound.

We are on shaky ground here with regard to theories and models of good organisations. Almost every one of us has our own idea as to what makes for a good organisation. We have naturally created our own mythologies about systems and structures that work and those that do not. Sometimes we are very attached to them.

We have opinions and views, not necessarily based on any accepted body of knowledge but rather based on our own experience or on what we have learnt from others. Systems Leadership has over many years endeavoured to create a body of knowledge, based on research and observed good practice, that helps people understand the principles that can be used in designing and in creating positive organisations that more effectively achieve the purpose.

While some think deeply about organisation, others might not think much about the organisation at all, especially if it is working quite well.

We do not particularly see it as a social construction but just somehow there. It is almost as if it has some sort of existence or reality that exists independent of us. We do tend to pay a lot more attention when things are not working very well, and when we see or experience wasted effort and resources that could be better used elsewhere. We may well have views about the quality of the leadership, and certainly the ways in which work is carried out and the sort of rules and regulations that operate and whether they are actually helpful in getting our work done.

# Structure

All schools have some sort of structure. Most of these structures can be represented in an organisational chart that shows people, or rather roles, with the various lines linking some roles to other roles. But there may be very different views as to the way that structure should be interpreted and what those lines and sometimes dotted lines actually mean. In our experience the guiding principles when creating a structure should include:

## CLEAR ROLE DESCRIPTIONS

That is, each role should have a specific role description (SRD) that describes the work expected of the person in the role, not merely a general one. For example, there are many principals of schools, but the work may vary significantly depending upon many variables such as the size of the school, demographic area, community and student body, history and reputation of the school and so on. In response it might be that these roles are put into categories, such as bands. While this may be useful, we would recommend the further step, which is to be specific about any role and what the work requirement of that role is at any one time. This is because the work of the role needs to be clear but it will also change over time, and we see these SRDs as forming a living document that can be used to review the work of the role, not simply describe it and then leave it to one side to be referred to hardly ever again. We will describe this in greater detail later in the book. However, the most important component is a clear purpose statement as we have argued previously.

## CLARITY OF AUTHORITY

There can be and is frequent misunderstanding about the nature of the authority that creates good working relationships. We will discuss this later in detail in Chapter 9. However, at the moment we propose that clarity around what authority there is between people in working relationships is essential for productive working relationships. What do the solid lines mean? Is everyone clear about the difference between the authority of a manager and supervisor? How else does authority in the organisation flow? Our observation is that structural diagrams are usually representative of managerial relationships but there are many other relationships that are needed if the school is to function effectively. These include supervisory relationships, advisory relationships and relationships where one role offers a service to someone in another role. Each carries its own particular authority and all parties need to be clear as to the nature of that authority. The alternative is simply to allow power to determine who is in charge and who can get people to do what, which may not suit the purpose or the productivity of an organisation, especially a school. It is interesting to observe that in schools we do try to be clear about the authority of the teacher in the classroom, but less so in the working relationships within the teaching part of the organisation and between teaching staff and the other staff that are essential to the running of the school.

We are not being prescriptive about any specific organisational structure or what those organisational relationships should be, merely that they should be clear, mutually understood and designed to enable the achievement of the purpose of the school. This is not an easy task, as anyone who has attempted to build an organisation or change an organisation will know.

## LEVELS OF REPORTING

We have found that it is easy to confuse managerial levels with grading structures, and, further, that some roles, although higher in terms of pay or title nevertheless do not warrant a full reporting relationship. Therefore we recommend that very careful thought be put into those reporting relationships, and those relationships are clearly distinguished. It is easy to have an apparently long "reporting" line but with several layers that are not actually adding any value. We have described the confusion and muddles that arise when the complexity of work is not understood (see Chapters 3 and 4). We do not need long lines of reporting, if by "reporting" we mean the role that is authorised to assign work, review the quality of that work and give recognition for performance. Thus we need to look very carefully and not assume that, because somebody is of higher grade or even has a particular title, they can assign tasks or review others. (For a fuller discussion of the different types of working relationships please see Macdonald, Burke and Stewart 2018.)

We will discuss this further in the chapter concerning the work of the principal (Chapter 13) and in the case studies (Chapter 16).

# Systems

As mentioned in the previous chapter, the systems are one of the three critical tools of leadership and include all the ways that people are expected to carry out work within any school. They cover all of the procedures and processes. Some use less complimentary words than others to describe the ways in which people are required to work. In *Systems Leadership: Creating Positive Organisations* (Macdonald, Burke and Stewart 2018) there is a significant amount of material that discusses both the importance of systems and how they can be designed effectively. We will not repeat all of that discussion here, but do emphasise the importance of systems with regard to influencing behaviour. Indeed, one of the authors of that book has coined the phrase "Systems drive behaviour." Systems also contribute significantly to the creation of mythologies, both positive and negative. All systems are in fact limits on behaviour and as such deliberately constrain discretion. We do not recommend systematising everything, since that can lead to an overly bureaucratic organisation. We also recognise the effort and complexity of the work that is required to design good systems. However, once the systems have been designed properly, they reduce workload significantly and can not only reduce waste but also variation, and potentially make a significant contribution to the overall purpose. A major problem that we have seen in organisations, including schools in the education system, is the lack of clarity around who should be doing the work of designing and or monitoring and redesigning systems. We can see from chapters 3 and 4 that system design is complex work and should not be delegated to someone who does not have the access to information or the mental processing ability to do that work.

For the purposes of this chapter we will discuss two types of systems and look at whether systems help or hinder the achievement of the purpose.

## SYSTEMS OF DIFFERENTIATION AND EQUALISATION

There are essentially two types of systems in any organisation including schools. First, there are systems of differentiation. These systems operate in a way that distinguishes roles or categories of roles from other roles or categories. Take a simple example: in schools roles are not all paid the same salary. Indeed, it would be very odd if they were. People are paid differently according to the work that they do and this differentiation on the basis of work is the basic rationale for any system of differentiation.

Systems of equalisation treat everybody the same. Again, to take a simple example: safety regulations apply to everybody. If particular equipment is to be worn in the science lab the same requirement will be made of a teacher and the students. The teacher is not excused because he or she is someone of higher authority.

Many systems in organisations are not so easy to place; should they be systems of equalisation or systems of differentiation? Should there be differentiated car parking, canteen facilities, uniforms or terms and conditions such as holidays or sick leave and so on? Our experience is that if systems are to be seen positively – that is, rated positively on the values continua – then any system of differentiation should be explained in terms of the work to be done. There should be a work reason why one role or group of roles gets a benefit compared to another. If the systems of differentiation are introduced where there is no work reason, or people do not understand the work reason, our experience is that people will rate that negatively on the values continua. This works the other way around, in that systems of equalisation might be seen as unfair because they do not recognise the need for differentiation due to work. We can see that in the example of salaries, where our prediction would be that people would regard it as negative if everyone were paid the same.

Systems of differentiation and equalisation have a huge impact on the social processes within the school. This is because the systems of equalisation bind us and could be characterised as reinforcing a collective experience. By definition, systems of differentiation show how we belong to separate groups and are therefore not the same. If we now consider the impact on the process of trying to build a productive culture, we can see how significant this can be. For example, it would be extremely difficult to build a socially cohesive culture if the only type of systems in the organisation were systems of differentiation. However, it would also be unrealistic to expect to build a socially cohesive culture solely based on systems of equalisation since the whole purpose of organisational arrangements is to define roles which distinguish some types of work from others.

The most symbolic system of differentiation in most organisations is exemplified by the titling system. The titling system clearly demonstrates that people's work is different in kind.

We have found it very useful to be aware of these two types of systems and to be very clear about whether the system should differentiate or equalise. One simple mistake people can make is to think that if a system applies to everybody it is a system of equalisation. This is not the case. There are many policies that apply to everybody, but we must look at whether the purpose is to differentiate. We have already mentioned the salary system, but we might also include the disciplinary system. The disciplinary system applies to everybody, but its purpose is to differentiate between people whose behaviour is acceptable and those whose behaviour is not acceptable. It is generally experienced to be very unfair to punish everybody for the transgression of one person.

People also underestimate the significance of changing a system from differentiation to equalisation or vice versa. In fact, you can guarantee an impact on the whole organisation by doing this. If you are not aware, you may be quite shocked by the response to apparently minor systems change. People respond very strongly and often emotionally when, for example, designated parking spaces are removed. This is because if you equalise where there has been differentiation then you are creating one group where there has been at least two, or vice versa if you are now differentiating. The emotional reactions can be very strong, especially when those systems of differentiation have been very powerful symbols of status. Think also about when people try to change titles of long-established roles.

Therefore it is really important to use this categorisation system when considering the design or redesign of systems and understanding whether such a change will help or hinder in creating the desired culture.

## THE SYSTEMS MATRIX

The other tool that we have found helpful when considering systems is the systems matrix (see Figure 7.1).

This diagram distinguishes between those systems in the organisation that are productive – that is, they are contributing to the creation of the desired culture – and those that are counter-productive; that is, they are

**Systems**

|  | Productive | Counter-productive |
|---|---|---|
| **Authorised** | A. Well-designed and Implemented | B. Restrictive practices which have been adopted by the organisation |
| **Unauthorised** | C. People "cutting corners" in order to get work done | D. Alternative leadership based on power, e.g. intimidation, racism, sexism, work quotas ... |

A All Right. B Area for Change. C Positive opportunities for change or education. D Must be addressed and challenged.

**Figure 7.1**    Distinguishing systems in the organisation that are productive/counter-productive and systems that are authorised/unauthorised

undermining the creation of such a culture. It also distinguishes between those systems that are authorised and those that are unauthorised. What we mean by this is that the authorised systems are the ways that we are meant to do the work and that have been approved, as opposed to ways where somebody is not following procedures, regulations and so on. Not all authorised systems have to be documented or formalised; they may exist through social custom and practice.

Ideally, we would clearly like all systems to be in box A. However, because no school is perfect and because the situation and context are changing all the time, this is highly unlikely. Many systems are in box B; that is, we are meant to do it like this but following the system wastes time and energy. This is what we often refer to as "red tape" or "bureaucracy". Because most people are trying to do their work and trying to be productive, we find it is not unusual for people to move into box C. We find ways around the system and try to get the work done despite the system. Unfortunately, this is all too common in education and causes great distress because of the box B systems. Operating in box C might even involve a personal cost. For example, many teachers will simply buy equipment or materials out of their own money because the bureaucratic systems involved in ordering or being paid for such purchases are far too cumbersome and/or unreliable.

Box D, however, is a completely different situation. Here people are being both counter-productive and unauthorised. This usually means they are gaining at the expense of the organisation. The most obvious example of this is theft or fraud. This also includes intimidation, racist or sexist behaviour and any systems operating for personal rather than organisational gain.

It is imperative that the leadership has zero tolerance for behaviour and systems in box D. It is also good leadership if behaviour and systems in box C are not automatically punished since they may often be creative responses to inadequate systems. Indeed, a measure of a good leader is someone who does not tolerate box D and learns from box C. We can predict that the leader who turns a blind eye to box D while rigidly enforcing box B systems will be seen as extremely negative on the values continua.

## HOW TO DESIGN SYSTEMS

We also have an approach that looks at the design of systems in more depth. This is explained more fully in *Systems Leadership: Creating Positive Organisations* (Macdonald, Burke and Stewart 2018). However, this is an approach that critiques any system by asking twenty questions. These include questions of purpose, ownership and interaction with other systems and will be referred to later in the book as we discuss implementation.

---

**Box 7.1    The twenty systems design questions**

1. What is the purpose of the system?
2. Who is/should be the owner?
3. Who is/should be the custodian/designer?
4. What is the underlying theory?
5. How is it to be measured?
6. Is it a system of differentiation or equalisation?
7. What are the current "benefits" of the poor system?
8. What are the boundaries of the system?
9. What are the linkages with other systems?
10. What structural boundaries does it cross?
11. Is the system one of transfer or transformation?
12. Are authorities and accountabilities consistent with roles?
13. Are there proper controls built into the system?
14. Is there an effective audit process?
15. Has the social process analysis been done?
16. Is there a fully outlined flowchart?
17. Is there a design plan that addresses the critical issues?
18. Is there full system documentation?
19. What is the implementation plan?
20. What is the final cost of design and implementation?

---

As mentioned, these questions are explained in much more depth in the main, general textbook on Systems Leadership.

However, the work of systems design and redesign has been fundamental to improvements as can be seen in the results chapter (Chapter 15) and the case studies. All the schools applied the twenty questions to both critique and redesign systems.

Below is an account of how each question in turn can be used in a school context.

1. The purpose of the system should be described in a single sentence without the conjunction "and". This question is probably the most important as it is pointless asking all the other questions unless you are clear about the purpose. The discussion of the purpose of the system is usually very interesting and it may be necessary to return to the definition of the purpose at a later stage. The purpose is finally defined by the owner. This is a really helpful discussion to have with a leadership team; for example, the principal and/or his or her direct reports. It is also worthwhile to explore this further with other stakeholders.

2. The owner of the system is the person in the role that has the authority to change or even remove the system. This might be the principal of the

school, but it may be that the system is owned outside of the school or college; for example, by a trust, academy, education department and so on. It is important to understand whether there is discretion to change the system and who has the authority to do so.

3. The custodian and designer may be people in different roles or may be the same role. The designer is the person in the role whose work it is to propose the system. Usually the system designer will be an expert in the field and will draw on the experience of others, especially actual or potential system users. Sometimes the designer is wrongly assumed to be the system owner. The system owner should always be in an executive position. The custodian of the system is the person in a role who makes sure that the system is operating as it should and collects information concerning its operation.

4. It is surprising that many systems are designed and implemented without questioning the underlying theory. This question is designed to ask why you think this system will encourage the behaviour that is intended. Think for a moment about pay for performance or bonus systems. On what basis are they supposed to encourage more productive or creative behaviour?

5. The measurement of the effectiveness of the system should be directly related to the purpose. We do not advocate a plethora of measures but rather several key measures that can clearly be connected to the purpose. Remember that measures do not all have to be quantitative; there should also be qualitative measures.

6. Whether the system is one of differentiation or equalisation is significant, as discussed above. Remember that this refers to the purpose of the system rather than whether it applies to everyone.

7. Many poor systems are nevertheless accepted because they provide benefits for some people. For example, poor-accountability systems may mean that some people can get away with doing very little or with poor attendance. Do not think you will always be praised for tightening up systems that shed light on unauthorised practices.

8. This question merely refers to where the system begins and ends. For example, we may have several small systems to manage morning break, lunchtime, afternoon break, leaving school and so on, or we may just have one system that covers all out-of-classroom activity. There is no right or wrong. The most important matter is that everyone knows where the boundaries are.

9. We often see that systems are designed and implemented in isolation. It is only after their implementation that we notice they are not compatible with other existing systems. This is especially so with IT systems, but not exclusively. In designing the system it is important to be aware of the interaction between systems.

10. When systems cross structural boundaries this can add complexity. Think of a system that operates in part of the school or across the whole school,

or even across several schools linked together, as in multi-academy trusts. Although larger systems can be more efficient, they are more difficult to design, as they have to take in a wider range of circumstances.

11. This question concerns whether a system is one that changes (transforms) whatever is going through it, or is intended to keep it the same. For example, education in itself should be a system of transformation. Education should result in changes in knowledge and behaviour. However, the systems that guide people round the school grounds should be one of transfer and children should go home in the same healthy state as they arrived.

12. This question merely checks that what somebody is asked to do by the system does not contradict or clash with his or her role in general. There could be an inconsistency in that the system requires more or less discretion than their current role. For example, a principal may have enormous discretion with regard to expenditure, but he or she may need to fill out numerous forms to authorise the use of a taxi.

13. Many systems are designed and implemented without any forms of control built into them. The controls in the system make sure it is operating within its limits, and provide information as to whether this is the case or not. (See above regarding the role of the custodian.) We sometimes implement systems, especially with regard to people, without knowing whether the system is actually being implemented as it was intended. We might introduce coaching but then not collect any systematic feedback from the coach or those being coached as to how this is being done.

14. Similarly all systems need an audit process. We refer to an audit as a process that tests whether the system is actually achieving its purpose and therefore is connected to the measures (see above). The audit should examine whether the controls are in place and review information as to what the system is achieving.

15. The social process analysis refers to the work that is needed to discover how the current situation is viewed (current mythologies) and the views or mythologies around any proposed changes. This needs to be done with great care as all assumptions need to be checked so that there are no surprises. This question helps in the consideration of how the implementation process might be handled.

16. We always recommend that there be an actual flowchart for the system. There are many different approaches that can be used in a flowchart and we do not specify any particular one. The flowchart is very useful as it helps to check the detail of the system and identifies if and where there are any gaps.

17. In relation to question 16 it is important that the design team identifies and addresses the critical issues. These issues may arise from any source but further help to design the implementation process. We describe critical issues in terms of "what ifs". These are the critical issues that, if

they are not addressed, will prevent the achievement of the purpose of the system. For example, what if significant stakeholders hold negative mythologies about the new system? How is this going to be addressed, and how are the context and purpose going to be explained to people? We do not recommend listing hundreds of critical issues; in our experience, there are usually three or four that are most important.

18. Sometimes the system documentation, or description of the system, is absent, or patchy at best. It is not advisable to write whole books on each system, but simply consider if someone new was coming into a role, is there a written account that would explain to the person how the system actually works?

19. All of the above can contribute to the implementation plan, especially the critical issues. We do recommend that there is such a plan, especially one that takes into account the proper resourcing of the process, and this leads to the final question.

20. This question is important not simply for accounting reasons but because sometimes the cost is higher than the realistic benefit that is to be gained from the system.

## Conclusion

This chapter has continued to examine how we can build productive cultures. We have looked at how people may have very different views as to what an organisation is and what makes for good organisation. We have expanded on how Systems Leadership helps to analyse and understand, through using various tools, what does actually work well, and predict what will not work well. The structure and systems in any organisation, including any educational organisations, will have a great impact on people's behaviour positively or negatively. This in fact can be underestimated, as can be the work to build a good organisation. This is leadership work. Those structures and systems are also rated on the values continua. This is not merely an intellectual process; people have very strong feelings as to their school systems. Leaders need to be aware not only how behaviour is rated but also how the structures and systems are rated, because changing a system that is fairly universally disliked is of course quite different from changing one that people are very attached to. Being aware by using the tools described above can make this work a lot easier and more successful.

# 8 Behaviour and symbols: how they are used to create change

In Chapter 6 we looked at the tools of leadership specifically systems, symbols and behaviour and how they can be used to create the desired culture. Then, in the last chapter we looked in more depth at systems and the structure to examine their impact on culture. This chapter looks in more depth at behaviour and symbols and their influence in an organisation and hence their impact on culture.

## Behaviour

There is a great deal written about the importance of behaviour, especially the behaviour of the leader. There is no doubt that the behaviour of a head teacher or a principal has a significant influence in the school. Anyone who has worked in a school in any role knows the importance of the behaviour of the head or principal and what a difference this can make to the effectiveness of the whole school.

The behaviour of all leaders in schools includes the need to behave consistently and according to the policies and espoused requirements. If a person preaches one message while behaving in a different way, we will always take the behaviour as the example of what really matters. As a child therapist once commented to distraught parents, "Don't worry if your children don't listen to you; they are watching you all the time!" In this way the leader's behaviour is also symbolic and seen as such by all other staff, pupils and all other stakeholders. For example, if the principal is walking around the school and walks past some litter lying on the ground then the message that this behaviour conveys is that it is not important to pick up litter. If, however, he or she deliberately picks that litter up and places it in the bin then that also sends a very clear message as to what is acceptable or unacceptable behaviour.

While we agree that behaviour, and especially the behaviour of leaders, is important and indeed critical, we also argue that when creating a desired culture it is a necessary but not sufficient condition. Indeed we would also argue that over the past decade or so there has been an over-idealisation of the importance of individual behaviour and individual leaders. In the West in general there tends to be a view that organisational problems can be solved simply by putting the right person into the leadership role. This is not restricted to education or the public service. The remuneration packages of CEOs of large organisations have increased dramatically over the last decade or so. Similarly when a sports team (especially a football team) starts to fail or underperform the answer always seems to be to sack the current manager and replace this person with another; even though often that person may have been sacked by their previous club! This desire for a saviour, while understandable, will rarely, if ever, on its own solve the organisational problem, especially over the longer term. We see so-called failing schools "saved" by the introduction of a so-called "super head", who is then expected to solve the problems almost on their own.

Systems Leadership proposes not only how to create a positive organisation but also how to sustain it. We have all seen charismatic leaders who have genuinely inspired people and improved organisational performance. However, the weakness in this approach is that we have also seen the consequences when that person leaves the organisation and that improved performance is not sustained, and indeed performance may decline. We do not think that it is healthy for any organisation or part of an organisation to be dependent on a particular person. That is why we argue that a positive organisation must be sustained by sound underlying systems, including a structure that includes clarity around work expectations.

Therefore we are arguing that although behaviour is very important it needs to be supported by systems and symbols if the organisation is going to be effective over time. The behaviour of leaders in an organisation certainly does send a clear message to all members of the organisation, and although it is not sufficient in itself to create a positive organisation it may be sufficient in itself to destroy a positive organisation. If the behaviour of the leader is inconsistent and is viewed negatively on the values continua by stakeholders we can predict significant disruption in the organisation. This can take various forms, and we have certainly seen unchecked behaviour leading to fragmented staff groups in conflict with one another and confused messages sent to pupils and community members. We do not underestimate the importance of the behaviour of the leader, but simply point out that this alone will not be sufficient to transform an organisation and sustain that transformation over time.

## Symbols

The third of the important leadership tools is the use of symbols. One of the interesting aspects of symbols is that we are often not consciously aware of their impact despite the fact that that impact may be significant. Leaders of some organisations are much more aware of the use of symbols than others. For example, the Christian church and indeed most religions are usually very conscious about the use of symbols. This does not mean that they necessarily use the same symbols in the same way. For example, Southern European and South American Catholic churches are very rich in the use of statues, colours, ornate decoration and very explicit and detailed ritual. However, Northern European Protestant churches, including Baptist and Methodist denominations, may be very particular in their plainness and the simplicity of their rituals, including the absence of statues or icons.

Armies are another example of organisations that constantly use symbols as a tool to create social cohesion. Regimental structures and the wearing of particular uniforms, including coloured berets, symbols of rank and particularly medals and flags, are used to give meaning both internally and externally.

All organisations use symbols to some extent. Most, indeed almost all, organisations have some sort of identifiable logo and/or brand. Some, such as Apple, Facebook or Google, have ubiquitous logos that are recognised around the world, as have other organisations such as the International Red Cross and Red Crescent Movement. All these organisations are very deliberately aware of their symbols and brands and how they are used.

Many schools are also well aware of the importance of symbols, rituals and traditions that are used to enhance their reputation and create positive mythologies among stakeholders. Think for a moment about school badges, school mottos, even school songs. While not all schools have uniforms, those that do may be highly specific in their design and requirements that may be quite strictly enforced. Schools may have end-of-year prize-giving, a Founder's Day and other events that are deliberately used to create social cohesion and send messages as to the nature and culture of the school.

The use of symbols, however, may extend beyond these more obvious examples. When we talk about symbolism we talk about anything that may be observed or experienced that sends a representative message about the organisation, in this case a school. So here we can consider a wide range of non-verbal communication; for example, the behaviour of children outside the school in the local community. This includes the school grounds. Are they clean and tidy? What about the signage around the school noticeboards, directions and car parking? How are people greeted at reception or simply by anyone in the school? What do classrooms look like? Are there displays? Are they colourful? Even the demeanour of staff and students as they go about daily life can convey very strong symbolic messages to others.

Of course many school leaders are aware of the importance of these symbols, and we underline that awareness and emphasise that it is the work of the leader to be aware and to think carefully about such symbols and whether they are encouraging or hindering the desired culture. It may sound obvious but requires conscious effort.

It is very difficult not to react to certain symbols and to draw conclusions even if those conclusions may not actually be justified. Such conclusions may be positive or negative. For example, a school may look very neat and tidy, and students may be very well behaved, but that does not necessarily mean that the quality of teaching is of the highest standard.

When attempting to create the desired culture it is a constant theme of this book that the work of leadership is constantly trying to see the world through other people's eyes. As human beings we are very adaptive. Over time we may not notice the slow deterioration of standards. We may get very used to viewing the world through our own eyes and thinking that what we see and experience as fair, respectful or loving is genuinely so. It is the work of leaders to consider how systems, symbols and behaviours are viewed through other people's eyes and then rated on the values continua. Although this may seem another obvious point it is genuinely difficult to do, especially if we are very attached to the particular approach or solution being put forward. We may disregard other people's perceptions and views, or just simply regard them as wrong.

The same symbols may well be viewed extremely positively or negatively depending upon our experience. If we have had a miserable time at school with little academic success and no great athletic achievement, then the school badge or motto may not be something that we cherish. On the other hand, if we have had a positive and successful experience the same symbols may be extremely precious to us.

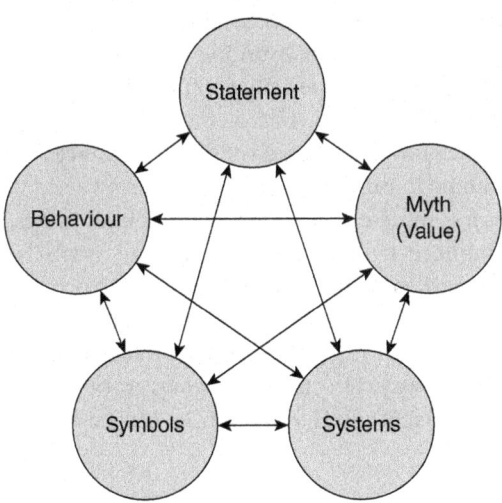

**Figure 8.1**      Understanding culture

Finally in this chapter, we include the model that connects all of these elements together.

Using this model we can start anywhere and see how any one element is connected to any other and all the other elements. For example, we might start with a "statement", that is the actual words that might be used. Someone might say, "I really like going to this school." We can then explore which of the values this might relate to. I might experience the school students as very respectful, or I might find the staff to be very trustworthy, for example. Then we could link that to systems that might underpin those positive values; for example, a school code of conduct that is effectively implemented by the leadership. This in turn leads us to be able to describe certain behaviours; for example, what exactly we mean by "somebody behaving in a respectful or trustworthy way", and then we can consider the symbols that represent that. However, we could start anywhere on the model – for example, with the system or a symbol – as long as we make all the connections with one another. This model then can be used to help us reflect upon what is going well and what is not going so well, and use it as a framework for identifying what we might need to change or indeed what we might need to sustain.

## Conclusion

When considering the tools of leadership all three are necessary to create the desired and positive culture. Behaviour may be the most obvious (and perhaps over-used) tool.

Systems are much less popular and for some leaders wearisome or just "more bureaucracy". This is often because understanding how to design and implement systems can be time-consuming in an organisation where no one seems to have any spare time, especially for Improvement work. However, systems do drive behaviour.

In this chapter we have also looked at the importance of symbols and how significant they can be in influencing behaviour. We would be surprised if this message comes as a completely new idea to any school leader, but what we are emphasising is the need to constantly review such symbols, and not merely the obvious ones, and look at them through other people's eyes. Also, the models presented provide a simple but disciplined approach to culture change. Often these ideas, although recognised as important, are not addressed in any coherent or integrated way. Effectiveness comes through using shared definitions and shared approaches so that the school can be much more effective in achieving its purpose.

CHAPTER

# 9 *Social process: authority and authoritarian*

In Chapter 2 we looked at the three domains of work: Social, Technical and Commercial. We discussed how in the Social Domain language definitions and meaning can be vague and certainly specific terms, such as "leadership", "culture", "collaboration" or "innovation", can be interpreted differently.

Of course all organisations, including schools, are social organisations in that they involve people coming together to work to achieve a purpose. As we have said, the way in which they then work together can have a profound effect on whether that purpose is achieved or not, and the well-being of those involved. Although people working in organisations may have very strong views about their organisations and how they are run, especially the quality of the leadership, understanding this and the work required to manage the impact of these organisational arrangements can be underestimated.

The Social Domain includes all of these arrangements, systems, structure, roles and so on. It also includes the social processes. These processes describe how people actually behave towards each other in ways that are more or less likely to result in a productive outcome.

If there is to be a productive outcome there needs to be clarity of purpose that is shared by all the staff and stakeholders. It seems somewhat unfair to hold someone to account if you have not been clear about what is expected, and by when.

Thus a school's primary purpose is to educate students, not primarily to provide employment for teachers or other staff. While this might seem obvious, many organisations, including schools, do end up designing their systems around the needs of staff. This is sometimes done inadvertently but can be an indication of confusion over purpose.

Another cause of confusion is the conflation of "authority" and "authoritarian". There is a reluctance to use the term "authority" lest it be interpreted as a statement of power.

However, in order for people to do work of the role then they must have authority as an integral part of their role. Indeed, an organisational chart can be seen as a map of authority. Roles carry authority: to use resources and equipment, to spend money, to access information or physical space. The key social process authorities (in an employment organisation) are to assign and review work. If no one has the authority to assign work the organisation cannot function in any predictable way and there can be no accountability. It is in effect a voluntary organisation. If work cannot be assigned or reviewed, in effect people can do what they want, which may or may not accord with the purpose of the organisation. The only way you can get work done in such circumstances is by personal persuasion and by gaining what is sometimes described as "buy in" (even though staff are already being paid).

However, we have observed that leaders (and others) in many organisations have become afraid of using authority.

In the last twenty years or so there has been a massive muddle between "authority" and "authoritarian". There has been a trend against "hierarchy", a fear of "command and control" and an anxiety about being too directive, judgemental or even just being a "boss". In education the GROW model or "purist" approach stresses a non-directive, non-judgemental approach (Whitmore 2009).

But this confuses two important but distinct issues. First is the very real and crucial authority that needs to be built into a role, and second the way that authority is enacted . . . exactly what we describe as social process.

*Social process* is defined as "the ability to interact with others at work to produce a productive outcome".

Social process can be likened to similar concepts such as "people skills", "interpersonal skills", "emotional intelligence", "soft skills" and the more recent and perhaps a little unnerving "soft power" (Nye 2004). While these items are quite similar, very few actually refer to the outcome but rather concentrate on the process itself. In Systems Leadership we are clear that such skills are directed to achieve a productive purpose. This area of people skills may also be confused with the ability "to get on with people". It can be quite easy to get on with people if you do not ask them to do much or never give any hard feedback about performance.

In Systems Leadership it is not an either/or. It is not appropriate to ask people to rely on social process skills alone and neither is it appropriate to rely only on the authority as built into the role alone. The way a person uses social process has a significant bearing on whether the authority is experienced to be reasonable or not.

Clearly not all roles carry the same authority; while one role may have the authority to assign and review work, another might have the authority to give advice or ask for a service. As such the social process skills required to be effective differ accordingly. Take, for example, the role of a principal. Here the person will have to interact with many different people and groups inside and outside the school. The demand for highly developed social process skills is significant.

Such skills need to be identified and made explicit prior to an appointment and be more specific than "must get on with a wide range of people". The role may succeed or fail on these skills being used effectively.

Being clear about authority and the appropriate use of social process skills leads to the acceptance of decisions without needing to resort to consensus (which assumes that everyone has equal authority) or voting (a similar assumption). If people did have equal authority, then this assumes they are not only doing the same work (for example, Members of Parliament), but also that they cannot be differentiated and as such should all be paid exactly the same (which appears not to be the case in schools). Thus in order for the people in any organisation, including schools, to do work, those people must have the authority to carry out the work of the role.

Social process skills can be used constructively or used destructively; that is, as a means of exercising power. The over-emphasis on social process skills (with a tacit denial of authority) can lead to a highly unsatisfactory working environment. Putting such emphasis on social process skills alone has avoided the very important issue about being clear what appropriate authority should be associated with any particular role. Our current, apparent anxiety and ambivalence about that term, "authority", has led to situations where because of strong social process skills some people can get others to do almost anything, while the others with lesser skills are unable to get people to do the work they are paid for even though it is central to their role and even though the person with the lesser skills is in a leadership position. This practice distributes leadership on the basis of social process skills rather than the work that needs to be done in each role:

- Step One is to identify the appropriate authority associated with any role relationship
- Step Two is to ensure that this authority is mutually understood
- Step Three is to help, where appropriate, to improve the social process skills needed to enact that authority in a way that is seen and felt to be fair and respectful of each person's dignity

It seems that too often it is assumed (rather stereotypically) that authority only flows downwards in an organisation. Actually it can, and should, flow in all directions since its purpose is to enable work and it is very important that there is clarity about this. Thus in Systems Leadership the team member has the authority to require the leader to explain the context and purpose of work. She or he can *demand a review*. This is not a simple authority, but a means whereby a team member can call the leader to account for their work as a leader . . . *command and control* it certainly is not (see the next chapter).

The other main area where people need to be clear about authority and social process is the enactment of systems. For example, a coach may be employed to offer advice as to the improvement of teaching practice or leadership. It must be clear what authority he or she has. Can she choose which person to observe/coach? When should she observe and advise? What are the consequences, if any, positive or negative? This should be clear in the system design and implementation and thereby set a transparent context.

Many people avoid addressing difficult situations because they do not have confidence in their social process skills. If the educational organisation does not have clarity about roles, the authority of the role and systems to monitor the use of authority, this avoidance can go unchecked. Social process paradoxically becomes the application of skills to avoid problems, not face difficult issues. Problems are continually smoothed over in the hope that *no one will notice*, as *it is necessary that no one be upset*, or that the problem *will just go away*. Meanwhile, social cohesion actually crumbles and the quality of work including teaching drops or remains variable.

## Authority and power

System Leadership is based on the proper use of authority in organisations. It is one of the most important concepts in creating positive organisations. We also recognise that power is used in organisations; sometimes for good, but more often to their detriment. While both these terms have been used primarily in the study of governments and politics, such terms are just as relevant in a school or college. Again these terms can be defined in different ways.

We use the following definitions:

---

**Box 9.1    Authority and power**

*Authority:* the exertion of will in the context of the mutual acceptance of agreed limits.

*Power:* the exertion of will while breaking one or more limits of authority.

A ------------------------- → B

In an organisation, if A wants B to do something that A wishes, then A is using authority when he or she is:

1. Requiring B to act within the limits of his/her role description
2. Requiring B to act within the limits of role relationships; that is, it is clear that A can require B to do something
3. Requiring B to act within the existing policies of the organisation
4. Requiring B to act within the limits of the law

---

5.  Requiring B to act within the ethical framework of the organisation or within custom and practice providing it does not breach 3 or 4 above

Further, the context of the relationship assumes that B has freely entered into the role; that is, B has not been coerced or appears to have no other choice. We will explore these elements below.

## POWER

If A uses power without authority to influence B to do something, then in bringing that influence to bear A breaks one or more of the five conditions above, or it is clear that B has unwillingly entered into the role:

1.  A has asked B to do something that is outside the limits of his/her role description
2.  A does not have a role relationship that acknowledges the right to ask for this action
3.  A requires B to violate one or more of the existing policies of the organisation
4.  A requires B to break the law
5.  A requires B to act unethically or outside existing custom and practice.

Both power and authority, as defined above, can be (and are) used in all organisations, including schools. Both can be used to achieve an objective but an organisation based on power takes a significant toll on its employees and is detrimental to psychological health. These are organisations with stressed employees. Organisations based on power require a lot of energy to protect one's turf, gain more turf, manipulate others to act and avoid accountability. This drains energy from the productive work of the school and causes burnout.

Power-based systems also alienate staff. It is debilitating and demoralising to have to deal with favouritism, power games, school politics, unclear accountabilities, blame-placing and decisions made on the basis of personal preference, not the work that needs to be done. The failure to understand these processes is causing teachers to become demoralised as they are often stretched by their workload anyway.

## ROYAL COURTS OR POSITIVE ORGANISATIONS?

We have observed that organisations that run on power often function like a royal court. At court the only thing that matters is what the monarch wants. It is critical to be "in favour" or "have the ear of the monarch". This encourages in-fighting, cliques and elites that become more concerned with power than achieving productive results. People advance on the basis of holding onto knowledge, manipulating others and starting and spreading rumours that denigrate rivals. While this can be fascinating (see *Game of Thrones*), it is hugely wasteful and damaging to many people.

Contrast this with the positive organisation: here people identify with the purpose of the organisation. Capability to do the work is paramount and working relationships and authorities are explicit and mutually understood. The overall purposes of the organisation and of the roles are more important than status and personal standing.

Our experience is that while the royal court produces much more intrigue, gossip and content suitable for television and film, it can be a most destructive place to work. The positive organisation is both productive and a healthy place to work and actually makes a real contribution to society.

## Conclusion

The Social Domain consists of all the behaviours and arrangements whereby people work together. Part of that includes the social process skills required to carry out the work of the role and enact the authorities associated with that role. The recent anxiety about confusing *authority* with *authoritarian* has blurred the clarity needed to design the appropriate authority into any role and its proper use in role relationships. Unless a role has the appropriate authority to carry out the work of the role, with regard to both people and resources, it is unfair to hold the person in the role to account for their work. The current "applied approach" (Blakey and Day 2012) has moved more towards an appreciation of the need for accountability and a need for systems thinking.

The muddle between exercising authority and being authoritarian has led to an avoidance of being clear about appropriate authority. People make up their own rules and boundaries and that in turn can lead to abuse.

We know of no organisations that can run without both authority and some form of hierarchy. That does not make them authoritarian. Rather, authoritarian approaches are due to poor social process skills and thus poor leadership. Substituting authority with the need to exercise brilliant social process skills is no answer either: we need both. The absence of clarity around authority and social process skills leads to organisations run on power – the basis of cliques, fragmented cultures, internal rivalry and favouritism which make it very difficult to deliver high-quality education.

# 10 *The work of team leadership and membership*

"Teamwork" is a term that has broad social usage and many different interpretations. It is simply not sufficient for leaders to exhort people to remember they are a team or to just work as a team unless there is a deeper and shared understanding as to what this means. What is the behaviour required from the leader and the team member? There are countless books written on team leadership (simply Google "leadership books" and see how many are listed). Certainly all these books emphasise different qualities, processes and even behaviour. There are far fewer books written about team membership and yet everyone in a school is a member of the team, but not everyone is in a leadership role. Again, if we ask somebody to be a good team member the interpretation of what this means can vary considerably.

Recently there has been a concern about the excessive use of teams and what is referred to as "collaborative overload". Data collected over two decades shows "the time spent by managers and employees in collaborative activities has ballooned by 50% or more" (Cross, Rebele and Grant 2016). They warn of the imbalance in contributions to teams and the excess demands this places on certain individuals. Their recommendations to improve the situation are similar to though less specific than ours: more clarity of roles, authorities and task assignments as well as appropriate recognition for both individual and team accomplishments.

## The false duality

Underlying much of this discussion is an implication, and at times the assertion, that there is some sort of basic choice between two types of organisation. One is the traditional hierarchy, and as we discussed in previous chapters, *hierarchy*, *authority* and *bureaucracy* have acquired negative connotations. The arguments put forward assert that these forms of organisation equate to command and control, top-down instruction, rigid structure and highly directive "manager–subordinate" relationships.

On the other hand, we are invited to believe in the organic, empowered, non- hierarchical, creative organisation. People in these forms of organisation, it is asserted, work willingly and unencumbered; teams form and reform, often without leaders. Actually, neither of these models is effective or efficient. It is misleading to present them as a choice. Social organisations need both structure and authority, clearly understood by all of their members, to be effective. Having a structure does not have to mean rigidity or inflexibility. Think of a fishing net or a flock of birds. People need to work together in teams if organisational goals are to be achieved. It is better to put aside this false duality and look at effective teamwork, what works and what does not.

Teamwork is about individuals collaborating for mutual benefit to achieve a purpose, clear about their mutual authority, their work and their relationship with each other and the leader. The word "team" is used very generally, as are many terms in management. We have a specific definition:

---

**Box 10.1    Definition of *team***

Team: a team is a group of people, including a leader, with a common purpose who must interact with each other in order to perform their individual tasks and thus achieve their common purpose.

---

There is nothing greatly contentious in this definition. However, the phrase "who must interact" is crucial. It demonstrates the mutual interdependency of the team members. This distinguishes the work of a team from a network where some members of it have no real relationship with some others, and there is no requirement for mutuality even if all the network members do have a common purpose. It also distinguishes the team from a group of people; say, passengers on a plane – all have a common purpose but do not need to interact to achieve it. We emphasise the need to interact and the mutuality. This is the difference between, for example, the members of a shift or project team and the group comprising all the employees of an organisation as a whole.

## Team tasks, goals and rewards

Confusion may be generated by the use of language, socially defined. Can a team have a task? Should a team be rewarded? Can a team be set goals?

In employment roles a team cannot be given a task. A task is given to an individual. If that individual is in a team leadership role, he or she may then actually say to the team members, "We have to make sure all the children get home safely from a school trip" or "We must establish good relationships with parents and improve the behaviour of school children in the local community."

This is an appropriate way for the leader to define the purpose but he or she may not simply walk away at this point, or even say, "Right, get on with it." The team members can only get on with it if they are clear about what their work is and what contribution they are expected to make.

The fact that there are team leaders does not mean that the organisation has to be authoritarian (see the previous chapter). An observer may at times find it difficult to spot the leader once an activity is underway, especially if everything is going well. This is not an argument against the need for leadership but rather an excellent example of how it should work.

## Team decisions

A rich area of confusion concerns the approach to decision making reflected in phrases like "the team decided", or "the team was against it". These are examples of poor or muddled leadership. Individuals are paid to make decisions; it is at the core of our understanding of work. It is an essential part of being a professional. This does not mean we do not confer, consult, discuss, suggest or recommend. Of course, good leaders listen to ideas and suggestions. A good leader will know whether members are comfortable with or even understand a proposed course of action and will not ride roughshod over team members. If the leader does lead badly, using poor social process, then an alternative leader will emerge over time or members will simply find ways to subvert the original leader. Good leadership and teamwork in a school is not, however, based on a system of individual veto or majority voting. A leadership role is far more than simply reflecting or representing members' views.

## Team processes

The team leader must also create and maintain the appropriate social processes in order to achieve the purpose. Team members need to establish constructive and cooperative work relationships with other team members. Below we describe some specific and practical steps to guide how this can be done. In particular we have developed a training course, Working Together (discussed further in Chapter 14), which helps people learn how to improve their understanding and practice of effective team processes. This experiential course uses exercises, which are filmed to help people see their behaviour so they may better recognise their own strengths and weaknesses, and to observe and learn what behaviour makes a good team and what behaviour detracts from this.

In 1992 Ian Macdonald articulated this into a complementary process (described below) outlining the steps and traps that team leaders and members can use (and avoid) to improve their contribution and effectiveness.

> **Box 10.2    Authority and teams**
>
> The team leadership and membership steps described below should be seen as authorities. Many organisations that have adopted this model require these steps from both leaders and members. They are part of work reviews and performance assessments. This demonstrates that, even in an executive hierarchy, authority does not simply flow downwards. Team members have the authority to require the leader to be clear about context, purpose and tasks, and can demand a review. This is a clear and proper flow of authority upwards. Also team members have authority with regard to each other requiring collaboration, information and feedback. This approach confounds the simplistic assertion that hierarchy is, by its nature, "authoritarian" or "top down".

## Leading a team

As we have mentioned there is a wealth of material on leadership and teamwork; theories and examples emphasise a range of qualities. There are debates about born leaders versus learning to lead. While there are many concepts, we have found it useful simply to describe what good leaders do, and consequently what is expected of someone in a leadership role. In our experience it is at best pointless and at worst dangerous to ask people to change their personalities, but you can ask someone to explain tasks clearly. The latter can be observed, recognised and improved. We are interested in behaviour, not "attitude" or "personality".

The following set of steps and frequently observed traps are set out in order but are not a rigid, linear process. It may be necessary to return to earlier steps to review and reassess a plan or a particular step. These are the steps and traps that formed the behavioural model used in the Working Together course in Far North Queensland. People put them into action while completing tasks relevant to their school and work. We demonstrated that when the model was used it resulted in much more effective and productive work that was both more enjoyable and satisfying.

The following is a practical guide to good leadership and perhaps even more importantly good team membership.

## Team leadership steps

### EXPLAIN THE CONTEXT AND PURPOSE

In setting the context for a task the leader needs to explain the situation: Why are we addressing a particular issue? How important is it? In public education there are many instances where a school might be changing significantly, such as becoming an academy or dividing into "upper" and "lower" schools. The reasons for this and the expected benefits and costs need to be explained to set the scene and provide the rationale so it can be discussed.

It is surprising how many team members are unsure why they have been brought into a team and what they are meant to achieve. It is not sufficient for the leader to assume they know. The leader must spell out a clear and overall purpose in a single statement without an "and". If leaders cannot do this, they probably do not understand that purpose clearly themselves.

A significant part of the context will be the constraints within which the team is working. These are known limits and may include safety, a budget, time limits, fixed resources, geographical boundaries, policy or the law. It is important at this stage to understand and communicate clearly what these explicit boundaries are.

## IDENTIFY AND ADDRESS THE CRITICAL ISSUES/PROBLEMS

It is important to identify, prior to action, the significant problems that will need to be overcome for the task to be completed successfully. This is not a case of listing everything that might go wrong (an infinite task) but selecting, in your judgement, what the key threats are likely to be and seeking proposals to overcome them if they do arise. As such this is similar to a risk analysis, often done for safety reasons, but we apply it generally.

A critical issue is something that threatens the purpose. People have described them as showstoppers. We describe them as what-ifs and we address them with "how-tos". For example, what if a key team member calls in sick? How do we cover all the classes in the school while we train some teachers in the new coaching system? The point here is not only to identify the critical issues, but also to work out a proposal of what to do if they occur. This is often called contingency planning.

In our experience there are usually only three or four critical issues, no matter what the task. They are the sorts of events that are revealed in enquiries after disasters, as issues that have, prior to the event, been mentioned or recognised but not acted upon.

Critical issues can be usefully categorised in terms of the Social, Technical and Commercial domains (see Chapter 2). It is recommended that each domain be considered as to whether there are critical issues associated with it.

For the process to operate well, it is also important to distinguish between critical issues and constraints. Constraints are known limitations. They would include the resources, laws, policies, time to completion and quality requirements. One participant on a course in California explained it well by saying, "So constraints are what you know, critical issues are what you have to work out."

## ENCOURAGE CONTRIBUTIONS

Most leaders need help in order to identify critical issues and contributions to their solution. Even if you, as the leader, do not think you need help, there is always a risk in going it alone. Not listening to others and therefore implying they have no contribution to make is almost always a mistake. The solution to the entire problem may come from another team member, but most often it is the solution to specific critical issues that come from different team members, and these need to be integrated into the solution for the whole problem. This is the work of the leader. Not being able to generate the complete solution personally is not a failure; the leader is being paid for his or her judgement.

## DECIDE AND ARTICULATE THE PLAN

Discussions with regard to critical issues and possible courses of action can continue for an inordinate amount of time and if not managed can result in going around in circles. Many meetings are like this, especially if the leader is overly sensitive in trying not to be authoritarian. Most team members find these discussions frustrating. On the other hand, the leader indeed may jump in too early and make a decision without properly listening to or considering the options. It is hard work and requires fine judgement to get the balance right between the Nike approach of "just do it" and the overly cautious approach, almost avoiding the decision altogether. It is important for the leader to clearly make a decision as well as giving the rationale for that decision and to articulate a plan, which then can be broken into tasks for individuals to complete.

## ASSIGN TASKS

Once the plan has been broken up into a number of tasks, these can be assigned to team members based on the leader's judgement of their capability. Team members must know what they are required to do. Using the task assignment model (CPQQRT) – that is, Context, Purpose, Quantity, Quality, Resources and Time (see Chapter 2) – team members must know:

1. What their tasks are – and what to do next
2. If and how their tasks complement other people's tasks
3. How their tasks will help to achieve the purpose and overcome problems – why they are doing these tasks

If team members cannot answer the questions above, the leader has failed and the team members will not know how and when to use their initiative when the situation changes (as it inevitably will!).

## MONITOR PROGRESS

The leader needs to do the work of monitoring progress of the team. If the leader does this, then team members are free to get on with their work. Progress is monitored along several dimensions (at once):

1.  Technical (the most obvious): Are the solutions working? Do they need to be modified? Will the methodology/plan actually solve the problem?
2.  Social: Is the team cohesive? Are people involved, using their initiative and interacting, or are they forming sub-groups, fragmenting, only doing "what is necessary"? Do they look interested? Engaged?
3.  Temporal: Is there a program, a timetable/schedule? Is it being achieved?
4.  Environmental: The leader does the work of monitoring the environment, allowing team members to concentrate on the task at hand. What is happening around the team and what intervention is required to help overcome problems?

Finally, if any or all of the above are going wrong, what contingency plan does the leader have? Can he or she answer this before a problem arises, even if only in outline? Here the leader may have to revisit critical issues, stop the process and re-evaluate.

## COACHING

As team members work, they may need help to complete their tasks or improve their methods. Leaders are helpers. This is a very sensitive area because the way in which a leader coaches will affect whether people will accept help. First, a leader must make it clear to the team member whether he or she is:

1.  Giving an instruction: telling someone to do something differently and expecting him or her to do it.
2.  Giving advice: suggesting a person think about using the leader's ideas but leaving it up to them.
3.  Teaching: showing/telling someone how to do something because they recognise that they do not know how. This area is critical to a leader as few people like being told how to do something while they are in the middle of work unless they think they are having problems. Consequently, do not be afraid to ask.
4.  Asking: gain information from members. For example, ask, "Why do you do that? Do you want any help?"

Although an important part of the leader's work is coaching, do not forget the leader may well learn from the team.

## REVIEW

At the end of the activity, whether the purpose has been achieved or not, the leader needs to review the process. This is the opportunity, when everything associated with the task is still fresh in people's minds, to give recognition to team members and to comment on the leader's perception of his or her leadership behaviour; in particular, those things that were not done as well as they might have been.

# Team leadership traps

There are some common traps that we have seen leaders fall into. In our experience these are the most common:

## NOT SEEING THE PROBLEM FROM THE MEMBERS' VIEWPOINT

This involves the leader making assumptions that team members know and see what he or she knows and sees. It does take a conscious effort at times, but a leader should be able, mentally, to step into someone else's shoes. What does the problem look like from their point of view? How anxious or confident are they?

## GETTING OVER-INVOLVED IN THE ACTION

There is a temptation, especially if there are problems, for the leader to dive in and take over. This not only interferes with team members' work and may well show that the leader has assigned tasks badly, but becoming over-involved in the action also prevents the monitoring work and good coaching. At times of great personal risk, it may be correct for a leader to demonstrate leading from the front. In most instances, however, it shows a lack of capability or confidence or both, and can result in dependency and/or resentment.

## FEELING YOU HAVE TO HAVE THE ANSWER

It is the leader's work to make sure the best solution is implemented. The solution to the entire problem may come from another team member. Not being able to generate the complete solution personally is not a failure – the leader is being paid for his or her judgement.

Often a leader fails to take note of an excellent suggestion as he or she is anxious because an answer has not come to mind or is too busy trying to make the present solution work.

## BEING THE TECHNICAL EXPERT

Like the trap above, this one arises because the leader behaves as though he or she has to know more than anyone else in the team. This is a particular risk if the problem or a critical issue has to do with a technical issue about which the leader does have some knowledge.

Superior technical knowledge and expertise is often mistaken for leadership by those who seek to demonstrate it, and by many observers, when in fact it masks poor social process and, at times, questionable capability. We argue that the leader does not have to be the best at any or all sub-tasks. The leader must, however, be able to understand and question the logic of technical proposals: "Explain to me, in simple language, how that is going to resolve the critical issue." The ability to give such an explanation is a real test of the depth of technical knowledge.

## IGNORING SOCIAL AND PROGRAMMING ISSUES

Part of the culture that emphasises technical knowledge also downgrades the importance of or difficulty in the other areas of social process and programming. In most cases the technical solutions can be found within the team. It is critical, however, that people have the opportunity to put forward their ideas and that there are time lines, controlled strictly by the leader, applied to the planning process and then to the performance of the task. Programming is not simply recording or telling the time but checking progress against a plan. At the same time, the team leader should be monitoring how the team members are relating to each other.

## ISSUE FIXATION

Often one problem area will gain enormous attention. It may be a critical issue but it gets blown up out of proportion. This may occur during the planning phase or during implementation. All resources are then directed toward the resolution of this issue, resulting in a failure to see how this affects other areas and what impact a new solution has on the rest of the problem. This also leads to a blindness to outside issues; there is not much point if, while changing a tyre, you get run over by a truck.

## NOT WILLING TO STAND OUT IN A CROWD

This is one of the most common and damaging traps – when a leader is reluctant to appear to be a leader. It is often perceived as against the grain to stand out, especially in a superior position. Consequently there is an over-dependence on consensus, an attempt to achieve a collective accountability, or leadership behaviour directed toward a merging with the group. The result is a rudderless slow approach that is conservative because it lacks direction and clear programming. Be reassured that groups/teams do like the leader to be decisive. Consult, certainly, but team members may become very frustrated with a leader who will not be decisive when a decision is required.

# Team membership steps

---

**Box 10.3    Membership**

Everyone is a team member but not everyone is a leader. However, very few people have a clear or shared idea about what behaviour makes for good team membership. The emphasis on team leadership overshadows the critical work of the team member. We hope to provide some clarity about what this means.

---

This section describes some of the constructive behaviour that all team members can demonstrate in order to achieve their common purpose.

The point about teams described here is that, from the viewpoint of each team member, in order to contribute effectively as a team member he or she is dependent upon others.

So how should team members behave and what are the traps? This section describes practical behaviour for all team members. It is described, as for team leadership, as a series of steps:

## CLARIFY CONTEXT AND PURPOSE

If you are a team member, and the great majority of people in school are, are you clear why you are at a meeting or an event? If you are not, then ask. If you are not clear what the purpose is, the chances are that others will also be unclear. How many times have you failed to ask a stupid question and found afterwards that other people were equally in the dark? If you do not ask, the leader will probably assume that you do understand.

## CONTRIBUTE TO THE "HOW"

If you think of problems and ways of solving them, then you have work to do to put these ideas forward. You may identify an apparently trivial point that is in fact crucial. It is for the leader to decide on the plan. Timing is critical if you want to be heard. Be available and accessible. Do not give up if not heard initially. However, do not continue to press a point if it has been recognised.

## LISTEN TO OTHERS

It is important to make a contribution, but equally important to listen to other points of view. It is difficult for the leader if all members are switched to "Send" and none to "Receive". You may find this difficult, especially if you think others are making apparently silly or trivial suggestions or ideas you had already thought of and dismissed. Listening is really hard work. It is not a passive process.

## ACCEPT DECISIONS

If you have had the opportunity to contribute and had the context and purpose explained, it is important to commit to the chosen path even if someone else has had his/her suggestions accepted. You are there to achieve the common purpose, not simply to prove that you are right. The ready and constructive acceptance of the ideas of others is much more likely if the team's social process prior to any decision has been handled well.

## CLARIFY YOUR TASKS

Are you sure:

1.  What you are meant to be doing (CPQQRT)?
2.  What you are meant to do next?
3.  How your effort contributes to the purpose (why)?
4.  How it fits with what others are doing?

If not, ask. Being a team member is an active process, not a matter of blind faith. People working in parallel are not a team. You must be in a position to use your initiative, especially if (or when!) something goes wrong (that is, not to plan). In short, can you think into your leader's head? If in doubt, ask.

## CONCENTRATE ON YOUR TASKS AND COOPERATE

Try to complete your tasks while ensuring that you help and cooperate with others. Be prepared to give information and feedback on your progress and give encouragement to fellow team members. Do not hide information or use it to exercise power.

## ACCEPT SOME COACHING

No one is perfect and you can learn from others. It may be uncomfortable at times but try to listen to other people's ideas as to how you might improve your work.

## DEMAND REVIEW

At the end of, and at times during, the process it is important to check and review your performance. You must ask the leader what he or she thought, and give your own view. It is also your work to suggest how it might be done better (next time). This does not mean proving your idea was right all along.

# Team membership traps

These are some of the most common traps for team members based upon what we have observed over time.

## KEEPING QUIET

This is where the team member does not ask questions or put forward ideas, behaving in a way that suggests that passive acceptance and blind obedience is what is required. It is not sufficient for a team member to assume that he or she will find things out from other team members after the briefing.

## NOT LISTENING

Allowing other people to speak does not equal listening. There is a difference between waiting for some idiot to finish and actively listening. It is remarkable how often we have seen people in meetings and on training courses repeat almost exactly the same point someone else has just made, thereby showing clearly they had not been listening. Women often note that when they put forward an idea, it is ignored; it is then repeated by a man in the team and everyone reacts by saying it is a great idea. Women do not take kindly to such inept social process, nor do minorities, who often confront the same issue.

## GETTING ON WITH MY JOB

This involves ignoring the situation and the needs of others and continuing to do your own work whatever the circumstances. This is a situation where a person isolates himself or herself and has nothing to do with the rest of the team: "It's not my problem."

## GETTING ON WITH OTHER PEOPLE'S JOBS

Some team members interfere with other people's tasks because they think they know better. This is sometimes because they do not know what they are supposed to be doing or because they are not capable of doing the work they were assigned. Such behaviour can also be an attempt to exercise power, disguised as cooperation, but is very different from cooperating.

## WANDERING OFF

We have seen team members wander off either mentally or physically and often both, exploring possibilities without reporting back and in doing so missing vital information. Often it is with good intention, or due to boredom. However, it causes distraction.

## FRAGMENTING THE TEAM

This is a variation of wandering off, and involves setting up ad hoc sub-groups to re-work the problems, changing the tasks and redefining the purpose, again without feedback. This is an exercise of power, setting up internal factions that polarise the team and undermine the leader.

## "I KNEW I WAS RIGHT"

Going along with the chosen plan while actually undermining it in order to prove it was bad may lead to its failure and the dubious satisfaction of seeing it fall apart. This behaviour is especially common when the team member is convinced he or she had had a better solution that was not adopted. This behaviour is also an exercise of power directed at destabilising the existing leadership and may be driven by an inflated ego.

## IGNORING COACHING

Being overly sensitive to questions from others (especially the leader) as to why you are doing something in a certain way. This may mean that you miss ways to improve. The statement "We have always done it like that" is usually an indicator that coaching will be ignored unless the leader or another team member forces the issue through the exercise of authority. It is also, unfortunately, an issue when safe work practice is being discussed: "No one's been hurt before."

## FEAR OF TAKING OVER

Holding back because you worry you might take over the leadership inhibits your potential and the team's resources. There are mechanisms – some subtle, some not so subtle – that fellow team members will use, apart from any intervention from the leader, that will tell you if you step out of line too much.

**Table 10.1**     Complementary roles of leaders and team members

| Leader | Member |
| --- | --- |
| Explain context and purpose | Clarify context and purpose |
| Identify critical issues | Contribute with the "how" |
| Encourage contributions | Listen |
| Make a decision about the plan | Accept decisions concerning which plan |
| Assign tasks | Clarify tasks |
| Monitor progress | Cooperate |
| Coach | Accept coaching |
| Review | Demand review |
| Avoid traps | Avoid traps |

While it is good not to dominate discussion, it is unlikely that the leader will be undermined if you are constructive in your behaviour.

## Process

It is important to emphasise that although we describe these as "steps" they are not necessarily a linear process. Depending upon the result of consideration we may go and revisit one or more steps. The critical issues may require a re-evaluation of purpose, and coaching may result in changing tasks and performance monitoring. The important aspect is that all of the steps are covered. They are linear in that one cannot logically start anywhere. It is not helpful to assign tasks before clarifying the purpose!

## Application

It should be fairly obvious from the descriptions above how to use this model. It can be used to monitor the process in any situation where a team is working together. In the context of schools and colleges we have found that when applied to staff meetings or indeed any meeting a great deal of time can be saved by following this process. On training courses where we have asked school leaders to work with their teams to address actual topics or run actual meetings, many reported that in a forty-five-minute exercise they achieved more, and made more and better-quality decisions, than they usually would in a three-hour meeting. It may seem awkward at first for team members to exercise their authority and raise questions about context and purpose. However, when groups agree explicitly to use this model this authorises the behaviour and the steps can literally be referred to. We see this model functioning well when, for example, a team member reminds the team leader, "Actually, we have not identified the critical issues or addressed them properly." Essentially it is a very practical tool that can be applied without cost and results in the saving of the most precious resource in schools; that is, time!

## Conclusion

In this chapter we have taken a very practical approach to understanding team processes. We have stressed that hierarchy and teamwork are not alternatives. We do not believe there is such an entity as a leaderless team. In all teams, leaders emerge. It is a question of whether they do so by authority or power.

"Teamwork" is an overworked and often vague term. We have been specific in terms of both definition and process. Good teamwork is an essential component of an effective organisation. It is at the heart of an organisation's social process. Without good teamwork and cooperative membership an organisation will fail even if it has excellent technical and commercial processes.

Our unique approach has been and is used to explain how the leadership role and membership role complement each other. This is a major reason why our model has been used so widely. The complementarity of the team leader and member steps can be seen clearly.

# PART 2 Implementing change

# 11 *The general context: critical issues in education*

This chapter examines general issues prevalent in education. This is not limited to Far North Queensland or even Australia.

Several factors cause confusion in schools and impact on the capability of school staff to do their work effectively in achieving the purpose of the school. As is evident in the ongoing discussion in the media and in the contest of ideas by political parties and various lobby groups, the purpose of the education system is unclear or certainly not shared. While we may say that the purpose is to educate young people, exactly what "educate" means can be very different. Simply using broad terms in a vision or mission statement does not take us far enough.

Throughout the history of the public service, strong unions have represented workers to achieve improved remuneration and conditions. "Public servants" are expected to work in the service of the public and as is the case with teachers also meet the expectations and responsibilities related to their profession. A tension may arise between a focus on staff needs and student needs. This materialises in the human resource systems that have developed in these circumstances. The purpose of the human resources system can be more aligned to caring for staff than to providing a service to students and their families.

For example, systems have developed that allow people to be selected for promotion according to seniority, nepotism, favouritism and protectionism rather than merit. Such systems are counterproductive. For example:

- Appointment as a senior teacher may be in reality determined by years of service rather than demonstrated capability to do the work of the role. In effect the position of senior teacher is a reward for longevity and essentially becomes another point on the teacher salary scale.
- In other cases there may be intense pressure to appoint friends or family members to roles rather than selecting a person on merit with demonstrated capability to do the work.

- Another requirement may be to retain permanent positions for people while they are on leave for a variety of reasons and sometimes for many years, causing uncertainty for the school and the people who act in these positions. Some "acting" roles may continue for months or even years.
- The level of work of the role (complexity; see Chapter 3) may not be correctly identified, and we have seen people with strong capability at Level II being appointed to a leadership role that requires Level III (systems) work. So this is the genuinely good classroom teacher with excellent relations with students and families being appointed to a head of department or even principal role. Everything becomes dealt with on a case-by-case basis and no underlying systemic causes are addressed.

Such systems result in the appointment of people who do not have the capability – knowledge, technical skills, social process skills, mental processing ability and application – or are not mentally or physically healthy enough to do the work of the role. People may be doing their best and with "the best intent" but the work they are doing may not be the work of the role and may not be the quality required to deliver the service. The authorities of people in leadership positions are muddled or constrained and as a result school performance plateaus.

Large government departments typically develop strategies, programs, frameworks, plans and models for schools to operationalise. Principals are expected to operationalise strategies, programs, frameworks, plans and models but in general this is not done by designing, implementing, maintaining and improving systems according to agreed criteria (see Chapter 7).

Principals and other school leaders have not been trained in a common methodology to design systems effectively. The absence of a consistent approach across schools results in a confused understanding of the fundamental question of any organisation: "What is the work?" In our view the core work of the principal should be creating and improving systems to achieve the purpose of the school.

Departments of education, be they state or national, have historically attempted to drive change at a high frequency with limited knowledge or consideration of the implications for the people at school level. The next change comes before the current initiative is implemented let alone embedded, causing change fatigue, disassociation and the development of counterproductive systems that drive counterproductive behaviour from staff who find ways to work around the changes. When people in organisations do not understand the work they are expected to do, they will act on their assumptions and this can result in a counterproductive culture of "create your own adventure". People have little choice to do what they can rather than what they should. This has a negative impact on well-being for both staff and students.

The regular churn of politically inspired priorities emphasises *what* should be achieved (targets and outcomes) but principals and their staff are not provided with a consistent and productive methodology for *how* to do their work. School leadership teams may consist of ex-classroom teachers who may have little background or training in operating a twenty-first-century organisation. A leader's development is often based on prior experience or comes from observing other leaders. It is often subject to the fads that come and go. It tends to focus on one aspect of a leader's work: devolved leadership, distributed leadership, entrepreneurial leadership, inclusive leadership, instructional leadership, empathetic leadership, experiential leadership, transactional leadership, transformational leadership. So much jargon and so little substance does not provide the clarity that people need in their roles and authorities.

Despite the efforts of individuals it is often the case that systems in schools drive the behaviour of teachers. Although schools are social entities, it is evident that teachers mostly work alone, both in their classrooms and when they are working in locations other than their classrooms. Many teachers organise their personal lives around a working day composed of timetabled teaching and designated meetings. Most of the working day is spent teaching at least twenty-five students at a time with rostered supervision duties for out-of-class hours. The way that work is organised in schools minimises the opportunities for teachers to work with others. Teachers even complete preparation and marking on their own.

Professional development for teachers usually occurs outside the classroom. The professional development most valued by teachers occurs outside of the school. Teachers do not believe they have been properly trained unless they have participated in a program operating outside of the school during school hours. This occurs at the expense of developing their capability – knowledge, technical skills, social process skills and application – to focus on their practice in the classroom. It is relatively uncommon for teachers to regularly observe other teachers teaching and it is rare for teachers to regularly observe themselves teaching. It is difficult for teachers to improve their capability in this system.

## Expectations: schools as whole systems

Nevertheless the expectations of teachers continue to increase. Teachers today are not only expected to teach but also to meet often strict, externally generated targets. At the same time, they have taken on responsibilities of parenting, social work and even policing. New expectations for being responsible for the mental health and well-being of students are being added. It is as if we, as a society, expect teachers to socialise our children while at the same time ensuring our children achieve academically.

Teachers' social status and reward have not increased. The well-being of teachers is insufficiently resourced, and consequently it is no wonder that more and more teachers consider leaving the profession. People may not appreciate the limited time teachers have to spend with students in a year, and consequently the limited time they have to influence student behaviour. Given these expectations, lack of clarity about work, authority, structure and systems only adds to this burden and wastes effort. Systems Leadership is designed to minimise such waste and to help staff use their creativity and energy in the most efficient and effective way.

In Australia schools operate on a very short year – typically about forty weeks, which becomes thirty-eight weeks after public holidays and student-free days are taken into account. This is similar to the situation in other developed countries.

- Students in Australia spend at best less than 14% of their life at school over a year, based on calculations of students attending for six hours a day, for five days each week, for thirty-nine weeks in a year.
- Students are engaged in lessons for at best less than 10.5% of their life over a year based on calculations of 280 minutes each day for five days each week and thirty-nine weeks each year.
- Students are in the care of parents or caregivers for the remaining 86% of their life each year and yet often parents/caregivers expect teachers to improve their child's behaviour.

School holidays occur four times a year for approximately ten or eleven weeks, depending on a school's location and the sector in which it operates. Students can have no contact with their school for more than seven weeks over the summer vacation in Australia. The majority of the roles in schools operating outside the classroom – for example, leaders such as heads of department, heads of specialist units, deputy principals and principals, or specialists such as heads of curriculum – share these leave entitlements. While some staff members work during the holidays to catch up on tasks, complete associated paperwork or plan for the following term, it is rare for school leaders to operate in teams on Improvement work. Even within a school there is limited time for the school leadership team to work together compared to other organisations. Indeed, we know of no other organisations that operate on such a basis.

Schools usually combine Improvement and support work with Service and Operation work. The day-by-day, hour-by-hour, minute-by-minute demands of the Operation work (teaching) and the Service work (student and business services), take precedence over the work of improvement – designing the future and improving systems. The quality of the Improvement work may be sacrificed or not done at all.

When work is being compacted into a very short and intense school year, it limits the opportunities for creativity, innovation and improvement.

The systems in schools should mitigate this by being designed to ensure that staff members' roles are clear and they do the work that will achieve the best learning outcomes for students. In addition to benefitting student learning, this clarity leads to improved working conditions and higher levels of satisfaction for staff members.

Unlike many other organisations, the vast majority of systems in a school are human. The exceptions are the information management systems. In many organisations there is a greater variety of systems and they are combinations of mechanical, electrical and information technology that are made and operated by people. The systems in a school to educate students involve people directly interacting with people: teachers interacting with students, students interacting with staff and staff interacting with staff. In a human system design, people use their mental processing ability to develop and apply the appropriate technical skill, knowledge and social processing skill. Our mental processing ability facilitates learning.

The design of a system must include an accurate analysis of the knowledge, technical skill and social processing skill that each person needs to do the work to the quality required. When the human system design is implemented without assessing and developing the capability required to do the work, it impacts negatively on the quality and quantity of the desired outputs.

The larger the school, the greater the number of leaders, specialists, support staff, teachers and teacher aides who must develop the specific knowledge, technical skill and/or social process skill required for systems to be effective and achieve their purpose. The complexity increases with the number of people who are involved in the system. Under these circumstances the principal must apply rigorous process management principles, utilise data to inform decision making and develop high-quality systems to consistently meet the educational needs of students in real time.

When the authorities of school leaders are unclear and systems are not effective, people use non-authorised and/or non-productive behaviour and use "power" and work to survive, rather than work to meet the purpose of the organisation. When people cannot predict their environment, it leads to anxiety and under-performance that further impacts negatively on the effectiveness of the organisation. The organisation becomes more like a royal court where people seek to please or depose the rulers rather than achieve the purpose of the organisation.

Public or state schools provide educational services to students and families from the entire population and students demonstrate the full range of capabilities. The work and systems required to operate a school can be arranged as follows:

1.  Teaching and learning services: these include the systems operated to provide a service to the majority of students who are educated by teachers the majority of the time in classrooms

2. Special education: systems operated to provide a service to students with special needs, verified or awaiting verification
3. Student services: systems operated to provide a service to teachers and students when students are outside classrooms for attendance, behaviour, social, emotional and/or academic reasons
4. Business services: systems operated to provide human resource, finance, facilities, admin, cleaning and infrastructure services to the whole school community

## Conclusion

When we look at the school as a whole system operating in its environment, the intrinsic complexity becomes apparent, as does the complexity of the work. However, people trying to run such systems are poorly served by methods and approaches to help them do so. It is to the credit but also the cost of such people that schools achieve what they do.

When systems are not designed for this context, then they will be counterproductive and limit performance and productivity. Principals and other leaders have not been trained to review and plan to make improvements in their schools. Limitations in resources, time and capability restrict principals and their leadership teams from designing and operating high-quality systems to develop the capability of teachers in classrooms where student learning happens. Systems Leadership is specifically intended to address these critical issues. The next chapters examine why and how Systems Leadership was implemented in Far North Queensland, Australia. Although this is a very particular context with specific challenges, we believe that similar issues exist in all education systems.

# 12 *The context of Far North Queensland*

This chapter looks at why Systems Leadership was introduced in the Far North region by the regional director. The need for change was evident from 2008 when state and national testing programs indicated that our students were not performing well in comparison with other students in those cohorts. The regional director had started searching for what could be done differently, especially in the core activity of schools, establishing a signature pedagogy and defining the role of principal as an instructional leader.

In the Far North region the key areas of concern included:

- The effect of poor school attendance on student learning
- The lack of time directed to quality teaching
- The poor outcomes of students in National Assessment Program Literacy and Numeracy (NAPLAN); in particular, those students failing in year 3 would be unlikely to ever "catch up" and participate in learning in later years
- The lack of an effective pedagogy being taught consistently
- The "churn" of school curriculum programs
- The limited capability to provide instructional leadership
- The absence of systems for school improvement
- The limited options for students in senior secondary school
- The inefficient use of resources

Systems Leadership had been used previously in the region, and Tony Tiplady, who had extensive practical experience with the successful application of Systems Leadership at manager level with Comalco (now Rio Tinto), was working in the Indigenous School Support Unit in Cairns. To his credit, Tony harassed the regional director until he finally recognised that Systems Leadership was at least worth investigating as a means of creating the sort of organisation that was needed.

A meeting in Brisbane between the three authors was spent unpacking what we were attempting to do. It became evident to the regional director that Systems Leadership offered a coherent theory of leadership and a comprehensive range of concepts, models and tools which could be learned and applied by people in the organisation. In comparison with any leadership or management program available at that time, it integrated concepts of leadership with structure, systems and capability and as such Systems Leadership was seen by the regional director as being much more than a grab bag of good ideas.

The story above is told as an introduction to this chapter because it raises a few issues worth noting. The regional director did not know what he did not know but someone else in the organisation could see a way forward and persisted until the matter was progressed or at least examined in depth. Sometimes it seems that these good things happen as a matter of chance, but it may be more the case that organisations attract like-minded people who want to share in the mythologies they see developing. When an organisation has a clear purpose it is easier for people, especially leaders, to decide what to do and others to contribute.

Other consultants in specialist areas were used to support the implementation of the five priority areas (explained in Chapter 14). They provided benefit because they identified with the purpose of the organisation, openly supported it and advocated for what the region was trying to do. Their work also offered a range of practices which people could be trained to use.

Despite the areas of concern before any of this work started, the region had a strong sense of identity and had developed a reputation for innovation and a "can do" attitude. This was based on constructive interpersonal relationships, a willingness to develop partnerships and a strategy of recognising and recruiting capable people in key positions.

In general, principals experienced more autonomy and consequently were more able to make decisions relating to school operations than principals in other regions of Queensland. It was the principal of Western Cape College who first used Systems Leadership in a school in a serious way to facilitate a significant change process and achieved improvements in student outcomes through restructuring the delivery of school education from pre-prep to year 12 across four sites in a remote area (this case study can be found at www. maconsultancy.com, the website associated with *Systems Leadership: Creating Positive Organisations*; Macdonald, Burke and Stewart 2018). It was principals in the remote areas who made the concept of student achievement more relevant by interpreting and naming it as "real life outcomes" that all students should achieve after thirteen years of school education.

# Purpose

The difference between the region before and after Systems Leadership originates in the purpose. Previously, the purpose of the region was: to deliver services to schools so that principals, teachers and other staff members could do their work. The purpose of schools was to organise the available resources to support teaching and learning. This was not written anywhere, nor would it have ever been stated as clearly as this, but it can be identified through the mythologies shared by people in the organisation at that time.

However, the data which became available through the NAPLAN, the analysis of year level assessment and state-wide collation of year 12 outcomes indicated that in spite of how effective we believed we were in delivering services and organising resources, our students were not achieving at a standard comparable to other students in Queensland and Australia.

The NAPLAN, which began in 2008, reports on standards of literacy and numeracy for students in years 3, 5, 7 and 9 in Australian schools. For the first time, every school, district and jurisdiction could compare the outcomes of their students in literacy and numeracy with students from across Australia. The NAPLAN results indicated that the outcomes for student cohorts in the Far North region were the lowest of any region in the state and Queensland was one of the poorest performing states in Australia (see Chapter 15).

In the region and generally across the nation, the performance of Aboriginal and Torres Strait Islander students was lower than non-Indigenous students. The NAPLAN data for Aboriginal and Torres Strait Islander students showed distinct differences for the students from three general geographic areas of Cairns city and suburbs, rural areas and the remote communities in the Torres Strait and Cape York. The students in the remote schools had the lowest achievement of all students in the NAPLAN, general assessment and in completion of year 12. The outcomes for Aboriginal and Torres Strait Islander students became a national concern and was a real issue in the region, where these students represented more than 30% of the enrolment.

In November 2008, the Council Of Australian Governments approved the National Indigenous Reform Agreement, which set out six Closing the Gap targets, three of which related directly to school education:

- To close the life expectancy gap within a generation
- To halve the gap in mortality rates for Indigenous children under five within a decade
- To ensure access to early childhood education for all Indigenous four-year-olds in remote communities within five years
- To halve the gap in reading, writing and numeracy achievements for children within a decade
- To halve the gap for Indigenous students in year 12 attainment rates by 2020
- To halve the gap in employment outcomes between Indigenous and non-Indigenous Australians within a decade.

From 2002 there were significant changes in the phases of learning in Queensland driven by the white paper "Queensland the Smart State: Education and Training Reforms for the Future" (State of Queensland 2002).

During the next decade pre-prep programs were introduced for four-year-olds across thirty-five identified Indigenous communities and a reform of senior schooling resulted in a legal requirement for young people to be enrolled in education and training until the age of 17, and increased training and education options for senior secondary students. These measures had significant implications in the Far North region in terms of additional resources and a general recognition that improving the outcomes for students in identified areas was a priority.

In this context it was apparent to the regional director that doing more of the same would result in declining outcomes and that the regional work units and schools needed to work differently if our students were to improve. The data provided the facts of the matter and a basis for identifying needs. This meant confronting the mythologies which had developed and determining the best ways to bring about the improvements required.

---

**Box 12.1    New purpose**

Our purpose needed to change from delivering and organising services to *improving the learning outcomes for all of our students.*

To move forward we needed to recognise what we had been doing and begin to explore what we needed to do to meet the new purpose. This had to be shared by the people working in offices, work units and schools across the region.

---

The most important lesson in this story is that Systems Leadership provides a comprehensive, coherent theory of organisational behaviour and a range of associated concepts, models and tools, which can be applied in a multi-layered organisation to achieve significant improvement on a large scale. It may have been one of four priorities and it may be difficult to untangle the effect of one on the other, but it is clear that the theory and practices of Systems Leadership permeate all aspects of the organisation and enhance the effectiveness of work in all priorities.

# Culture

From the 1970s as teacher preparation transferred from training colleges to the faculties of universities, education struggled for recognition as a profession and a contrived collegiality and congeniality developed among educators to reinforce their own belief in the efficacy of practice in spite of the evidence.

In this state of group think or cognitive bias, as Irving Janis (1971) explains, "there are numerous indications pointing to the development of group norms that bolster morale at the expense of critical thinking". Educators have been captured by the needs of their profession at the expense of their students' learning. This is evident in mythologies about how children learn, how the background of children determines their success at school, the role of the school in society, how schools are managed and the role and the authority of the teacher and principal. Even in the face of limited improvement in student outcomes in literacy and numeracy the professional dialogue is consumed by criticism of the test and resourcing levels rather than a discussion of how to improve teacher practice.

At a broader level, large-scale reform has failed to generate significant improvements in student learning in Australia. In a paper, "Exploding the Myths of School Reform", written for the Centre for Strategic Education in Victoria, David Hopkins (2013) identified the myths of school reform and explained why so many educational reforms fail to impact on student learning. Hopkins uses the term "myths" to mean "unfounded assumptions", and that is different from the meaning that Systems Leadership attributes to "mythology" as the rationale for judging behaviour (see Chapter 5). Hopkins sets out ten myths:

Myth 1    The myth that achievement cannot be realised at scale for all students

Myth 2    The myth of school autonomy

Myth 3    The myth that poverty is a determinant of student and school performance

Myth 4    The myth that it is the curriculum rather than the learning that counts

Myth 5    The myth that teaching is either an art or a science

Myth 6    The myth that external accountability results in sustained school reform

Myth 7    The myth that innovation and networking always add value to school reform

Myth 8    The myth of the contribution of charismatic leadership to school reform

Myth 9    The myth that 'one size fits all' in implementing school reform

Myth 10   The myth that market forces drive educational excellence

By 2013, Systems Leadership had been used widely in the Far North region and people were familiar with the meaning and implications of the term "mythology". From one to ten, the myths identified by Hopkins were relevant to the region and the broader context of school education in Australia. The beliefs that had been held in the education community generally and in the schools and work units of the Far North region did not align with the purpose of improving the learning outcomes of all of our students.

In education it is not uncommon for the purpose of a program or initiative to change over time. In most cases this is not a deliberate choice resulting from feedback or recognition of changing circumstances; it happens because of poor planning. The purpose of a program or initiative is not always clear to begin with, so it is open to interpretation. Contributions are not sought from the people who are expected to do the work so that there are significant gaps in the understanding of the context, which leads to poor planning. Critical issues are not identified, especially implications for the classroom, and teachers make the best of a bad situation. The quality indicators are not clearly defined so that time and energy is wasted on the wrong work.

People became used to the shifting sands and as a result the staff of schools learned to wait and see before committing to a new initiative, because who knows what they are signing up for or how long it will last? There is a rule in schools to either commit early and receive the benefit of the resources that flow in the first phase of a program or wait and see because by the time it comes around to your turn it may have been modified or abandoned or may not happen at all.

We cannot emphasise enough how essential it is to have a clearly stated purpose which is understood by everyone involved. The purpose provides clarity and acts as a reference point for all the decisions that need to be made about what to do and how to do it. Our newly defined purpose focused on the outcomes of all of our students rather than services, schools or employees and it applied to all work units and schools in the region.

# Leadership

The work of leadership is to improve the culture of the organisation (see Chapter 5). This leads to encouraging behaviours which are aligned to the purpose of the organisation. People working in the Far North region needed to have high expectations of our students and to believe they could achieve as well as any other student in Queensland.

When we challenge existing mythologies it causes dissonance. Confronted by the facts, there is a tendency for people to defend the beliefs in which they have invested time, energy and reputation. In the Far North region the mythologies were based on patterns of behaviour which had developed over many years and were shared by other service providers which operated in remote communities; a benign benevolence which supported staff members to maintain the status quo of deteriorating life outcomes.

While regions are organised according to the structure of central office directorates and represent mostly education and corporate services, there is no common organisational structure in schools other than that represented through the hierarchy of principal, deputy principal and heads of department/ curriculum. The number of school leadership positions grew from the 1960s through various additions and bolt-ons in an attempt to cater for changing and expanding needs.

The recruitment and selection of principals and other classified officers reflects the complexity of positions but in schools the levels of work and the authorities of people at different levels are not clear. Organisational charts should reflect levels of work and the authorities of roles. A common mistake is that of having staff members report to more than one supervisor.

Organisational thinking is typically seen as being operational or strategic, with strategic deemed to be more important and the operational a lesser cause for those who enjoy delving in the detail. At central office and region level the conversation is about the "strategic" and principals are selected on their ability to be "strategic". Little wonder teachers are driven mad by their many bosses at all levels of the department, running around being strategic when all the teachers really want is for things to work well. If work is not organised in systems and does not have a clear purpose it results in negative consequences for principals, teachers, students and members of school communities.

During the 1990s, formal planning became important as more decisions and resources were devolved to schools, although it was not always clear what "planning" actually meant in practice. Principals and members of the school communities were introduced to the concepts of the vision or mission statement, which relate to where the organisation sees itself in the future and what the organisation believes to be important. We emphasise the articulation of purpose because it focuses directly on what we intend to achieve and can be used when planning work at various levels of the organisation, whether developing a four-year strategic plan or setting a specific task to be completed.

School leaders were trained to manage the additional planning and accountability measures, their role changed and mythologies developed. Teachers were professionals and did not require intervention in their work. Principals were meant to play a strategic role and therefore should not be involved in the classroom. We believed it to be a mistake for the development of their technical knowledge and skills as instructional leaders to not be a priority.

For a generation of principals, their most important work was interpreted to be planning, budgeting, implementing, monitoring and reporting on human resources, finance, facilities and later information technology. This work aligned to the previous purpose of organising resources to support teaching and learning. However, we judged that it would not be enough to improve the learning outcomes of all of our students. Principals had been deskilled in a capability essential to their role.

## Systems thinking

The term "system" is more likely used to describe the department or sector as "the system" than it is to be used in organising work. Although good teachers and good principals typically use systems to do their work there is limited appreciation of systems and how they contribute to achieving purpose. Without a coherent theory of leadership and management, there is a lack of clarity in our understanding and the language we use. The terms "process", "framework", "policy", "procedure", "guideline" and "system" are used interchangeably and can mean anything anyone wants them to.

Systems are the means of putting policies into action. In remote areas we identified that new teaching systems were required in order that inexperienced teachers, often in their first teaching job and living away from home for the first time, could begin teaching effectively from the day they walked in to the classroom. Data had to be collected and analysed to understand the progress our students made and to target additional or specialist support. With systems in place we have a way to improve what we do, rather than hoping individuals will cope or a miracle will occur.

To meet our purpose and improve the effectiveness of schools, work should be organised in systems. In most schools these would include planning and accountability, teaching and learning, student services and business services. In large schools there will be several sub-systems coming from these. Small schools should be organised along these lines and their principals trained in thinking and working in systems to develop their capability.

## Work

Systems leadership theory is about the work. In education as in many other industries, generic position descriptions are used to describe the work that a person is expected to do. Position descriptions are used in selecting new staff members and existing employees for vacant positions. Position descriptions do not adequately describe the work that a person is expected to do in a specific role, in a specific context.

It is difficult for people to be effective if they do not understand the purpose of their roles and the work they are expected to do. A newly recruited person requires induction into the role and may need training in some aspects of the work. A supervisor and an employee should have the opportunity to clarify the expectations of a role, the reporting relationships and how the work they do relates to other work being done.

In education, there is almost a hesitancy to spend time ensuring that a new employee is clear on the work they are expected to do. Once a person is appointed, they are often left to sort it out. Perhaps this results from the belief that "the professional is responsible for their own work and free from outside interference" or it may be a misguided display of support to display confidence in their ability. In highly relational occupations such as teaching, it is a priority to maintain harmony with coworkers and avoid situations which may cause conflict. This can come at the expense of achieving the intended purpose.

Planning, accountability and business services have grown rapidly as more resources and decision making have been devolved to schools over a relatively short time. Student services, including meeting the needs of students with a range of special needs, are significantly busier across all schools.

## Curriculum, teaching and learning

*Curriculum* refers to the content of a course or program. Principals referred to themselves as curriculum leaders. Secondary teachers, some primary specialist teachers and the support roles in primary and secondary schools are predominantly defined by subject area. Decades of curriculum renewal and development reinforced a belief in the minds of people in schools that it was the most important factor in improving student learning. Resources were devoted to interpreting each syllabus to develop school curriculum programs from which teachers were expected to develop units and lessons. The professional learning accompanying the implementation of a new syllabus aimed to make teachers familiar with the documentation and the intent of the syllabus. Curriculum development became an end in itself and the syllabus was a mystery to be solved.

Even if the syllabus is the best ever developed and describes perfectly what students should learn, there needs to be an improvement in teaching if there is to be an improvement in student learning. The time spent interpreting curriculum documents and rewriting school and class plans meant less time and energy was spent on improving teaching.

Working on curriculum involves discussion, planning, writing and problem solving using documents and other artefacts. The professional learning which typically takes place outside of the classroom at staff meetings, workshops or conferences through presentations and discussion is relatively non-threatening. Improving teaching and learning to the extent that it will result in better student outcomes requires teachers to engage with others directly in their work, through modelling, coaching and feedback.

Teachers and principals in the Far North region shared these mythologies of curriculum. When students did not achieve at a level comparable to other students in Queensland then it could be the fault of the curriculum or the fault of the students. There were several options for resolving the issue. The first was to dumb down the curriculum and have lower expectations of students. This meant teaching work at a lower standard or from a lower year level. For many children who fell behind it meant being withdrawn from classrooms for remedial teaching in small groups. Special curricula were developed to cater for the needs of students. For Aboriginal and Torres Strait Islander students this meant a superficial inclusion of culture.

These patterns of behaviour are difficult to change. The roles which were previously devoted to curriculum work needed to be directed towards improving teaching and learning. Principals needed to develop the role of "instructional leader" so their work was focused on improving teaching and learning.

Current improvement strategies are based on collaboration, where teachers work together in variations of models of enquiry to solve problems of practice. For decades collaboration has been the "holy grail" for educators wishing to emulate other professions to develop their knowledge and practice. In education collaboration is often an end in itself and becomes the work. If these exercises were to be of benefit to the student and not merely entertainment for facilitators they would need to be focused on the right work and matched to the developmental stage of the teachers involved.

## Conclusion

Despite the evidence that students in the region were not achieving to their potential, the underlying mythologies were supporting the current ways of doing things. The regional director did not want to support the status quo and had identified approaches and methods that he thought could improve the situation, especially around a new clearer purpose. Convincing others and testing his hypotheses was the next stage. What if staff saw Systems Leadership as another "initiative", another "fad" that would fade soon enough? It was now up to the regional director to put this to the test.

# 13 *The work of the principal*

The role of a school principal is complex and the workload seems to be ever increasing. Catchphrases like "work smarter, not harder" do not amount to much in reality and promises to "reduce red tape" and "streamline work" wither long before the next initiative arrives. The unofficial guidelines for principal survival advise that when someone, especially a senior officer or a politician, announces that the principal is the most important person in the whole department and possibly the world, it is time to duck for cover or run for the hills, whichever provides the most protection. These appeals to the collective goodwill of school leaders are code for "there is more work coming and it's the principal who will be doing it".

This chapter cannot be and is not the magical "five easy steps to becoming a great school leader", but it will help solve the mystery of how principals can lead their school to be more effective while also improving the working lives of themselves and others. Systems Leadership argues *the leader's work is to create a single, productive culture*. This chapter outlines how the concepts of Systems Leadership are applied in practical ways to clarify the level, type and nature of work; the nature of authority; the impact of the principle "the right person, in the right role, doing the right work"; and the role of teams, team leadership and team membership.

Initially, school leaders are selected on the basis of the capability they demonstrate as a teacher. Successful teachers have well-developed social processing skills to interact with a range of people and good technical knowledge and skills in teaching and learning. Teachers must be capable managers who plan and review their work and use systems to get their work done. While the pool of teachers provides a number of people who may be motivated to become school leaders, there are specific capabilities they will need to develop to be successful in these roles.

The professional development of principals occurs through a smorgasbord of approaches based on eclectic theories of leadership. In attending conferences, participating in workshops, completing courses and picking through the flotsam and jetsam of professional learning, it is rare for the gap between theory and practice to close sufficiently for the school leader to be confident that the outcomes will be worth the expenditure of time and effort.

In Far North Queensland we recognised that developing capability had to be aligned to our priorities if we were to make significant progress. The professional learning being offered through the department of education was useful to train people in policy and departmental systems, but the training provided in the technical aspects of teaching and learning had not resulted in any significant improvement in student outcomes and there was no consistent and sequential approach to developing the capability of school leaders. It was difficult to develop partnerships with universities because the theoretical underpinning of their leadership programs did not align with the direction we were developing and did not provide the level of practical application needed.

Capability development should align to the key priorities, be evidence based and provide a coherent theory and the models, tools, practices and behaviour required to do the work. When the leaders within a group of schools or within a school itself learn to use these elements it boosts their effectiveness. It makes a difference when thinking is based on common understandings, communication on a common language and work on common practices.

## Levels of work

Schools undertake the work required to teach students a curriculum, which is developed within parameters prescribed by government and intended to meet a range of community expectations. State or public schools typically cater for students from across the social and economic spectrum of society, although even within each sector there are marked differences between one school and the next. The correlation between postcode and student achievement can drive parents to buy the family home in the catchment area of a favoured school.

Schools are complex organisations in their own right and may be part of a larger organisation in the form of a department or a school sector or part of a trust/academy. Within a school there should be levels of management that clarify the authorities of managers to make decisions about work and how it will be done. The principal will assign tasks to deputy principals and the business manager. The deputy principal will have the authority to assign tasks to heads of curriculum and heads of department. The business manager will have the authority to assign tasks to the administration officer, cleaners and groundsman. We found that in many instances these authorities were not clear or were understood differently, and as we have discussed, people were reluctant to use to their authority for fear of being "authoritarian". As such there was wide variation in practice and outcomes. In short, work was unclear.

As we have discussed, work is made up of tasks that can be differentiated by their complexity. Systems Leadership proposes that a person must have the mental processing ability required to deal with the complexity of work if they are to complete it successfully. Descriptors of the complexity of tasks and mental processing ability are combined to describe levels of work that are applicable to organisations in general (see earlier chapters).

Level I work involves completion of concrete, hands-on tasks. Examples of these roles in schools include administration officers, laboratory assistants, groundsmen, teachers' aides and cleaners. There can be a clear understanding of the work to be done and there are known steps to be taken in completing the work. This work is essential for the school to operate efficiently and will be set out in manuals as standards, procedures and schedules. Even so it cannot be taken for granted that people will automatically know what work they are supposed to do; a specific role description should clearly set the work the person is expected to do.

The role of the teacher has undergone significant change in recent decades. Today the teacher must have the technical knowledge and skill required to ensure that their students achieve to their potential and meet or exceed benchmarks. It is not about teaching content, testing the students and assuming that some will fail. Teachers differentiate the learning for students to ensure they are successful and improve. This is Level II work in our model.

Teachers need to be effective classroom managers who implement systems, follow processes and diagnose problems when they occur and remedy them. They collaborate with other staff and work effectively as team members in a variety of tasks across the school. Teachers develop partnerships with parents and caregivers to support their children's learning. Increasingly teachers are involved with support staff and the representatives of other agencies to deliver services to students and families.

Teachers who have taught for some time feel the changing expectations. Their role is no longer confined to the classroom, following procedures, teaching according to set methods, administering tests and shutting up shop at three o'clock. As professionals they are expected to be responsible for meeting the changing demands of their role. The work of the teacher requires Level II complexity mental processing.

In a small school, the principal is accountable for the services delivered in the school and at the same time may be directly involved in delivering those services. The small-school principal should be an effective teacher and manager who can develop school-wide systems albeit in a less complex setting. He or she provides leadership within the broader school community, demonstrating effective social processing to engage with a small number of support staff, service providers and community members. The position of small-school principal is an entry point to formal leadership and, similar to the classroom teacher, is at Level II.

As the complexity of the work increases, there are more variables involved and an increasing interaction between these variables. A principal working at Level III should be able to design and implement a school-wide system to achieve an intended purpose. The principal is aware of the systems that operate across the school but may not engage with them all at the same time. The principal uses the available data and feedback to draw conclusions as to why a problem may be occurring and has the ability to design a response, which will take into account the factors required to achieve the desired purpose. The principal at Level III is going beyond the individual case. This ability to discern the systemic from the special cause is critical for success in the role. Principals that keep addressing issues as "cases" will fail to design or redesign the underlying systems that are causing the problem. They may be very busy but they are not effective.

Principals in medium and large schools need to have the mental processing ability to work at Level III. Principals of small and medium schools may demonstrate the capability to work at a higher level. In practical terms this may become evident as they develop new systems, extend their role to work more broadly in the community or develop partnerships across schools or with external organisations.

It became evident in the first years of the improvement agenda in Far North Queensland that small schools with an enrolment of less than 300 or 400 students generally achieved the greatest improvements in the National Assessment Program of Literacy and Numeracy. One obvious reason is that it is simply easier to manage work and make things happen in a small school where there are fewer students and fewer staff members. In a small school the principal may be the only teacher or one of a small number of teachers, and even in a school with an enrolment of a few hundred students the principal usually does not have to work through layers of management. As long as the principal has good social processing skills, the direct supervision of a limited number of class teachers, specialist teachers and support staff may mean that expectations are more easily shared and roles are clearer because the principal has greater direct influence.

Generally, as the size of the school grows, so too does the complexity. In more complex organisations, the results of work may not be seen immediately, and it is more difficult to draw a line between the work done and the results achieved. The principal working at Level IV can see the relationships between systems and understand the impact that one system may have on another. The principal realises in some cases a decision regarding one system may mean a reduction in service in one area in order to improve a service delivered in another system. Principals also need to have highly developed social processing skills, which he or she uses to engage the school in the broader community.

The focus of Level V work is shaping and managing an organisation within its environment. It involves understanding the environment to determine the operations of the organisation into the future and to minimise any negative impact those changes might have on the organisation. This may involve introducing complex organisational projects such as a totally new information management system. To work effectively at this level a principal would need to have the authority to manage the school and make the type of decisions that have far-reaching consequences.

The principal working at Level V may be evident in some large schools and in the private and government sectors where the position is described as an executive principal or similar and is the equivalent of a senior officer in a government department. In reality there are very few principals who truly operate at this level. In many cases the position of executive principal is recognition for principals who are prepared to cope with the extra stress and workload associated with this position rather than qualitatively higher-order complexity.

Level VI work is concerned with shaping the organisation of the future and even influencing the global environment. It could be considered to be the work of directors general in government departments like education. Experience at least in recent times indicates that directors general tend to work at Level V to ensure the department is operating successfully within its environment. It is the exception for a director general/chief executive officer to work at Level VI.

Lack of mental processing ability is one of the main reasons why a person may not work effectively in their role; people who, having invested time and energy in attaining a new position, find they cannot meet the demands of more complex work. The teacher aide who loves children, devotes time and energy to work, is encouraged by others to study to be a teacher but finds that after all, the day is full of problems and planning for a week or a term is impossible. The teacher who has aspirations to work in a leadership role but as a deputy principal finds it difficult to design and implement systems, intervenes directly instead and is always busy trying to do the work by himself or herself. The principal who performs well in a small school but in a larger school focuses on one area of work to the detriment of the whole school and finds it difficult to make decisions when there are so many competing demands.

In such cases, the problem would probably be diagnosed and dealt with in terms of the issues that presented; for example, "He needs some help with planning"; "She should learn to delegate"; "She doesn't know how to handle people." Ensure the person clearly understands their role and what is expected of them. Provide training and development to develop the person's capability to do the work.

An analysis of how the person conceptualises the work may indicate that he or she does not have the capability to match the complexity of the work expected in that role and even with support, improvement will be piecemeal and unsustainable. Again, this has a significant bearing on well-being. It seems there is a reluctance to address this and the departmental systems are lacking. Instead of acknowledging the problem, people are directed to complete professional development and training, which results in little improvement if the problem is really mental processing ability. This in turn creates stress and then an understandable request for stress leave that may continue for some time. Denial of this issue is hugely costly for both the person and the organisation.

## Levels of work and role

A larger school has layers of management representing levels of work and including the various roles required to do the work required for the school to achieve its purpose. These might be generally represented as:

- Level I: teachers' aides, cleaners, administration officers, specialist and support staff
- Level II: teachers, heads of curriculum, heads of department
- Level III: business services manager, deputy principals, small-school principal
- Level IV: large-school or college principal.

Deputy principals may work at Level III if they are involved in the design of a whole school system. In Far North Queensland, schools were organised and managed through systems for planning and accountability, education services (teaching and learning), student services and business services. Deputy principals managed student services and education services, supervised teachers and managed processes in coaching, data analysis, curriculum planning and moderation in a section of the school. Aligning the roles of the deputy principals with the key systems provided clarity for deputy principals in their work and allowed the principal to concentrate on doing the work of his or her role.

The role of head of department (HOD) or head of curriculum (HOC) is seen as an entry point for leadership in schools but is primarily designed as a support or improvement role. The authors have observed that the expectations of the people in these roles are often not clear. In some cases HODs and HOCs are expected to supervise teachers. As an opportunity to develop their capability or because of a strength they demonstrate, HODs and HOCs can be allocated whole-of-school tasks that cross the boundaries of various systems and require the authority normally associated with a deputy principal. They are the last point of "delegation" outside of the classroom and can end up doing random jobs that deputy principals and principals are too busy to do or do not want to do. The work and the authorities of the role must be clear to avoid confusion that can impact negatively on social cohesion and the quality of the work.

The authority to supervise teachers should rest with deputy principals or with the principal in a smaller school. A deputy principal in a large school or the principal in a smaller school should supervise HODs and HOCs. Deputy principals need to maintain currency in their knowledge and skill of teaching and learning while developing their capabilities to lead and manage. These roles require high-level social processing skills to work effectively with teachers, their supervisor, people external to the school and other school leaders. Their role includes influencing school decision making through providing their principal with the information they require to make informed decisions. The devolution of operations to schools has increased the scope and complexity of the work of school leaders; none more so than the business manager, whose role has changed significantly since their widespread introduction in the 1990s. They design and implement school-based systems and processes to ensure that the corporate services systems operate effectively and meet legislative and policy requirements.

In smaller schools the administration officer may work at Level I to complete administrative tasks under the direct supervision of the principal. The work of business managers varies from Level II in smaller schools where there is still a reliance on the principal to Level III in larger schools where the business manager supervises a large number of people in a variety of roles and manages complex systems of service delivery.

## The authority of the principal

Good principals lead and influence the people in the school and community through using excellent social processing skills. The principal's authority depends on "mutuality" – the extent to which the people who are being led are willing to enter into this relationship with the leader.

When people are committed to achieving the purpose of the school, see that work is organised accordingly and believe they are being treated fairly, they will actively support the principal's leadership. On the other hand, if the people who work in the school feel they are being treated unfairly or there is a misalignment between the way work is organised and the purpose of the school, this will manifest itself in their behaviour and they may temper or withdraw their support.

In organisations there are boundaries around the authority of the leader. Systems Leadership identifies some of these as being:

1. The operating limits of the role and role relationships
2. The policies and procedures of the organisation
3. The law (local, national and international)
4. The ethical framework of the organisation, often expressed as "custom and practice" or "the way we treat people", providing it does not breach 1, 2 or 3 above.

This understanding of authority extends to relationships developed with people from other organisations and members of the broader school community. People expect the principal to work within boundaries. When a principal seeks to extend the influence of the school into non-traditional areas, the parties involved must establish mutually agreed boundaries that provide the authority required to lead that initiative.

The principal's behaviour, the decisions made and what is said and done are under constant scrutiny. In schools there are policies and guidelines that govern people's behaviour and there are systems and processes for dealing with people who operate outside the boundaries set by the organisation. When someone abuses or steps beyond their authority it is often described as "bullying". It is behaviour that falls outside of what both parties might understand is an acceptable way to treat other people.

It is no accident that the most successful principals demonstrate excellent social processing. These principals understand they are able to use their authority and influence to optimise the effectiveness of the school to the benefit of students. Both the work and the authority of the principal need to be clear.

## The tools of leadership

Systems Leadership argues the work of the leader is "to create, maintain and improve a group of people so that they achieve objectives and continue to do so over time".

A useful model that principals can use to develop a single productive culture is illustrated in Chapter 6. To understand the culture of the school the principal must unpack the "mythologies"; that is, the assumptions and beliefs held by the people who are part of the school. This includes employees, volunteers, students, parents and members of the broader school community who are connected to the school. This is the stuff that school reputations are made of: how people see the school, what people believe about the school and the assumptions they make about the school.

In addition to the mythologies concerning the school as a whole there are the subcultures of the school. The special education unit, prep classes, physical education department, school administration, library and parent group are ripe for developing mythologies of their own and for having mythologies developed about them. Understanding the mythologies of these groups can assist the principal in understanding why people behave the way they do.

This is particularly useful when a principal is appointed to a school or is planning for improvement. In the early stages of planning significant work, the principal needs to develop a clear understanding of the context; that is, the situation in which the work is occurring. To understand the context of the school the principal talks to people, observes the behaviour of people in the school, collects information and examines data. The principal uses social processing skills to engage people in the school community to contribute to an understanding of the context.

Mythologies can often be at odds with reality. There may be a belief that the school does the very best for students in preparing them for the future, but data from testing programs indicates many students fail to achieve benchmarks in learning and in fact are not being prepared for their future. Exit data indicates that students do not transition to work or further education. Conversations with past students tell of disappointment that their expectations were not realised.

Mythologies can be very comforting because they help us to predict our environment and when a principal challenges them, people will experience dissonance. This must occur if there is to be change. Some people may choose to ignore the data or go into a state of denial, and some may see challenging data as merely an aberration. These people are generally a minority and faced with the facts most people will test their beliefs and assumptions against the information provided. Some people welcome the information and the new understanding it generates.

It is the work of the principal to engage members of the school community to identify and establish new mythologies that align with the purpose of the school and will create a productive culture. As identified in Chapter 6, three tools that the principal can use to develop a productive culture are symbols, systems and behaviour. The principal must apply these consistently and be prepared to persist with them until the new mythologies are established.

## SYMBOLS

Uniforms, school colours and mottos exist to develop a sense of belonging and contribute to what is commonly described as the student morale. They are examples of symbols that reflect the school's culture.

During the days of the school inspector, the first heading on the inspection report related to the general condition of the school and grounds. In this section the inspector of schools would describe the appearance of the school buildings, the classrooms and grounds. Any improvement, outstanding feature or extra effort resulted in a commendation. Similarly, any deficiency in the appearance, condition, upkeep and tidiness was recorded. Symbols provide a strong indication of what a school is like, what is valued and what it must be like to study or to work there.

Schools may require students to wear a uniform. What is the purpose of requiring students to wear a uniform to school? If it is to develop the students' sense of pride in their school but uniforms are a ragtag collection of odds and ends, there may be a disconnect between students and the culture of the school.

Similarly, if the purpose of a classroom is to facilitate student learning then it should be designed and furnished with that purpose in mind. The displays in the classroom should relate to student learning. The furniture should be arranged to facilitate learning. The classroom should be tidy to allow student learning.

Behaviour can also be symbolic. When walking around the school, do staff and students greet each other? Do students move about the school in their classes in a calm and organised way? Is the principal out in the school grounds during break times and meeting parents at the school gate after school, at pick-up time?

Symbols are a rich source of information. Principals who are active observers and participants in the life of the school are attentive to symbols and understand their meaning. They utilise strategies like "walk throughs" to regularly and informally take the pulse of the school through observing symbols and behaviour.

## SYSTEMS

If a principal could provide only one thing to a school, then maybe "clarity" should be the choice. The starting point would be clarity of purpose. When principals learn to think in systems it makes a world of difference to people's work. Systems organise work and drive the behaviour required to achieve an intended purpose.

In most cases the principal has the authority to implement a system in a school and will be the owner. The custodian of a system is the person responsible for monitoring the system to ensure it works as intended and achieves its purpose. In larger schools the deputy principals and the business services manager will be the custodians of systems.

Broadly speaking, a school requires these systems:

- Planning and accountability systems include the processes of planning, monitoring, reviewing and reporting the work of the school
- Education services include teaching and learning, assessment, data and school curriculum planning systems
- Student services include systems to optimise student engagement in learning such as behaviour management, attendance, well-being and special needs
- Business services include systems to plan, review and report and deliver corporate services – human resources, finance, infrastructure and school administration
- School operations include the day-to-day organisation of people and resources to support effective teaching and learning.

The language used to describe how work is organised in schools is not precise. Terms like "framework", "policy", "system", "process", "procedure", "initiative" and "program" are used interchangeably without much thought given to the intended purpose of each. In Systems Leadership, systems are used to organise the work to enact policy. They direct the flows of people, money, resources and information to drive behaviour and they may incorporate frameworks, flowcharts and schedules to do this.

To improve student outcomes, teaching and learning is developed as a system rather than being a collection of practices from which teachers choose what they might do. A teaching system ensures that the most effective practices, based on research, are used consistently to achieve improved outcomes. Data systems organise the collection and analysis of specified student learning data to inform and improve teaching and learning. School curriculum planning systems ensure that learning experiences are organised to meet the needs of students.

An example of the tasks set for principals comes from a PowerPoint presentation at the regional director's regional business meeting in 2011. This slide outlined the systems to be established in every school:

Systems development:

- Selection and recruitment of staff by principals
- Student attendance
- Explicit teaching in every classroom
- Coaching
- Intervention
- Connecting parents.

Systems Leadership is a key driver of staying consistently focused and making all the other dimensions of schooling work in the service of teaching and learning. Training in Systems Leadership provides school leaders and regional leaders with the skills and tools they need to make schools and work places more effective and better places to work.

## BEHAVIOUR

If the purpose of the school is to maximise the learning outcomes of all students then the behaviour of the principal and other members of the school community must be seen to be consistent. A key reference which informed the understanding of the work required, *Leadership for Learning: A Research-based Model and Taxonomy of Behaviours* (Murphy et al. 2007), draws on research of the previous thirty years to explain the work required of school leaders to improve their schools to achieve better outcomes for students. It argues "a particular type of leadership is especially visible in high performing school districts – 'leadership for learning', 'instructionally focussed leadership' or 'leadership for school improvement.'"

The paper explains that

the touchstones for this type of leadership include the ability of leaders:

a) To stay consistently focused on the right stuff – the core technology of schooling, or learning, teaching, curriculum and assessment and
b) To make all the other dimensions of schooling (e.g. administration, organization, finance) work in the service of a more robust core technology and improved student learning.

This indicates that the role of the principal has two dimensions. The first is focused on the principal's technical capability in teaching and learning and the second on managing to improve the quality of teaching and learning.

In recent decades principals have been distracted from the focus on teaching and learning to concentrate on being effective managers even though no coherent and consistent approach was ever used to develop their capability to perform either aspect of the role. The development of principal capability has been either discouraged or neglected. The de facto focus on developing principals as instructional leaders became "the principal as curriculum leader", a strategy which has limited impact on the quality of teaching.

## Instructional leadership

In addition to developing capability in the core technology of teaching and learning, principals need to develop their capability to be instructional leaders. This involves the behaviour and practices that a principal will use in working with other school leaders and teachers to improve teaching and learning. The focus of the work is the improvement of teaching and learning, the core business of the school. Principals need to understand what effective teaching is and be able to coach other school leaders to be effective coaches and teachers to improve their practice.

The principal and school leaders support improvement across the whole school context through instructional coaching. Teachers need regular, affirming and informative feedback to improve their teaching. Coaching provides teachers with insightful and intensive opportunities to reflect and construct their understanding about teaching to improve student performance.

In Far North Queensland the regional coaching system was aligned with the principles of key policies and guidelines of the department of education: the Developing Performance Framework, Principal Capability and Leadership Framework, and Principal Performance and Development Plan (Education Queensland 2018; n.d.; n.d.).

The regional coaching system incorporated the following qualities:

- Acknowledges that student learning is the heart of our work
- Aligns teacher development priorities with school and regional strategies
- Includes the process of prompt feedback, inquiry and reflection in order to meet individual needs of adult learning
- Reflects and respects the alternative ways individuals learn, in order to aid instruction to students using the best research and practices
- Emphasises improved performance of students, teaching colleagues and the region
- Achieves positive change throughout the region's education system by facilitating individualised learning
- Learning is most likely to occur when the learner is in the first instance given high degrees of support, then gradually assumes more responsibility for new skills through guided practice and finally independent control of the strategy.

## Instructional coaches

The work involved requires the following capabilities:

- Pedagogical knowledge
  A thorough understanding of developing and implementing effective instructional strategies.

- Content expertise
  A thorough understanding of the subject they are coaching and a working knowledge of the curriculum

- Interpersonal capabilities
  Highly developed social processing skills, including the capability to build relationships, establish trust and credibility and tailor assistance to individual adult learning needs.

Finally, the principal should use the team leadership and team membership model described in Chapter 10.

Leadership is a social process. In Systems Leadership, the team leadership steps outline what the team leader does to lead the team to plan and complete work. In this context the team leader is a person who has the authority to do the work. The role of the principal is to use the team leadership steps in teams he or she leads and model them for other team leaders in the school.

In a school, the team leaders will be the custodians of the systems and sub-systems and in some cases other people who have been assigned a task which requires a team to complete. When the team leadership steps are used consistently throughout the school the process becomes second nature to team leaders and team members, and in the authors' experience the initial planning of quite complex pieces of work can be completed in a short period of time, sometimes as little as an hour.

Detailed information on team leadership and team membership is available in *Systems Leadership: Creating Positive Organisations* (Macdonald, Burke and Stewart 2018). Team leadership and membership are also incorporated in practical tasks in Working Together courses. As in other models and tools of Systems Leadership the steps begin with the context and purpose.

---

### Box 13.1    Team leadership steps

*EXPLAIN THE CONTEXT AND PURPOSE*

Explain the situation, including constraints, and state a clear, overall purpose in a single statement. Constraints are the known limits; for example, budget, safety, time, resources, legislation.

*IDENTIFY AND ADDRESS THE CRITICAL ISSUES/PROBLEMS*

Constraints are what you know. The critical issues are what you need to work out with the team.

Identify and communicate the key threats and what you will do if they arise.

A critical issue threatens the purpose. It is a "showstopper". Usually there will be three or four critical issues. Describe a critical issue by saying "what if"; for example, "What if the resources we ordered aren't available?"

*ENCOURAGE CONTRIBUTIONS*

The team leader explains the context and gives team members time to think.

Ensure that everyone is positioned so that you are accessible to all team members.

Give each team member the opportunity to contribute.

Be sensitive to non-verbal indicators.

*MAKE A DECISION ABOUT THE PLANNED ACTION*

End the discussion stage and articulate the plan to team members.

Make clear the intended actions, the critical issues and how they will be dealt with.

Outline why some ideas have not been used.

*ASSIGN TASKS*

Team members should know what they are meant to do to achieve the purpose.

Use the task assignment model tell each member:

- Their task – what they have to do
- What they need to do next
- If and how their task complements other team members' tasks
- How their task will help to achieve the purpose
- The timeline.

## MONITOR PROGRESS

- Technical considerations – Are the solutions working? Do they need to be modified?
- Social considerations – Are team members engaged, using their initiative and interacting?
- Temporal considerations – Is the timeline being met?
- Environmental considerations – The team leader should monitor the environment to ensure that team members can work effectively.

## COACHING

The team leader helps team members complete their tasks:

- Give an instruction – to direct a team member to do something
- Give advice – suggest how to do something
- Teach – show and tell how to do something
- Ask – to gain information.

## REVIEW

At the end, the leader should review the plan – whether the purpose has been achieved – and give feedback to team members on team membership and leadership behaviour.

Some principals who have used the team leadership steps have included professional learning as an additional element.

The team leader identifies the professional learning required by team members to complete this task:

- Knowledge
- Technical skills
- Social processing skills.

# Team membership

While people in schools speak of the need for teams and teamwork, more often than not they call these "committees" rather than "teams". Ian Macdonald, one of the current authors, takes great pains to point out the essential difference between the two is that a committee is a meeting of equals who with the assistance of a chairperson have the authority to make decisions on behalf of themselves and colleagues. In a school the social committee is one of a few examples of a true committee structure.

Schools should be meritocracies and teams have leaders who have the necessary authority to ensure the task is completed and is accountable for the outcomes. Team members are selected on the basis of their potential to contribute to the work and achieve the team's purpose.

Systems Leadership outlines the practical behaviour that all team members should demonstrate and aligns them to the team leadership steps.

---

**Box 13.2    Team membership steps**

*CLARIFY CONTEXT AND PURPOSE*

The team member must ensure they are clear on the purpose and be prepared to ask questions if they are not.

*CONTRIBUTE TO THE HOW*

Team members should contribute their ideas, and put forward problems they think of and ways to solve them. Team members should be aware of the social process and ensure they are accessible and available within the sight of the leader.

*LISTEN TO OTHERS*

Team members should listen to other team members' points of view.

*ACCEPT DECISIONS*

If the team member has been able to contribute ideas and the leader has considered them, then the team member should accept the decisions that the leader makes and commit to the chosen path.

*CLARIFY YOUR TASKS*

Team members need to be sure:

- What the team member is meant to be doing
- What the team member is meant to be doing next
- How this fits with what other team members are doing.

*CONCENTRATE ON YOUR TASKS AND COOPERATE*

Team members should encourage other team members, help them and cooperate with them to complete the work. Provide the team leader with feedback on your progress.

*ACCEPT SOME COACHING*

Team members should listen to other team members, and learn from them to improve your work.

> *DEMAND REVIEW*
>
> Team members should review their performance and ask their team leader for feedback. Suggest how it might be improved to work better next time.

# Summary

Throughout this book the authors have presented the concepts, models and tools of Systems Leadership and endeavoured to link them to the work expected of people in schools.

In Systems Leadership the role of the principal is considered in terms of the work that a principal will do to ensure the school achieves its purpose.

Systems Leadership provides a simple but thorough understanding of capability and a theory of levels of work in an organisation. These two elements inform a variety of systems including recruitment and selection, school management and performance development. School leaders must have the mental processing ability to deal with the complexity of the work of their roles and the capability to complete the work expected.

The tools of leadership – symbols, systems and behaviour – are part and parcel of the work of the teacher in the classroom and the principal in the school. The team leadership steps and team membership steps provide a means to achieve purposeful collaboration on the important work of the school.

Although it is unlikely that the pace of change will slow and the expectations of schools will become any clearer any time soon, Systems Leadership provides principals with the concepts, models and tools they can use to lead and manage their schools to be more productive. Principals can apply Systems Leadership to understand the external environment and how it may impact on the work of the school. There is nothing more satisfying than listening to principals speaking up, to give their contributions on a new "initiative/priority/program"; to question the context that led to the work; to seek clarity about its purpose; or to identify the critical issues, the authorities and resources required and the outputs expected. Principals have considerable authority in their role and can influence the behaviour of other people through their social processing skills. This can extend to influencing their supervisor to be the sort of leader they need them to be.

Our analysis reinforced the idea that for any change to be successful the work of the principal was crucial. However, this perhaps obvious point was interesting to explore as we discovered that the work and role of the principal was not clear, and we needed to address that first.

# **14** *Implementing change*

This chapter explains how we implemented Systems Leadership in order to improve the way that schools were organised and operated and in turn improve student outcomes. This included raising awareness; gaining commitment; implementing training programs; developing the coaching capability of managers at all levels; developing and implementing new systems; and establishing consistent regional requirements with reference to the Technical, Social and Commercial domains.

The improvements were made in the region over a five-year period. As the work developed, more information became available and more ideas and questions were generated about what else could be done. New thinking often creates dissonance and there is a tension between maintaining successful work and what needs to be done to meet higher targets.

## Understanding the context

Understanding the context is an important first step in planning significant work. Good leaders do this as a matter of course, especially when they begin in a new role or consider a major change. A principal who is new to a school will often spend a term or semester understanding the context before embarking on new projects or significant work.

Context is an element of the models and tools used in Systems Leadership. It is the first step in developing a task assignment and in the team leadership model. Leaders need to understand the context to develop a purpose that clearly states what the organisation wants to achieve. Using the contributions of team members in developing context provides a more thorough understanding and indicates to team members that their contributions are valued.

When a task needs to be completed immediately – for example, in the case of an accident or emergency – the context may be explored and developed in a matter of minutes. For longer-term and more complex work, leaders may spend months clarifying the context to ensure it is a sound basis for developing a purpose and planning the work. The leader must be open to the views of others and be skilled in questioning, listening and observing. The leader may not always agree with the contribution they receive but they should provide others with the opportunity to have their say.

When gathering information for the writing of this book, discussions with principals revealed that the presentation of student data was the catalyst that created the dissonance that led them to commit to change. As shown in the analysis of data in Chapter 15, many of the students in Far North Queensland were failing at the most basic levels. In the early years, a high proportion of our students were not achieving to even a minimum standard in literacy and numeracy and after thirteen years of school education many young people left with nothing to assist them in gaining entry to further education, training or employment.

This compelling case is reflected in the purpose that was developed for the region and became the basis for a narrative that was used and retold in many forms in many contexts over the next few years. It drove the consistency and persistence required to make and sustain change.

## Purpose

Our purpose was always clear: to improve the learning outcomes for all our students.

## Critical issues

We identified several critical issues that would need to be addressed, if we were to achieve our purpose. The three most important were:

1.  What if staff members did not see any need to change?
2.  What if the work was not clear?
3.  What if staff members did not have the capability to do the work required?

## Developing a vision for the region and schools

The support of principals is critical to the success of large-scale improvement because of their key role in leading school communities. Previously, principals had not been brought together on a regular basis by the region for professional learning or to plan work and conduct business. When principals did meet it was typically for one-off workshops and meetings called by the central office to meet accountability requirements on policy and procedures.

To signal that change was required, things needed to be done differently from the start. In contrast to the culture of "choose your own adventure", senior officers and managers from the regional offices and the principals of medium and large schools – eighty participants – were asked to attend a two-day workshop to plan how we would improve the outcomes of our students. Neil Carrington and John Edwards, consultants in leadership and organisational development, were engaged to facilitate the workshop. Using external facilitators allowed the leaders to participate fully in workshops and to produce the documentation that was available for participants to take away.

The actual outcome of the workshop is in the document "Far North Queensland – Leading for Learning", shown in Box 14.1.

---

### Box 14.1    Far North Queensland: leading for learning

The Far North Queensland [FNQ] region has a *shared vision* which gives us clear direction and alignment of purpose. Our schools are student centered [*sic*] and we all share a passionate belief in the potential of every child.

Respect, trust, honesty, resilience and integrity are the *values* which underpin the way we work together, relate to each other and get the best out of each other on a daily basis. As leaders we value autonomy and are skilled at flexibly meeting the diverse needs of learners. We are committed to public education and act on a strong belief that every child in FNQ can achieve to the best of his or her ability.

Far North Queensland is networked to ensure that *communications* are efficient, effective and functional. We use sophisticated, multi-modal technology which is reliable and easy to use in the diverse settings of our region. Our authentic feedback culture embedded in practice promotes continuous improvement, risk taking and the freedom to be flexible yet accountable. Our policies and practices are purposeful, performance driven and clearly aligned with our vision.

*Decision making* is decentralised and our school leaders are integral members of regional decision making forums and processes which prioritise programs and resource allocation. We advocate strongly for appropriate resources to meet the needs and challenges of schools and clusters. We know our schools and communities and value flexible processes and structures. Resources are allocated differentially and transparently. Our principals determine the most appropriate staffing arrangements to facilitate learning in their schools.

In our region we ensure that our practice is aligned with our vision. We prioritise our work to ensure that what we do is relevant, necessary and implemented efficiently. We lead change through collaboration and make strong evidence-based decisions to improve school effectiveness.

We have a clear understanding of the need for *professional learning* communities and professional development that impacts teaching and learning. Coaching and mentoring models ensure the transfer of theory into practice. Professional learning is data-driven and aligned with school needs and FNQ priorities. The required time, money, experience and expertise are provided to facilitate professional learning.

Our *Service Commitment* is clear and collectively owned by everyone in our schools and region. The whole school community has clear confirmed responsibilities, roles and targets to provide student pathways and community partnerships. High yield [*sic*] teaching and learning practices ensure that every student continues to improve. Our destination data proves how successful we are in achieving the Service Commitment.

# Establishing priorities

Priorities were identified and teams were established to investigate each one to determine the work required to make it happen. The priorities that were developed in this workshop were maintained in the schools and region from 2010 until 2014. During that time the wording changed as the work developed and more was understood, but essentially the priorities that we began with remained the same five years later.

The regional priorities were:

- Principals as instructional leaders
- Explicit teaching
- Data-based decision making
- Organisational improvement
- Connecting parents/caregivers to their children's learning.

Setting priorities was a first step to finding out what was needed to turn intention into reality and to ensure that time, energy and resources were directed to making them happen.

It was apparent that the demands of the job were having a deleterious effect on the well-being of principals and other school leaders. The way forward was to ensure there was a clear purpose and priorities for work, and the work was organised and supported to ensure it was completed to the quality required.

In education in general, we argue it is the lack of clarity of purpose and the continuing misalignment between what are the stated priorities and the reality of day-to-day expectations and experience of teachers, principals and other staff members that causes stress. In the preparation for the writing of this book, interviews with principals indicated that establishing and maintaining priorities over five years provided them with the clarity and consistency they needed to effectively plan and implement the work required. Identifying the right work and sticking to it was a key factor in achieving improved performance.

# Developing a purpose

The senior leaders in the region had developed a shared understanding of the context of education in Far North Queensland and a vision of what education should be like. In strategic planning models it is common to develop a mission statement that is derived from the vision. A mission statement talks about who we are as an organisation and where we are going. It is the sort of thing that can be found on websites, letterheads and posters – a proud declaration of our place in the world.

During the 1990s, the idea of a mission statement had been introduced in school planning but had not really taken hold. Mission statements were created and displayed and people often could relate to the sentiments expressed, but there was no direct connection between what was written and the work people were expected to do. A mission statement may serve as the shorthand version of the vision but does not bridge the gap between intention and reality.

Systems Leadership uses the concept of "purpose", which specifies what is to be achieved by accomplishing this task. Determining the purpose of an organisation is a very practical way of providing people with a clear under-standing of what they need to achieve. This in turn gives people clarity about the work they need to do.

Developing a purpose is at the heart of the tools of Systems Leadership; for example, when developing a system, assigning a task and using the team lead-ership and membership steps. When people become familiar with the concept of purpose, they will apply it to their day-to-day work activities; for example, *the purpose of our meeting, the purpose of our various school communications* or *the purpose of a workshop.*

With the knowledge that Systems Leadership brought to the region, we defined our purpose as "to improve the learning outcomes for all of our stu-dents". In terms of a practical application the purpose was described through a service commitment to students. The idea of the service commitment origi-nated with principals working in the remote schools on Cape York and in the Torres Strait as a means of focusing the work of schools to ensure that every student left school with what became described as a "real life opportunity".

Good ideas and smart responses often emerge from the most difficult contexts where people are struggling the hardest to get ahead. This was dem-onstrated by, for example, the outstanding leadership of people such as Ross Clark, a previous regional director, and Don Anderson, an executive direc-tor and principal, both of whom had the capability to understand context, develop clear purpose and translate it into action.

The service commitment was described in the Far North region as a commitment that 100% of students in our state schools would graduate as confident, healthy, young Australians and achieve:

- An Overall Position (OP) score and enter university, or
- A clear Vocational Education and Training pathway to employment, or
- Paid employment of at least 25 hours per week, or
- Alternative pathways (for students with special needs).

The service commitment was adopted in the region because of its practical, all-encompassing nature and its focus on student outcomes, and because it had proven to be successful when adopted by some remote schools. Although the commitment focused on the outcomes for students leaving school at year 12, the ability of the students to achieve an outcome depended on the contribution of all the phases of schooling from the early years through to secondary education.

This straightforward, concise, targeted commitment was relevant to various stakeholders in state education and the broader community of Far North Queensland.

As a result of the service commitment:

- In schools, systems were developed and services were provided to ensure that all of the students would achieve the service commitment. In the senior secondary school, individual student learning accounts were negotiated with the assistance of mentors and the input of parents and caregivers. It was important to monitor students' progress during their school education but there was an added expectation that schools would monitor each student's destination when they completed year 12. In some schools, such as Tagai State College in the Torres Strait, 100% of students achieved the service commitment because the school continued to work with students even after they had completed year 12 to ensure they achieved a worthwhile pathway.
- In the regional office and other work units, systems were developed and services provided to support the delivery of the service commitment. The capacity to deliver services can be enhanced when systems differentiate between what can be best delivered by a region or district on behalf of a group of schools and what needs to be delivered by individual schools. Scaling up the delivery of some services such as capability development can be more cost effective and lead to greater consistency in practice. At the same time, coaching and feedback systems are required to operate at an individual level in schools to improve the performance of teachers and other staff members.
- Students came to understand they had a role in achieving a real life outcome – be on time, be prepared for learning, complete tasks, attend school every day. The service commitment was a reciprocal arrangement that depended as much on the commitment of the student to his or her learning as it did on the provision of services to the student. This became evident, especially with the development of explicit teaching. Just as teachers developed their teaching practice, students developed their

learning practices. Learning was no longer a mystery. Students understood what they needed to do to maximise their learning.

- Parents could be called upon to support their child to be the best student they could, by providing good nutrition, ensuring enough sleep, assisting with homework, ensuring regular attendance, purchasing equipment, negotiating their child's learning program and attending school functions.
- Businesses could be co-opted to support the school through providing work placements and sponsorships, supporting attendance programs and participating in school governance.
- Other government departments and non-government agencies clarified how they worked most effectively with schools to meet their purpose and maximise the outcomes for students across a range of areas.

The Far North region implemented a system of education and training which delivered the service commitment to students and met the training and skilling needs of population, industries and communities in Far North Queensland. Above all, there was a clear message that if everyone worked together to support all of our children to achieve a real life opportunity then we would all benefit from a stronger, more productive community. The service commitment made sense to people and was used as the basis for marketing state education in Far North Queensland.

Below is a page from a brochure used to market state education in Far North Queensland. The common messages of the service commitment, explicit teaching, real life outcomes and more effective and efficient management are evident on this page. Brochures were distributed to every family of students in our schools and at community and business events.

The service commitment caused dissonance with some principals because it challenged the existing culture and had direct implications for school operations. It was no longer acceptable to allow students to continue to fail from one semester to the next without intervention. Schools could not focus almost exclusively on the students who performed well in the academic stream when many would not go on to tertiary study and needed to be prepared for employment or training.

During 2013 a significant task was undertaken to develop region-wide systems for key areas of performance: attendance, behaviour and explicit teaching to achieve more consistency and greater improvement. These systems were developed by teams composed of people from schools and the regional office. Capability development was focused on the knowledge and skills that people needed to do the work and the implementation was planned to include trial and review.

It is important to emphasise the complexity of this task and the heavy workload involved. Systems Leadership helped participants to understand the nature and complexity of this work and provided the tools and models to assist team members in completing the task.

## Box 14.2    Poster

*FROM CRAYONS TO CAREERS*

*FAR NORTH QUEENSLAND'S SERVICE COMMITMENT*

Four years ago Far North Queensland Education made a bold "Service Commitment": 100% of students in our schools will graduate as confident and healthy young Australians and achieve:

Far North Queensland state schools are committed to delivering education, training and skills needs of students as well as industry and the diverse FNQ community.

- an Overall Position (OP) and enter university; or
- a Vocational Education and Training (VET) pathway to employment; or
- paid employment of 25+ hours per week; or
- alternative pathways for some students with special needs.

Since the introduction of our Service Commitment there has been:

- an 18% increase in students achieving the Queensland Certificate of Education
- improvement to Far North Queensland's NAPLAN scores across all areas – particularly in the early years where scores have increased by 10%
- dramatically improved Aboriginal and Torres Strait Islander NAPLAN scores – in some instances scores have improved by 18%.

A key to these students' improvements has been the introduction of explicit teaching which is often referred to as: I do (teacher demonstrates), we do (class participates), you do (individual student does activity).

State school education in the Far North covers over 273,000 square kilometres from Cardwell to Thursday Island. There are over 100 state schools providing services ranging from early childhood and primary school, to distance education high school and college where a range of vocational and academic pathways are offered, such as TAFE and university subjects.

As part of the region's strategy to ensure our 34,000 students have the best opportunity to achieve real life outcomes we have developed a Charter of High Expectations. Additionally, we have done a lot of work with school leaders, asking the question, "What can we do better?" One of the outcomes of this was the development of management tools to help us run our schools more effectively and efficiently.

We are on a journey of improvement and I am proud of the significant progress we have made in a short time. I encourage the whole community: parents, carers and service providers to join us on this journey to continue improving the education and job opportunities of our young people – our future.

Clive Dixon
REGIONAL DIRECTOR

# Implementing Systems Leadership to help us achieve our purpose

## PURPOSE

The purpose of implementing Systems Leadership in the Far North region was to develop the capability of school and regional leaders to improve the organisational effectiveness of schools and work units to achieve improved outcomes for our students.

## PROCESS

Systems Leadership was implemented in stages:

1.  Raising awareness
2.  Developing the capability of leaders
3.  Developing and implementing region-wide systems.

The starting point for introducing Systems Leadership was training the regional management team, which included people at manager level and higher from regional offices and work units representing education, corporate and support services. In effect these people led the teams that delivered services to schools. Managers reported to the regional director and met as the regional management team once a month to plan the implementation of the strategies coming from central office and to manage issues arising in the schools or region.

In the region and across the department, people were in a general state of "busyness", reacting to issues at the level of an emergency response even for everyday matters. Within large departments and depending on the leadership and the degree and type of political engagement, risk-averse behaviour can become all-consuming. Much of the work each and every day was directed towards meeting the demands of external players and organisations. The more you feed this insatiable monster the more its appetite grows, the busier you become and the less effective you are in doing what should be the work of your role.

There was little support for Systems Leadership in the regional management team. Some people approached it with an open mind but mythologies that had developed when it was used at Western Cape College were largely negative and in people's minds it was associated with the mining industry, and therefore it was concluded that it probably was not suitable for education and would not work. In actual fact Systems Leadership originated from work in the public sector in the United Kingdom, in particular in health and social services (Jaques 1976). It was developed in the mining sector much later.

As an introduction to Systems Leadership, the regional management team completed a modified two-day Working Together course led by a trained consultant at an off-site venue with accommodation provided. This deliberate choice removed people from their normal workplace to minimise distractions and focus minds on the work at hand. Mobile phones were off and instructions were that, short of disaster, participants were not to contact their offices and nor were offices to contact them.

In addition to presentations on the concepts of Systems Leadership, participants completed practical tasks in small teams, made observations and received feedback through analysis of videos taken during the activities. This was quite confronting as mythologies were exposed and people reacted, sometimes with frustration and sometimes surprise at what was possible. For the most part it was working together, uninterrupted for a sustained period of time, using the tools and models that made a difference to how people viewed each other and their understanding of team leadership and team membership.

When initiatives were introduced in the department, it seemed that it was always the teachers and principals who were expected to change what they were doing. People in schools developed a sense that "they are doing this to us". In fact it was the leadership of the organisation that had to work differently in the first instance, if the region was to achieve its purpose.

In the early stages of change, people test the boundaries to see if it is really happening as the leader has said.

- *Are the leader's behaviour and actions consistent with what he or she has said?*
- *Is there any room for team members to continue their existing behaviour or to introduce their own version of what might be required?*

The leader must gain the commitment of team members and be aware how each team member views the proposed changes so that the decisions that are made and the actions taken are sensitive to the needs of individuals even though the changes may continue to challenge their mythologies.

Readers who have a teaching background may see similarities to beginning the school year with a new class. Teachers have high expectations of their students. Lessons are very structured and the teacher spends time establishing systems for the classroom and teaching the students how to behave so they understand what is expected in different types of lessons, at break time and when moving around the school. When students test the boundaries of the behaviour expected, the teacher reinforces the desired behaviour and ensures their behaviour is consistent in every circumstance. In order to establish patterns of behaviour the teacher must be consistent and persistent over time.

# Organisational domains

Systems Leadership identifies three inter-related domains or streams of work in organisations. All three domains must be addressed to bring about sustainable change.

The Social Domain includes all the arrangements of how work is organised and people work together. These are the structures, roles, organisational systems and practices. It relates to what is meant by "work", "leadership", "culture", "management" and the authority to do that work. It includes if and how people are held to account and how they are developed and recognised for work. In most organisations this domain is not treated with the same rigour, discipline or clarity as the other two. The social element can play a dominant role in schools and education departments and can often be unproductive.

Ensuring the right person is in the right role doing the right work is at the core of Systems Leadership. While it seems a reasonable and even obvious requirement, this alignment is not always the case in many organisations, including schools. This mantra is handy to have in mind when developing the three elements: the person, the role and the work and can be a useful place to start if things are not working well.

Systems Leadership provides tools for the principal to use to ensure that the right person is in the right role doing the right work. The right work could be identified by having systems in place that answer the three questions at work for all employees:

1.   What am I meant to do?
2.   How well am I doing?
3.   What future do I have?

# Question 1: What am I meant to do?

### ESSENTIAL SYSTEMS

In the first stage of implementing Systems Leadership, the manager of organisational effectiveness provided internal support to design systems:

- Organisational charts
- Specific role descriptions
- Action plans and task assignments.

The manager worked directly with principals and school teams to teach them how to develop and use each of these tools. This provided consistency in an area where previously there had been none.

Organisational charts were often not available and in many cases where they had been developed, they did not represent the structure of the school or work unit, the levels of work and the lines of supervision. They were often not clear because the arrangements being represented were not clear to the people who worked in the school or work unit.

An organisational chart can tell the story of how things may not work, as much as it tells the story of how things should work. A large number of people reporting directly to one person or people at different levels reporting directly to one person can indicate problems with the management structure. They may be compensating for someone who is not completing their role effectively or it may be because authorities are not articulated clearly.

A common example is the principal who has too many direct reports – deputy principals, business services manager, head of special education, heads of department or curriculum, guidance officer and other services/support staff reporting directly to him or her. This will restrict the ability of the principal to do his or her own work and make it difficult for other people to exercise the authority they need to get their work done. It may indicate that the principal does not think in systems, does not understand the levels of work or is unwilling to give people the authority they need to do their job.

It is common in schools for people to take on additional work, not included in their specific role description, to compensate for others who are not doing their work satisfactorily. The culture of schools is highly relational and there is a reluctance to address unsatisfactory performance through the authorised system. When we develop strategies to compensate for the shortcomings of systems or lack of capability in some people, it puts a strain on the other people who under normal circumstances would have the capability to do the work of their role. People may become used to ineffectiveness or react when expectations are not met with an unauthorised response that causes further problems.

Systems Leadership brought an understanding of levels of work, as discussed in detail in Chapter 3. The expectations and authorities of heads of curriculum, heads of departments, deputy principals and principals were clear, and an understanding of service and support roles helped to clarify the relationships between roles in what previously had been described broadly as "line management". Training in developing organisational charts resulted in clear lines of supervision and clarity in reporting relationships.

To test the effectiveness of an organisational chart, ask a sample of people two simple questions:

- *To whom do you report?*
- *Who reports to you?*

The organisational chart should be reviewed regularly, especially when changes are made to roles or additional positions are created. It is an essential tool to provide clarity in reporting relationships and is a reference for the specific role description.

Specific role descriptions were developed initially for managers and school leaders. The position descriptions used in the department are a description of the type of work that can be expected of a person at a level. In large organisations generic position descriptions are used for groups and bands of employees. With the increasing complexity of schools there is a greater variety of positions, and their roles become more specialised. In reality, a person at a particular level could be appointed to a position and be expected to do much different work because of the context in which that role exists.

A specific role description is developed so that an employee has a clear understanding of the role they are undertaking and the work they are required to do in a particular context. Some of the key questions that can be considered through the specific role description include:

- *What is the purpose of this role?*
- *Who is your supervisor?*
- *Which other roles inside and outside of the school does this role interact with?*
- *What capabilities and experience are required to complete the work expected in this role?*
- *Where is the role based and what environment does it encompass?*
- *What work are you expected to complete?*

A specific role description is developed for the recruitment and selection of a new staff member. It informs the induction of a new staff member and assists in identifying professional learning and training. The induction of new staff members will often focus on the physical features (where things are) and personnel (who everyone is) rather than on the work (what you are expected to do). The new staff member's line manager should spend time with her or him to discuss their work and the indicators of performance. The staff member should be encouraged to engage in the discussion to ensure they clearly understand the work they are expected to do. In turn this process informs performance development and planning.

Specific role descriptions should be developed, made available and used by all staff members in planning for and conducting work progress reviews. Some schools post copies of specific role descriptions on their portals and in newsletters to make them available to the whole school community. The principal's specific role description acts as a model for staff members and develops consistency across the school. Combined with an annual action plan, the principal's specific role description is a reference for the development of the deputy principals' and business services manager's specific role description. In turn, the deputy principals and business services manager work with the people who report directly to them to develop their specific role descriptions to ensure consistency and alignment with the expectations and priorities of the school.

Schools engage with other departments, private providers, non-government agencies and community groups. The specific role description is very useful in clarifying the roles of volunteers who work in the school, the office-bearers of school councils, parents' and citizens' associations and people they may employ. See an example of a specific role description in Tables 14.1 and 14.2.

A slide from a PowerPoint presentation to principals at a business meeting in 2011 included these expectations of all schools:

- Specific role descriptions aligned at all levels
- Annual action plans aligned at all levels
- Work progress reviews conducted at all levels.

Task assignments were introduced in the second phase of the implementation of Systems Leadership. It became more important as the recognition of the need for clarity increased with the development of specific role descriptions and annual action plans. Managers use task assignments to set out the work that is required and the boundaries within which the work should be completed. Managers assess a situation and determine what is to be done, why it is to be done, the deadline for its completion, the resources available to perform the task and the limits within which it must be completed.

Leaders can develop the habit of writing task assignments to clarify their own thinking. A page can be set up on the laptop or in a daybook so the task can be revisited as your ideas develop and more information becomes available. This is the type of work that can be done in spare moments between activities; for example, while travelling. Many times the thoughts behind tasks have been scribbled on the backs of boarding passes and in the margins of programs and agendas as they came to mind.

The leader may work with the person who is assigned the task to gain their contributions and refine it further. A leader can engage a team to develop a task assignment to ensure that team members' contributions are included and that all team members clearly understand what is to be achieved and what is expected of them.

In a school the principal will typically assign tasks to people reporting directly to him or her, such as deputy principals, the business manager, consultants and people who are offline for a period of time to undertake projects in specific areas. In turn, deputy principals and business services managers use task assignments to allocate work to the people who report directly to them.

**Table 14.1** A sample specific role description

| SPECIFIC ROLE DESCRIPTION | | |
|---|---|---|
| **Atherton SHS Principal** | | |
| **Supervisor:** Assistant Regional Director | **SoR:** Regional Director | **Band:** SL 6 |
| **Requisite Role Authorities** | | |
| **Team:** ASHS Management | | |
| **SoR:** HoDs, AO's, Cleaners, SO's, Specialists | **Supervisor:** Deputy Principals, BSMs, HOSES, HoS OCAS | |
| **Program Manager :** Management | **Team Member:** Management Team | |
| **Purpose:** Lead Atherton SHS to deliver the school purpose | | |

**Authorities**

Team Leadership steps
Team membership steps
Veto of selection within departmental limits
Assign tasks
Review, recognise and reward work performance
Initiate removal from role
One School, WH&S, HR authorities of role
Credit card limit $20,000
Exclusion and suspension

## Person Specification:

### Qualifications & Experience:

- Lead the school community to develop, articulate and commit to a shared educational vision focused on providing quality learning outcomes for all students
- Uphold the principalship as a values-based, ethical and moral activity
- Uphold the principalship as a values-based, ethical and moral activity.
- Embed socially just practices in daily school life.
- Set high standards for student and staff performance.
- Actively participate in lifelong learning and ongoing professional development.
- Form partnerships with parents, other government agencies, community groups, industry and business.
- Be futures oriented and strategic.
- Understand the legislation and policies that impact on schooling.
- Manage resources to achieve goals.

## Role Relationships:

**Professional** – Cluster Principals, Tablelands Secondary Principals, ISSU staff, Regional Office Staff, Regional Secondary Principals, HOCS, HODS, BSM, teaching staff, support staff & ancillary staff.
**Parents & Community** – P&C, Parents, Indigenous Elders, TRC, Atherton Tablelands Chamber of Commerce.
**Students** – General student population.

## Role Environment:

The role is based at Atherton State High School in the Atherton Cluster. The Atherton cluster includes Atherton SS, Kairi SS, Herberton SS, Irvinebank SS, Tinaroo EEC, Tolga SS, Yungaburra SS.

Organisational chart: Deputy Director General → Regional Director → Assistant Regional Director → Principal, Principal

**Table 14.2**  A sample appendix for a specific role description.

| Key Result Area | Accountability | Performance Indicator |
|---|---|---|
| Leadership | ***The Atherton High Way* – our desired culture** | |
| | Identify and model behaviour that represents *The Atherton High Way* | 100% of the time |
| | Create symbols that represent *The Atherton High Way* | Number/type of symbols |
| | Develop capability of leadership team | Goals achieved |
| | Review, revise and plan sustaining and improvement work | AIP completed to schedule |
| | Lead and monitor project completion as per Annual Improvement Plans | Reports completed to schedule |
| | Review and revise SRDs | Completed to schedule |
| | Monitor leader usage and quality of Annual Action Plans | Reports completed to schedule |
| | Review and revise Organisational Chart | Org Chart published to schedule |
| | Monitor and endorse timetable | Completed to schedule |
| | Monitor revision and implementation of Annual Performance Review system | Completed to schedule |
| | Assign tasks using SL model | Number of tasks |
| | Lead Atherton SHS ISR | Completed to schedule |
| | Model and apply team leader steps in meetings with fidelity | 0 traps |
| | Model and apply team member steps in meetings with fidelity | 0 traps |
| | Lead and report data at meetings | Completed to schedule |
| | Attend staffrooms, work spaces and team meetings | Number of times completed |
| | Review and revise meeting system | Completed to schedule |
| | Review and revise planning system | Completed to schedule |
| | Prepare for SATE implementation | Completed to schedule |
| | Design House Cup | Completed to schedule |

| | |
|---|---|
| Monitor the revision of the Sport System | Completed to schedule |
| Investigate IT solution to provide DBDM reports for staff about their work | Completed to schedule |
| Investigate, plan and stage the implementation of Teaching and Learning IT provision | Completed to schedule |
| Review, revise and implement professional development system | Completed to schedule |
| Clarify authority across sectors at all levels | Number of incidents |
| Lead annual report publications | |
| School Annual Report | Published to schedule |
| Next steps | |
| Investing for Success | |
| Audit(s) | |
| Monitor regional/external partnerships | |
| Contribution to Regional SLA committee | Completed to schedule |
| Contribution to and engagement in Regional/State Principal events | Number of events/contributions |
| Contribution to and engagement in Cluster/District Principal events | Number of events/contributions |
| Monitor the custodianship of Atherton SHS extra-curricular activities system | |
| Complete Professional Development | |
| Number of PD events | |
| Facilitation – Allan Parker | Completed to schedule |
| School Budget Solution | Completed to schedule |
| SL accreditation/master classes | Completed to schedule |
| Lead compliance with DET audit controls | Control self-assessment to schedule |
| Design and implement *The Atherton High Way* interface | Completed to schedule |
| Monitor and review design of OCAS | Completed to schedule |

(continued)

**Table 14.2** *(continued)*

| | | |
|---|---|---|
| **Teaching & Learning** | Monitor TL Deputy Principal AIP project completion | Completed to schedule |
| | Improving Teacher Capability System | |
| | Design and implementation of Atherton SHS T&L Standard Operating Procedures (SOPs) | |
| | Systematic Curriculum Delivery | |
| | Design NAPLAN system | |
| | Monitor HOSES AIP project completion | |
| | Monitor custodianship of TL Deputy Principal and HOSES | Completed to schedule |
| | Audit teaching quality | Completed to schedule |
| **Student Services** | Monitor SS Deputy Principal AIP project completion | Completed to schedule |
| | Revise behaviour system | |
| | Revise attendance system | |
| | Design, implement and review an ICP system | |
| | Design, implement and review a Learning Support System for Students Educationally at Risk (U2B, L2B) | |
| | Review and revise Standard Operating Procedures | |
| | Monitor custodianship of SS Deputy Principal | Completed to schedule |
| | Lead student executive capability development, meetings and events | Student targets achieved, completed to schedule |

| Community Engagement | | |
|---|---|---|
| Develop and sustain exemplary working relationships with P&C, Council and partners to deliver annual and strategic plans | | |
| | Develop plan for ASH School Council | Completed to schedule |
| | Develop plan for ASHS P&C | Completed to schedule |
| Deliver reports | | |
| | School Council | Completed to schedule |
| | Parents and Citizens' Assn | Completed to schedule |
| Lead events | | |
| | Welcome ceremony | Completed to schedule |
| | ANZAC ceremony | Completed to schedule |
| | Meet and Greet | Completed to schedule |
| | NAIDOC ceremony | Completed to schedule |
| | Graduation Ceremony | Completed to schedule |
| Lead and publish marketing information | | |
| | Electronic media | Website, Facebook and Q Parents published to schedule |
| | Newsletter | To schedule |
| | Newspaper | Number of articles published |

(continued)

**Table 14.2**  *(continued)*

| | Activity | Measure |
|---|---|---|
| **Finance** | Monitor F & F BSM AIP project completion | |
| | Review, revise and implement School Budget Solution | |
| | Revise and upload Budget to the Atherton High Way standard | Completed to schedule |
| | Monitor publication of annual budget system | Completed to schedule |
| | Lead budget development and allocations | Completed to schedule |
| | Monitor budget expenditure | Budget expenditure to plan |
| | Lead annual review and improvement of student resource scheme | Number of parents who join and pay |
| **Facilities** | Monitor planned and unplanned facility maintenance | Completed to schedule |
| | Monitor improvement and sustain work for annual stocktake | Completed to schedule |
| | Monitor Facilities upgrades | Completed to schedule |
| | Monitor identified BSM improvement work | |
| **HR** | Monitor HR BSM AIP project completion | Number of staff completing training annually |
| | Complete design of Internal Relief system to Atherton High Way Standard | |
| | Develop payroll Standards Operating Procedures | |
| | Review, revise and implement professional development system | |
| | Review and revise and implement support staff replacement process | |
| | Lead and monitor completion of mandatory training | |
| | Monitor return to work system | Number of staff successful |
| | Monitor ASHS HR systems – Timesheets, leave with fidelity | Completed to schedule |

| WH&S | Lead and monitor the improvement and sustaining work of the WH&S systems at Atherton SHS aligned to departmental standards | | |
|---|---|---|---|
| | BEMIR system (inc contractor induction) | Number of WAAPs |
| | Emergency Management Plan | Completed to schedule |
| | Chemical maintenance | Completed to schedule |
| | Curriculum Activity Risk Assessment | Number of CARAs completed |
| | Excursions | Number of excursions |
| | WH&S team meetings | Completed to schedule |
| | Incidents and hazards recorded and actioned in My HR WH&S | Number of incidents |
| | PGD | Completed to schedule |
| | Visitor Sign in | All visitors |
| | Lead/participate in wellness activities | Number of activities |

Task assignment is a valuable process because it assists the manager in determining clearly what needs to be achieved and the best way of going about it, considering the limits. A good task assignment clearly establishes the authorities the person has to complete the task and allows the person the scope to apply managerial judgement and creativity. The leader should assess whether the person can complete the task given their current workload.

Tasks are assigned for work that will have a significant impact on the performance of the organisation. Principals engage the school leadership team to gain their contributions in developing significant tasks that might have implications for other systems and the work of various team members. As an example, a task relating to the development of a whole-of-school information and communication technology plan will have implications for the budget, school curriculum planning, facilities and staffing, so it would be useful to have contributions from the custodians of those systems – for example, deputy principals and the business services manager – in developing the task. Working together to develop a task assignment is an excellent way of breaking down the "silos" that often develop in school leadership teams.

Writing a task assignment is a skill in itself and requires a level of mental processing ability of at least Level II. In addition to the training provided through Working Together courses, the manager of organisational effectiveness provided support to principals, managers and other school leaders to develop their capability to develop task assignments. A major consideration in every task assignment is whether the quality aspect of the task requires the inclusion of professional learning for those people who are assigned the task and those people who are expected to complete the work.

Schools do not operate in isolation and increasingly collaborate with the agencies of other departments, private providers and community groups. These partnerships can be the most difficult to manage because each organisation has a different culture and purpose and anticipates different outcomes. Developing a task assignment together has been proven to be an effective means of clarifying the authorities and contributions of the partners and the boundaries of the activity.

- Context: the circumstances in which the task is to be performed and the background explaining why the task has to be done and its relationship to any other tasks.
- Purpose: what is to be achieved by completing the task; a single idea, expressed in a one sentence that does not use "and".
- The quantity and quality of output is stated.
- Resources: the funding, people, facilities available to be utilised in completing the task.
- Time: milestones for completion of the task including those for specific outputs.

# Question 2: How well am I doing?

## ESSENTIAL SYSTEMS

- Coaching
- Work progress review
- Task review.

Coaching was identified as a key strategy to improve the capability of people at all levels of the organisation. The regional director had engaged a coach to work with him for the three years prior to his appointment to the position. From 2010 to 2013 Ian Macdonald (external consultant) and Tony Tiplady (manager, organisational effectiveness) provided coaching to the regional director and other senior officers to support the implementation of Systems Leadership.

In schools and educations systems, professional learning typically takes place in conferences and workshops. For the most part, the transfer of knowledge or skills to the workplace depends on the motivation and initiative of the individual. Coaching individuals in their work and in their workplace has not been a priority until recently.

In Systems Leadership, monitoring and coaching are key components of the team leadership and team membership steps and relate directly to the capability model outlined in Chapter 4. Senior officers and school leaders were trained as coaches and expected to provide coaching to develop the capability of the people they supervised. Likewise it was expected that staff members would accept coaching to improve their capability. Coaching impacted most on the work of principals as instructional leaders and on teachers in their pedagogy.

In most education systems there is a position at the level of "superintendent" that relates to the supervision of principals. In the Queensland Department of Education this role has had various titles but at the time it was "assistant regional director" (ARD). The department has vacillated between declaring the role to be supervisor, coach or a combination of the two. It was essential for the ARDs in the Far North region to adopt the approach of Systems Leadership and accept that for a supervisor, coaching was a necessary part of the role. Likewise, as the supervisors of teachers, principals and schools leaders had to accept that coaching was an essential part of their role.

Work progress reviews were introduced as a regular discussion between a supervisor and their team members about the progress he or she had made in the work outlined in their specific role description. The work progress review answered three questions for the employee:

1. How well am I doing?
2. What assistance do I need to improve my work?
3. What are my future prospects?

This created a direct relationship between work, performance and capability. It was more useful and meaningful than a review conducted in performance development systems where the employee planned and was assessed against a developmental framework based on knowledge and skills required for a generic role. The supervisor and the employee discussed the work of the role with the focus being on improvement.

# Question 3: What future do I have?

## ESSENTIAL SYSTEMS

- Work progress review
- Internal school reviews
- Quadrennial school review.

The planning and review system that was developed for schools and work units had two main components for planning. The annual plan was a one-page document based on the regional priorities. Principals completed the plan by listing the strategies they would implement to address each priority. The second component was an annual action plan that each school leader or manager used to organise the work required they were required to do to implement the strategies from the annual plan.

An internal school review was held in the final term of the school year. It took anything from a couple of hours to two days depending on the size and complexity of the school. Deputy principals and other middle managers reported on the work completed and the outcomes achieved in the twelve months against the work that was outlined in the action plan and the targets set by the region. The principal led the review and the principals' supervisor (the ARD), school councillors, parent and community representatives participated.

The purpose of the internal school review is to review the progress of each role in achieving their current implementation plan to inform the development of the school implementation plan in the following year:

- Analysis of student and school outcomes (achievement, improvement, opinion) against performance measures and targets
- Assessment of the effectiveness of planned strategies/actions
- Assessment of the success of annual implementation plan strategies and actions

- Assessment of school context, curriculum, pedagogy, student diversity, workforce, resource management and other planning requirements
- Identification of the resources available for the year, including funds carried forward from the previous year, grants and other income allocated to school outcomes.

The internal school review was tied directly to the work planned. The regional director led an internal review of the progress of the region as a whole with the managers of work units in the regional office. Each manager reported on delivering planned work and achieving targets set in key performance areas. A written report of the information and conclusions reached was published and made available to principals. The data from the internal review was used to set targets and develop the next annual plan.

## Quadrennial school review

The quadrennial school review includes the internal review for the current year and also takes into account the previous three internal reviews to inform the development of the next four-year plan.

These elements were developed as a planning and accountability system. The purpose was to ensure that in every school and work unit we planned and reviewed the work from our priorities to achieve the targets we had set.

---

**Box 14.3    Planning and accountability**

Make appropriate changes to your annual action plan to:

- Develop your instructional leadership consistent with the region and the centre
- Develop systems in your school that generate school improvement
- Develop and implement a charter of expectations
- Implement coaching and feedback with schools, leaders and teachers
- Use the task assignment model in planning
- Meet as a group to report on completion of tasks at the end of Term 3.

---

## The right people in the right roles, doing the right work

The region was restructured to provide services to schools through Education Services, Corporate Services, Student Services and Regional Services. There were various arrangements in schools, loosely based on the regional services and ultimately determined by the principal. Principals were encouraged to restructure their school's operations into Education Services (Teaching and Learning), Student Services and Business Services to achieve more effective service delivery.

New roles were developed to meet emerging needs:

- A manager was appointed to lead the "My Futures Team" to develop a system to assist year 12 students to meet the service commitment in the 26 weeks after leaving school.
- An information and complaints manager was tasked with developing a system to effectively manage the complaints that were lodged with the regional office. Complaints management is very complex and can have deleterious effects on individuals, schools and the organisation when not done properly. It concerns very complex issues that involve people inside and outside of the organisation in school and non-school settings.
- A manager of communication and marketing was appointed to ensure that the work of schools and the service commitment was understood and recognised in the broader community. In recent decades there has been a significant increase in the number of options for private school education.
- An executive director led the development of a regional data management system to articulate regional baseline data in teaching and learning, human resources and finance.
- The role of the manager of organisational effectiveness was developed to support Systems Leadership training and the development and implementation of systems in schools and work units.

The majority of people in leadership roles in schools and regional offices have spent most of their working lives in schools and university. As a result they have not had the opportunity to develop their capability – knowledge, technical skills, social processing skills and application – to lead and manage a modern organisation at a high standard.

The manager of organisational effectiveness was appointed to address these gaps in capability. Tony Tiplady, who is a co-author of this book, has worked as a teacher and deputy principal and importantly has twenty-one years' experience working in a large multi-national company developing the capability that would be critical to improving performance in the region:

- Training and application of Systems Leadership in a range of senior leadership roles
- Training and application of process management and improvement methodologies, including McKinsey's Breakthrough process and Six Sigma, which require rigorous data-based decision making and planning

- Training and application of rigorous systemic processes, such as environment and safety international standards; for example, ISO 14001, DuPont's Safety Systems and Root Cause Analysis
- Training and completion of high-quality planning.

This role had accountability for:

- Coaching and advising the regional director, principals and other leaders
- Custodianship of Systems Leadership implementation throughout the region
- Training and coaching regional managers, principals and other school leaders
- Designing regional systems, including planning and accountability, attendance, teaching and student services.

# Working Together courses

The region committed to running three-day residential Working Together courses for principals and regional managers to ensure a critical mass of leaders were trained. The regional director or an executive director introduced every Working Together course to emphasise symbolically the importance of participating in the training. The regional director welcomed participants, outlined the context and purpose of the training and made links to the research relating to school improvement.

The Working Together courses were designed to develop the capability of our leaders to use the concepts, tools and models of Systems Leadership to improve the effectiveness of our schools and regional work units. Team leadership and team membership skills were emphasised in the practical activities.

The purpose of the Working Together course was "To develop the skills and capabilities of principals as Instructional Leaders to improve student achievement".

To illustrate the nature of the tasks from Working Together, it may be worthwhile and possibly amusing to describe one of the more challenging activities, the "mystery box" – a rectangular plastic storage box containing an interconnecting arrangement of three pieces of plywood supported by six lengths of PVC pipe suspended through holes drilled in the walls of the box. Teams of six or five had a short time to study this arrangement (which appeared to be deceptively simple) and decide how to disassemble and reassemble it as quickly as they could. This was attempted many times, before most breaks in the program over the two days, with the aim of completing the task in the shortest possible time. After the first attempt, teams were asked to predict the best time they thought they would be able to achieve. Over the course of the workshop, the teams applied and practised the principles and behaviour they learned, and inevitably their predictions were slashed from minutes to a matter of seconds. The best effort recorded to disassemble and reassemble the mystery box in the Working Together courses that were conducted over five years with hundreds of participants was 19.36 seconds.

The mystery box task illustrated the importance of:

- Understanding the context
- Clarity of purpose
- Using team members' contributions
- Identifying critical issues
- Allocating tasks
- Using feedback and review.

When a critical mass of principals and managers had completed the training, the focus of the Working Together courses changed to training leadership teams from schools and teams from work units. These courses were planned by the principal/manager with Ian Macdonald, so that the work of the school or unit became the content of the course. Team members learned how to use the concepts, models and tools to progress the work they were tasked to do in their role.

Ian Macdonald worked in the region at least twice each year to lead the Working Together courses and to run workshops for principals, school leaders and regional leaders. Tony Tiplady did the essential job of managing the training system. He liaised with principals, managers and Ian to organise the courses. He developed schedules and managed the logistics of venues, travel, accommodation and finance. Tony co-presented courses with Ian and ensured the work was aligned to the regional context.

Before Ian's visits to the region, Tony met with the regional director to discuss the work to be completed. Ian met with the regional director prior to beginning work each time. Tony and Ian provided feedback to the regional director after every course and any issues or possibilities that had arisen were discussed. The effective relationship which developed between the consultant who had the expertise the region needed, the manager who was responsible for planning and supporting the implementation of the work and the officer with the authority to require the work to be done was essential for its success.

Within the context of improvements in the Social Domain we were able to address the Technical and Commercial domains because work and authority had become clearer.

## Developing capability

To "launch" Systems Leadership in the region as the preferred means of addressing the priority of improving organisational effectiveness, Ian Macdonald presented a two-day workshop in August 2010 for more than 120 school leaders and senior managers from across the region. The purpose of the workshop was to provide senior leaders with an introduction to the principles of Systems Leadership and its application in an organisation.

It was symbolic that every principal and senior manager was expected to attend. This was as much about developing new mythologies as it was about exposing everyone to the content of Systems Leadership. This was everyone's work – a challenge to the existing mythology of "choose your own adventure".

In a symbolic change to how business was done in the region, regional business meetings were held each term and all principals and senior officers were required to attend. The agenda was organised with a third of the time for professional learning for principals and senior officers in the work from our priorities, a third for business planning and a third for departmental priorities. This maintained focus on our purpose and restricted the interference of associations, the central office, private providers and other departments that enjoyed nothing more than making their work ours.

The Technical is the domain that concerns the specialist/professional or core work of the organisation. Therefore, in schools this concerns systems, processes and practices focused on curriculum and pedagogy. It is the "technical" approach of how we choose to teach. Usually it is assumed that there needs to be rigour, discipline and clarity around this element.

In fact this is not always the case. As argued previously, when school staff members are able to create and run their own adventure and within schools pedagogy is seen to be the sole responsibility of the individual teacher, there is no guarantee of a consistent, effective pedagogy. Privatised practice aided and abetted the development of curriculum becoming the de facto technical work of schools.

In Far North Queensland explicit teaching and data-based decision making were two of the regional priorities. It was important to achieve a balance between the work in curriculum (what we teach) and pedagogy (how we teach) so that schools spent less time rehashing curriculum and more time on implementing explicit teaching and analysing student learning data to inform their teaching.

Ken Maclean, who was the principal of Northern Peninsula Area College, had followed the traditional approaches to curriculum and pedagogy over two years and found these did not achieve any real improvement in student learning. Ken was drawn to the work of John Fleming and the model of explicit instruction that John had developed when he was principal at Bellfield Primary School in North Melbourne.

Implementing this model at Northern Peninsula Area College brought improved results in the NAPLAN within one year. Over three years the college achieved the best results of any remote school in the Australia.

The effectiveness of explicit teaching had been identified in the findings of national research conducted in Australia, New Zealand, the United Kingdom and United States. The results achieved by John Fleming at Bellfield

Primary School and the positive feedback on the work at Northern Peninsula Area College indicated that explicit teaching was the best option for what was termed in the region as "high-yield teaching".

There were two areas of technical capability that were required to implement explicit teaching. One related to teachers learning how to teach explicitly and the other involved principals and other school leaders learning to be instructional leaders who could lead implementation in the region and schools.

John Fleming's model was conceptually sound and provided the practices teachers and principals would use to implement explicit teaching. The work aligned to the priorities, which in turn aligned to the purpose of the region: to improve the outcomes of all of our students.

Initially twenty-five principals nominated their schools to engage in a pilot to implement explicit teaching. John Fleming was engaged as a consultant to train principals and teachers through a combination of workshops and on-the-job coaching and feedback. The implementation was led by the ARDs, who learned the required skills and strategies through working with John and the principals.

After the success of the pilot a second group of schools was included in the next phase of implementation, and the strategies and experiences that were learned through the pilot were adapted by the region and used as standards of practice for all schools. It was not until this work was well underway that the importance of data-based decision making became evident and a system and practices were developed.

An example of a practice that was trialled and then extended to all schools was the charter of expectations (see below). It is the exemplar adapted from the work of John Fleming and distributed to schools in an update of the key improvement strategies for 2012. Principals used this to develop a charter of expectations for their own school. Developing this with staff reinforced the need for consistency in the improvement strategies while also encouraging the inclusion of individual school characteristics.

---

**Box 14.4  Charter of expectations**

Every school in Far North Queensland has a charter of expectations which aligns with the region's charter:

1.  The school has a culture of care and of high expectations, inside and outside the classroom.

    - All students matter, every day
    - All students can achieve high academic results
    - Practices within the school enhance the learning climate and tone
    - Feedback for learning is valued and practised at all levels
    - There are high standards of student behaviour (positive school-wide behaviour, orderly student movement, high student engagement and motivation within the classroom)

- There is an emphasis on the uniform and dress code
- There is an emphasis on achieving consistently high student attendance.

2. Curriculum delivery is underpinned by highly effective explicit teaching.
3. There is a high level of community engagement and support.
4. There are strong relationships between parents and their children's teachers.
5. School leaders actively coach and support teachers in their skill development.
6. Staff members share collective accountability for all student outcomes.

*CHARTER OF EXPECTATIONS FOR TEACHING AND LEARNING*

School-wide pedagogy

Each teacher:

- Builds effective relationships with each student
- Accepts accountability for each student's learning
- Uses data to inform teaching and monitor student learning
- Plans and teaches each lesson using the agreed explicit teaching model
- Uses differentiation strategies to eliminate the tail and cater for high achievers
- Uses revision strategies to move student knowledge from short-term to long-term memory.

*LEARNING ENVIRONMENT*

Each teacher:

- Sets a positive classroom learning tone
- Establishes an atmosphere of high expectations
- Focuses on high standards of student presentation and handwriting
- Regularly corrects student work and provides feedback to each student
- Has a high standard of classroom display that is relevant and education-ally stimulating.

*STUDENT ENGAGEMENT*

Each teacher:

- Ensures that each student feels valued and respected by them
- Ensures that each student is given work and other learning experiences at their ability level
- Supports each student to have friends at school
- Engages each student in their progress towards their annual learning goals.

Professional development and training funds that were provided to the region were used in a very targeted strategy to develop capability. Education advisors were employed to develop a series of modules designed to train teachers in explicit teaching. The education advisors delivered the modules to teachers in schools across the region and provided in-class support, modelling, coaching and feedback.

The emphasis on explicit teaching led principals, teachers and ARDs to examine the work of other people:

- Anita Archer's workshops on explicit instruction and the book *Explicit Instruction: Effective and Efficient Teaching* (Archer and Hughes 2010) became favourites.
- Anne Bayetto is a lecturer in undergraduate and postgraduate studies at Flinders University. She presented workshops in the region on the "big six" of reading: Oral Language, Phonological Awareness, Letter–Sound Relationships (phonics), Vocabulary, Fluency and Comprehension.

As teachers and principals saw improvement happening, they searched for other sources of information on related practices.

Senior officers from the region had identified the need for "high-yield teaching" to overcome the deficit in children's learning. The work initiated by Ken Maclean at Northern Peninsula Area College to implement explicit teaching provided a way forward that could be trialled and improved by groups of schools. Successful practices and strategies were incorporated into the training and became standards of practice for schools. The geographical clusters of schools provided a means of bringing principals together to focus on improving teaching, and learning and resources were used more effectively to target priorities.

Once the teaching system began to take shape, the development of a data system made a lot more sense. Schools organised for data from the key areas of student learning – for example, the big six – to be collected and reviewed by school leaders and teachers in "data conversations" every five weeks. This emerging "professional dialogue" focused on student learning and achievement. Teachers used these conversations to inform their planning for teaching and to determine interventions required by groups and individual students.

If data conversations are treated as a supervisory measure – that is, a means of checking up on teachers – then they will be of limited benefit and can sometimes be counterproductive. If the purpose of the data system is something along the lines of "use the information generated through teaching and learning to improve our capability to maximise the achievement of our students" and the data system is designed accordingly, then it will be a major contributor to school improvement.

Through the data system school leaders can assess progress across year-level cohorts and from one year level to the next. Regular data conversations with teachers provide feedback on the effectiveness of strategies being used in sections of the school or the whole school and allow school leaders to be responsive to emerging trends. This could mean coaching for an individual, training teachers or other staff members in a particular skill or strategy, or it could mean adjusting how a strategy is being implemented.

While this may involve changing the way something is being done, or more predictably slowing things down, we found that it is essential to recognise when it is time to raise expectations. This particularly relates to student learning. Teaching has been directed to the middle ground – the average student and a lot of resources are directed to assisting students who are falling behind.

A widespread mythology of teachers is that when a student masters learning, the appropriate response is to expand learning laterally – in other words, provide more learning experiences at that level. Improvement requires teachers to recognise when students and cohorts have mastered learning, raise the standard and accelerate learning. Similarly the school leader must recognise when performance plateaus, and set targets to a higher standard.

It is vital to reinforce high expectations, set targets and revise them when it becomes evident that they are being achieved. In addition to the targets the Far North region set for key performance indicators such as the NAPLAN, targets were also set for specific standards in students' learning. An example is year-level targets that students were expected to reach in the structured reading series. Each year these were revised to increase the expectation of what our students could achieve.

---

**Box 14.5    Weighing the pig**

The "weighing the pig doesn't make it any fatter" anecdote became a regular feature of presentations from the time that consistent and comparable data became available for all schools. The English Language & Usage website (https://english.stackexchange.com/) indicates it originated in the year 2000, and notes that the majority of references to weighing the pig can be found in books and articles related to education. It is particularly useful for people hoping to draw an analogy with standardised testing of students. The argument goes that just as weighing the pig does not make it any fatter, testing the students does not improve their outcomes.

But is that the purpose of testing the students? Testing students provides point-in-time information on their achievement. Teachers can apply their professional knowledge and skill and use the information to develop teaching strategies and learning experiences to improve their students' outcomes. At the school level, testing provides feedback on the effectiveness of learning and teaching systems. The system receives feedback on the effectiveness of programs, resourcing and capability development.

The irony of the "weighing the pig" anecdote is that in stating the obvious, the whole question of what will fatten the pig is laid bare. Ignoring the information provided by testing programs means that knowledge of student capability is the sole remit of the teacher. Testing students provides objective information to improve performance of teachers, schools and systems.

These systems were implemented in a rigorous way using the modelling of Systems Leadership. Often such systems are "rolled out" with a lack of consistency and wide variation. In such circumstances people are likely to pay only lip service to implementation.

The Commercial Domain of an organisation includes all the systems, processes and practices concerned with revenue and costs. The department of education has systems to facilitate finance and other corporate services. There are ways of carrying out and measuring the effectiveness of this element.

Efficient and effective systems provide the people in the organisation with the boundaries within which they can work. This provides them with the certainty they need to do their work, and in a sense protects them from misusing resources. This can also be a constraint if the systems are not designed to match the purpose or meet the qualities required. Because the strategies of the region were different from other regions and more specific than usual, the managers of corporate services had to ensure that, where possible, resources were delivered to support regional strategies.

There is a latency of inertia in large departments and organisations. Funding is locked in to support ongoing operations and when new funding does become available it is tied to deliver specified outputs in a program. Claims of innovation and responsiveness – "Our people are our greatest asset" – can be difficult to support with resources, especially at start-up, and it is often difficult to know what is meant by this and what work is required.

There is a role for the principal to advocate on behalf of the school for resources and to ensure that resources are directed to the priority work. There is a role for the principals' supervisor to advocate on behalf of students and schools for the resources required to do priority work, and to ensure that the system for allocating and accounting for resources is not so onerous that it impacts negatively on the work of the school.

Partnerships with business, universities, other government departments and providers are one way that schools can access external funding sources, expertise and bigger markets to expand their operations and expand the options available to their students. This work must be led by the principal of the school and is most successful when he or she engages a coalition of key people in the school and community to champion the purpose, support the work and guide decision making.

In a partnership the principal's role is extended beyond the traditional limits of their commercial authority. A successful partnership is dependent on the principal's capability, especially their social processing skills. In addition to leading the implementation in the school, the principal will need to "manage up" to meet the expectations of the immediate supervisor and mitigate possible interference in order to gain their support. The principal will work "laterally" to develop productive relationships with partners in an environment where he or she has no formal authority.

A large-scale project can take five to ten years or longer to bring to fruition. Even when a principal has the capability to deal with the complexity, a major disruptor can be the turnover of people in key positions within the school and in the partnership organisations. This problem extends to departments of education and other education authorities where there can be a regular churn of ministers, directors general or chief executive officers.

The two initiatives described below are examples of partnerships led by principals doing the work of their role to maximise the capacity of their schools to provide opportunities for students. In both cases the initiatives are continuing to develop after more than ten years.

---

### Box 14.6    The Tropical North Learning Academy

The Tropical North Learning Academy (TNLA) is a strategic partnership between Trinity Beach State School, Smithfield State High School and James Cook University (JCU). A seamless educational pathway is delivered from the early phase of learning to university and adult life. TNLA partners work together to provide a range of "learning enhancements", called academies, for students at all stages of learning. Partners ensure smooth transitions occur for students at the key junctures of schooling.

The signature programs are:

- Academic Excellence: specialist JCU learning academies for high-achieving, tertiary aspirants from years 5 to 12
- Philosophy in Action: explore future life in the tropics using the disciplines of philosophy and critical thinking
- Jazz and Contemporary Music: a jazz academy for talented and aspiring musicians
- Early Years: on-site Montessori early childhood programs for children up to 3 years
- Soccer and Baseball Academies: for talented sportsmen and sportswomen
- Vocational Training: a diverse suite of accredited Cert III and IV courses.

---

### Box 14.7    Transforming education: the Atherton High way

The Student Informed Learning Management System (SILMS) was designed by David Platz using active and flipped pedagogical methodology with significant input from students about how they learn best. Atherton State High School (SHS) and its university partners with the full endorsement of the Atherton SHS communities have successfully designed, piloted, trialled and operationalised the SILMS since 2010 through the Online College of Advanced STEM (Science, Technology, Engineering and Maths; OCAS) and the Open High

School Education (OHSE) system on a small scale, which has demonstrated the capability to transform school education and contribute significantly to addressing issues with teacher well-being and a range of national educational goals, specifically:

1.  Reversing Australia's declining performance in education
2.  Demonstrating innovation in twenty-first-century education delivery
3.  Redefining eLearning in the education sector
4.  Delivering new and innovative learning pathways for students to prepare them for future STEM careers
5.  Providing seamless transitions between education sectors for staff and students (primary, secondary, tertiary, international)
6.  Developing teacher capability in twenty-first-century pedagogy using twenty-first-century learning management systems
7.  Minimising educational disengagement of highly capable and other "at risk" students.

## THE STUDENT INFORMED LEARNING MANAGEMENT SYSTEM

The SILMS underpins both the OCAS and OHSE. It was developed to:

*   Improve teacher well-being through a unique transformative twenty-first-century way of educating that improves students achieving their individual learning goals
*   Improve student achievement of their individual learning goals by providing them with a unique transformative twenty-first-century way of learning.

The SILMS design includes a full suite of cutting-edge twenty-first-century systems which will contribute significantly to addressing a range of national educational goals, specifically:

*   An automated course publishing system for facilitators and teachers (Moodle)
*   A learning system for teachers and all students that contains all of the required resources for all courses and units of work (Moodle; SCORM for exporting and resynchronising materials for offline study)
*   Videoconferencing with the highest possible levels of student security and safety
*   A server with robust levels of storage, student security and safety (Queensland Cyber Infrastructure Foundation server).

## THE ONLINE COLLEGE OF ADVANCED STEM

From its conception in 2004 as the School of Astronomy and Astrophysics, the OCAS was developed with the purpose of delivering world's best practice, advanced STEM education to high capability high school students online. In this way, the OCAS STEM system design differs from other high school STEM initiatives as it delivers independent self-paced learning to high school students and teachers in STEM education across Queensland – as well as interstate and overseas – online 365 days of the year, 24 hours per day. This initiative is a paradigm shift in that highly capable high school students, anywhere in the world, at any time, can engage flexibly in advanced STEM learning online, equipping them for direct university entry into twenty-first-century STEM careers.

From 2010 to 2018, online enrolments have grown from eight to 107 highly capable students, with most coming from fifty-one Australian public and private schools and eight being international students. OCAS now has three schools: Astronomy and Astrophysics, Computational Sciences and Earth Sciences. The range of courses currently on offer includes Senior Astronomy, Advanced Astrophysics, Senior Coding, Data Science Applications and Fisheries Resilience for the Future. OCAS has demonstrated the capability to expand further into various fields of advanced STEM education.

OCAS courses are government-accredited, university-endorsed and moderated, and contribute towards a students' Queensland Certificate of Education.

*OPEN HIGH SCHOOL EDUCATION*

The system was developed with the purpose of liberating students' potential to best prepare them for direct university entry to twenty-first-century STEM careers through unprecedented online, self-paced, advanced STEM that activates individual and collective innovative learning.

From 2014 to 2017, strong high school collaborations were established to trial, then operationalise, the effectiveness of the system for these students. The trials with 237 students in two Queensland public high schools and one private school in New South Wales demonstrated that the SILMS could successfully deliver OHSE capability to deliver online/eLearning education solutions for high school teachers to successfully teach and or facilitate learning, even when they do not have subject specific expertise.

**Table 14.3**   OHSE results

| OHSE: Year 10 Astronomy Trinity Bay SHS | | | OHSE: Year 11 Physics Atherton SHS | | | | |
|---|---|---|---|---|---|---|---|
| Grade | A | B | C | A | B | C | D | E |
| 2014 | 21 | 5 | | 3 | 3 | 8 | 3 | 1 |
| 2015 | 16 | 10 | 1 | | | | | |
| 2016 | 23 | 3 | 2 | | | | | |
| 2017 | 21 | 5 | 2 | | | | | |

The successes in this are underpinned by design and implementation based on Systems Leadership concepts and models.

# Working within a department

Systems Leadership emphasises a leader's use of social process to achieve the purpose of the organisation. *Social process* is defined as "the ability to interact with others at work to produce a productive outcome". A leader demonstrates they are aligned to the purpose of the organisation through their behaviour, what they say and the work that they do.

As discussed in Chapter 9, social process can be likened to similar concepts such as "people skills", "interpersonal skills", "emotional intelligence", "soft skills" and "soft power". Systems Leadership is clear that such skills are directed to achieve a productive purpose.

In Systems Leadership this is *not* an either/or. People cannot rely solely on social process skills, nor can they rely only on the authority described in their role. The way a person uses social processing has a significant bearing on whether the authority is experienced to be reasonable or not.

The term "managing up" is often used when a person tries to influence their supervisor to ensure she understands and supports the work that they are doing. It is a common-sense approach which means you must not only be aware of how you are viewed by team members but also how you are viewed by your supervisor. In addition, you must understand what your supervisor is trying to do and how you can help them achieve it.

Systems Leadership points to the "mutuality" of the relationship between the leader and those who are led. People will follow a leader if the leader works within mutually accepted boundaries. Systems Leadership describes the behaviour available to leaders:

- *Influence is "the ability to exert one's will in social context".*
- *Authority is "the mutual acceptance of agreed limits in exerting one's will".*
- *Power is "the exertion of will while breaking one or more limits of authority".*

It is just as important to predict how your supervisor will perceive particular changes as it is to understand how staff members will react. Mythologies are shared across organisations and some reside within groups, departments and levels of an organisation. It is important for the leader to understand these mythologies and how they may impact on the planned work. This is the essence of the work of the leader as described in more detail elsewhere in this text: using the three tools of leadership – symbols, systems and behaviour – to change the culture of the organisation.

The leader must develop and use a strong narrative that reflects the purpose of the organisation and reinforces the importance of the work that is being done. The ongoing narrative provides feedback to the people in the organisation on what we are doing, why we are doing it, how we are going and what we expect we need to be doing next.

One director general during the time of this work encouraged regional directors to use initiative and implement strategies that would account for the different circumstances in each region and achieve improved outcomes for students in specified elements. The results of the NAPLAN and in particular the percentage of students achieving the national minimum standard was the most prominent measure used to demonstrate improvement. This provided the clarity for regional directors to determine what they were required to do according to the context in which they worked.

The purpose of the Far North region was aligned to the purpose of the department of education.

- The service commitment, discussed earlier in this chapter, included the goals of early education, primary education, secondary education and training.
- Systems Leadership provided the means for the regional office and schools to improve the performance of all aspects of the organisation.
- The performance of the region was measured in terms of the improved performance of students in the NAPLAN and a number of elements identified by the department.

It did not matter whether the audience comprised teachers, principals, parents, students, community members or representatives of the department of education; the service commitment provided the thread for a narrative in the Far North region.

An organisation may have multiple goals and the purpose may not seem to be clear. People in schools have become used to a churn of events, priorities, initiatives and programs. Governments can include schools in multi-agency partnerships to address child and family issues or more general social issues. As important as the intent of these programs may be, they reduce the time available in school for teaching and learning and add to the workload of the people in schools. The children who attend schools and their families are the clients of a multitude of organisations that see the school as a means of accessing them. In terms of the commercial element, businesses are increasingly looking to engage with students and families through their school. The leader must minimise distractions and maximise the quantity of time and the quality of teaching.

Regional and school leaders play a vital role in ensuring that local factors are considered when planning and implementing change. An effective leader must be responsive to the changes that occur in the department as a whole and in the teams, work units and schools.

# Summary

Implementation was not easy. It required us to use all the elements in the culture change model: the tools of leadership. We had to articulate a clear purpose, and what that purpose would look like in reality rather than relying on general fuzzy statements. It had to be observable. We had to understand our current culture; where would there be support, concern or cynicism. We carefully described the behaviour we wanted to encourage and how they connected to the purpose. We had to design appropriate productive systems using a shared methodology. Such work takes time, effort and an ability to deal with complexity. At times it can be very frustrating and wearing.

We had to understand, reinforce or change symbols to underpin this work at both the regional and school levels. We had to create dissonance and proceed with persistence and consistency. We did not try to get "buy in" because staff members were already being paid. If we had a clear and shared purpose and we could link behaviour, symbols and systems to that purpose we found that staff would engage. If staff members are encouraged to contribute, to identify critical issues and give feedback they will over time use the material even if they are not directed externally.

The next chapters report the results and case studies that show how this approach becomes embedded and, rather than an initiative or program, become just the way we do our work.

# 3 *Results and outcomes*

PART

3

Results and
outcomes

# 15 *Regional data*

## Introduction

As can be seen in previous chapters, there is no point in implementing a program unless the outcomes are assessed. We have seen so many initiatives that are never evaluated. There are assertions and exhortations but not always data to back up the claims. We had clearly rewritten the regional purpose to focus on student outcomes, so that is what we will now look at. In doing so, we look at scores and quantitative data. We do not think that these are the only measures that matter. We also include case studies that describe broader results and outcomes as well. From 2008 until 2013 the work implemented in the Far North region improved the effectiveness of the organisation to deliver significant improvements in the outcomes for all our students. In this chapter we present the data from the National Assessment Program of Literacy and Numeracy (NAPLAN) and other key indicators of performance in year 12, which is the final year of school education in Queensland.

The NAPLAN was introduced in 2008. On the web page of the Australian Curriculum, Assessment and Reporting Authority (ACARA; www.acara.edu.au/) providing information to parents, the NAPLAN is said to test

> the sorts of skills that are essential for every child to progress through school and life, such as reading, writing, spelling, grammar and numeracy. It is important to remember that NAPLAN is not about passing or failing, but about assessing learning progress. At the classroom level it is one of a number of important tools used by teachers to measure student progress.

Student results in the NAPLAN are measured against an assessment scale in each of the areas tested: reading, writing, spelling, grammar and punctuation, and numeracy. Students receive a score for each assessment domain, called the NAPLAN scale score, which is between 0 and 1,000. The scales cover the year levels from year 3 to year 9, and are divided into ten bands. A national minimum standard is identified on the assessment scale for each year level. Band 2 is the minimum standard for year 3, band 4 is the minimum standard for year 5, band 5 is the minimum standard for year 7 and band 6 is the minimum standard for year 9. These standards represent increasingly challenging skills and require increasingly higher scores on the NAPLAN scale. The "upper two bands" is the measure used to report on the percentage of students achieving higher scores for their year level in each domain.

More information on the NAPLAN can be found on the ACARA website.

# Improvements achieved in the Far North region in the NAPLAN from 2008 to 2013

From 2008 to 2013 the Far North region demonstrated a strong improvement trend across year 3, year 5 and year 7 in the results of the NAPLAN in the national minimum standard, mean scale score and upper two bands.

The regional director decided that the number and the percentage of students at or above the national minimum standard would be the initial focus of the improvement strategies in the region. Although the national minimum standard could be considered a very low level, it was essential for our staff members throughout the region to develop the capability to educate students to achieve to a recognised standard through the implementation of regional strategies. As capability developed and improvement followed, more emphasis was given to increasing the percentage of students in the upper two bands.

The work of improvement in the region focused initially on the early years to ensure that these students had the necessary skills to progress through their school education. Before looking at the data more broadly there are a few specific examples provided to illustrate the scale of the improvement in what is arguably the most important skill: reading.

## TARGETS FOR STUDENT OUTCOMES

A slide from a PowerPoint presentation used by the regional director to explain the context of the region at a workshop to induct principals in 2011 is included in this chapter (see Box 15.1). The slide lists the targets that all schools were expected to achieve to provide a consistent message to principals.

Even though the state-wide targets had previously amounted to small, incremental improvements – for example, a 3% annual increase in students at or above the national minimum standard – they were not achieved state-wide. On the other hand, the targets set by the region called for huge improvements and were seen by some to be aspirational and by some as unrealistic. However, the data presented here shows the region achieved improvements of 20% and more in some elements of the NAPLAN and reached or bettered the target in others.

Rather than determining the targets in terms of what may be an acceptable or reasonable increase, the regional director set the targets based on a calculation of the achievement that could be expected if capability was improved and the work was completed as planned. As the results improved, the targets in some areas were increased. For example, by 2012 our expectation was that at least 40% of students should be achieving in the upper two bands.

---

**Box 15.1    Regional targets**

- Students achieving national minimum standard in the NAPLAN – 90%
- Students represented in top two bands of the NAPLAN – 25%
- Students achieving Queensland Certificate of Education – 95%
- Student attendance – 90%
- Confidence in state schools – QLD [Queensland]
- Student Disciplinary Absences – QLD.

---

Achieving the Queensland Certificate of Education was selected as the target for year 12 students because it aligned with the intent of the service commitment. It represented student achievement in a range of areas and reinforced the need for schools to provide pathways to meaningful opportunities in employment, training and further education. It was necessary for our students to achieve to a recognised standard and for us to be able to compare the achievement of our students against others across schools in Queensland.

A target was set to emphasise the role of schools in maximising the attendance of students. With the right teaching, we should expect that students would learn successfully, if they attended school regularly. With an attendance rate of 90% or better, schools should improve student outcomes significantly. School leaders were required to do more than promote attendance; they needed to implement systems and work with students, families, agencies and other departments to improve attendance and student outcomes. In reality an attendance rate of 80% meant that a student was absent from school on average one day every week. Lack of continuity hinders learning.

The school satisfaction survey of staff, students and parents/caregivers was conducted annually in all state schools in Queensland. From the many questions included in the survey, two were selected as targets. First, *confidence in state schools* went to the heart of how our schools were considered by stakeholders, and second, the *rate of student disciplinary absences* reflected the impact of a host of factors: the engagement of students in learning, the effectiveness of student support and the level of teacher capability. Student disciplinary absences impacted on attendance. If students were not at school, they were not learning, and the more school they missed, the more difficult it was for them to engage in school.

## THE SCALE OF IMPROVEMENT

Before reviewing the range of available data there are a few specific examples from the test element of reading in the NAPLAN that illustrate the scale of the improvement in the Far North region. These are presented as simple statements of comparison. Reading has been selected because of its essential relevance to children's learning and although there is variation across the elements, the improvements in the results for reading are indicative of what was achieved in general. The reader will note that in some cases the regional targets that were discussed earlier were achieved or exceeded.

## ALL STUDENTS' READING OUTCOMES

These statements compare the performance of year 3 students in 2008 with the performance of year 3 students in 2013 in reading in the NAPLAN:

- The percentage of students at or above the national minimum standard in year 3 reading improved from 76.3% for the 2008 cohort to 90.3% for the 2013 cohort. The target of 90% was achieved.
- The mean scale score for year 3 reading improved from 333.2 in 2008 to 382.8 in 2013.
- The percentage of students in the upper two bands for year 3 reading improved from 18.4% of students in 2008 to 28.6% of students in 2013. The target was exceeded.

Similarly, comparing the performance of the year 5 students in 2008 with the performance of year 5 students in 2013 shows significant improvement:

- The percentage of students at or above national minimum standard in year 5 reading improved from 70.3% for the 2008 cohort to 92.5% for the 2013 cohort. The target was exceeded.
- The mean scale score for year 5 reading improved from 430.4 in 2008 to 471.3 in 2013.
- The percentage of students in the upper two bands for year 5 reading improved from 12.5% of students in 2008 to 20.4% in 2013.

## ABORIGINAL AND TORRES STRAIT ISLANDER STUDENTS' READING OUTCOMES

While the cohort of "all students" in the Far North region improved over the period, the cohort of Aboriginal and Torres Strait Islander students achieved greater improvements. "Closing the gap" was achieved through consistently applying highly effective teaching strategies to all students. There was no specific teaching program implemented for Aboriginal and Torres Strait Islander students. In fact, schools were advised not to use some programs specifically designed for use with teaching Aboriginal and Torres Strait Islander students, because experience had shown they had achieved little, if any, improvement. As an example, the band scales for Aboriginal and Torres Strait Islander Learners had been introduced in the early 2000s and involved excessive amounts of energy and time to implement for no discernible improvement in outcomes.

The following data highlights the significant improvements in the percentage of Aboriginal and Torres Strait Islander students achieving the national minimum standard from 2008 to 2013 in the Far North region:

- The percentage at or above the national minimum standard in year 3 reading improved from 58.5% for the cohort in 2008 to 82.9% for the 2013 cohort.
- The percentage at or above the national minimum standard in year 5 reading improved from 42.7% for the cohort in 2008 to 85.1% for the 2013 cohort.
- The percentage at or above the national minimum standard in year 7 reading improved from 62.6% for the cohort in 2008 to 68% for the 2013 cohort.
- The percentage at or above the national minimum standard in year 9 reading improved from 58.5% for the cohort 2008 to 71.4% for the 2013 cohort.

The following graphs illustrate the improvement in the percentage of year 3 students and year 5 students at or above the national minimum standard in reading from 2008 to 2013. As explained earlier in this chapter, the national minimum

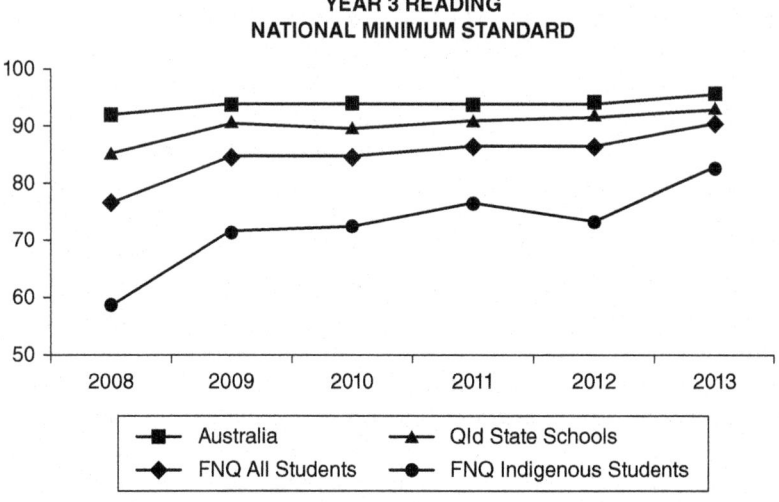

YEAR 3 READING
NATIONAL MINIMUM STANDARD

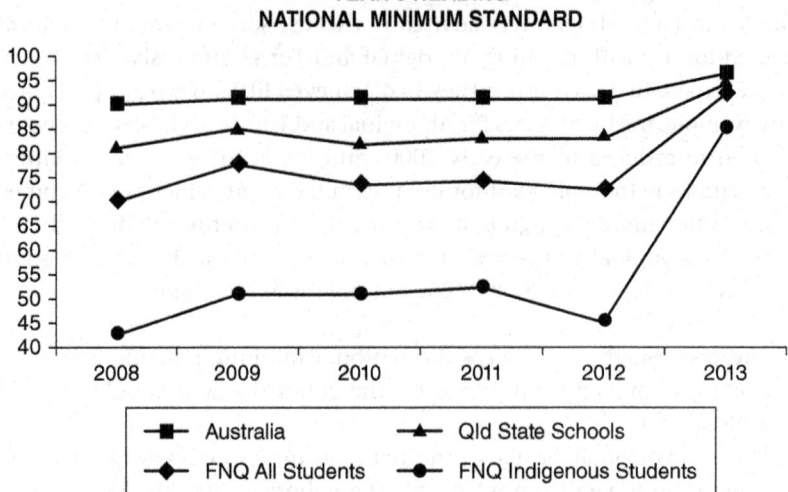

standard was the initial focus of our work. These two test areas show examples of the most significant improvement achieved, especially for Aboriginal and Torres Strait Islander students (described as FNQ Indigenous on these graphs).

## FAR NORTH REGIONAL DATA TRENDS FROM 2008 TO 2013

To illustrate the improved performance of the region over time, comparisons are made between the performance of the Far North region and the other six regions in Queensland and between the average performance of state schools in the Far North region with the average performance of all Queensland state schools. The sixteen elements mentioned in these comparisons are composed of reading, spelling, writing conventions (grammar and punctuation) and numeracy across the four year levels in which the test is completed: years 3, 5, 7 and 9. Writing is not included because changes to the test between the years of 2008 to 2010 and 2011 to 2013 make comparisons invalid.

In the national minimum standard the improvement for students in the Far North region was greater than the average improvement of all Queensland state schools in fifteen of the sixteen areas. In five of these areas the improvement was greater than 4%. The Far North region improved in more areas of the national minimum standard than any other region.

The mean scale score is a good indicator of overall performance, as it represents the average score for each cohort. The improvement in the mean scale score for students in the Far North region from 2008 until 2013 was greater than the average improvement of students in all Queensland state schools in thirteen of the sixteen areas. In eleven of these areas the improvement was greater than 4%. Only one other region in Queensland improved in more areas than did the Far North region.

In the upper two bands the improvement for students in the Far North region was greater than the improvement for students in Queensland state schools in eight of sixteen areas. In one of these areas the improvement was greater than 4%. Only one other region in Queensland improved in more areas than did the Far North region.

## IMPROVEMENTS ACHIEVED IN THE FAR NORTH REGION IN YEAR 12 OUTCOMES FROM 2008 TO 2013

The service commitment is described more fully in Chapter 14. Suffice to say here that it provided clarity of purpose for leaders in the organisation and clear indicators of success for students completing year 12. The service commitment in the Far North region was that 100% of students in our state schools would graduate as confident, healthy, young Australians and achieve:

- An Overall Position (OP) score and enter university, or
- A clear Vocational Education and Training (VET) pathway to employment, or
- Paid employment of at least 25 hours per week, or
- Alternate pathways (for students with special needs)

The elements of the service commitment could be linked to the data sets used by secondary schools across the department. Before looking at the data more broadly, there are a few specific examples to illustrate the scale of the improvement in year 12 outcomes in the Far North region:

- The percentage of students achieving the Queensland Certificate of Education:
  - In 2008, 53% of year 12 students achieved a QCE.
  - In 2013, 79.6% of year 12 students achieved a QCE.

- The percentage of OP-eligible students achieving an Overall Position Score of 1–15:
  - In 2008, 67% of OP-eligible year 12 students achieved an OP 1–15.
  - In 2013, 72.3% of OP-eligible students achieved and OP 1–15.

- The percentage of students achieving a VET certificate:
  - In 2008, 34% of students achieved a VET certificate.
  - In 2013, 73.7% of students achieved a VET certificate.

- The percentage of students achieving a SAT, QCE, IBD, VET or OP:
  - In 2008, 77.8% of students achieved a SAT, QCE, IBD, VET or OP.
  - In 2013, 93.4% of students achieved a SAT, QCE, IBD, VET or OP.
  - In 2013 89.2% of Aboriginal and Torres Strait Islander students achieved a SAT, QCE, IBD, VET or OP.

An explanation of the terms used here is provided in Box 15.2.

---

**Box 15.2    Terms used**

*OVERALL POSITION SCORE*

An OP is a student's position in a state-wide rank order based on their overall achievement in authority subjects. It indicates how well a student has done in comparison to all other OP-eligible students in Queensland and is used for tertiary entrance purposes only. Students are placed in one of 25 OP bands, from OP1 (highest) to OP25 (lowest).

*QUEENSLAND CERTIFICATE OF EDUCATION*

The QCE is Queensland's senior school qualification, which is usually awarded to eligible students at the end of year 12. The QCE recognises broad learning options and offers flexibility in what, where and when learning occurs.

*SAT*

School-based Apprenticeship/Traineeship.

*VET*

Vocational education and training qualifications, including Certificate I, II, III, IV, Diploma or Advanced Diploma.

*IBD*

International Baccalaureate Diploma.

(Source: website of the Queensland Curriculum and Assessment Authority.)

---

# Regional data presentation: graphs

These graphs illustrate the improvement in the mean scale score of state school students in years 3, 5, 7 and 9 in reading and numeracy in the years from 2008 until 2013. Although using the national minimum standard may have illustrated more dramatic improvements, the mean scale score is used because it is a good indicator of overall performance, as it represents the average score for each cohort. Reading and numeracy were selected as the two test areas to graph in this section as representative of the degree of improvement achieved.

## YEAR 3 READING 2008–2013 MEAN SCALE SCORE

The improvement in the results for students in Far North Queensland in each year from 2008 to 2013 is greater than the improvement for students in Queensland state schools and Australia. The gap between the performance of Aboriginal and Torres Strait Islander students and Australia was reduced in 2013.

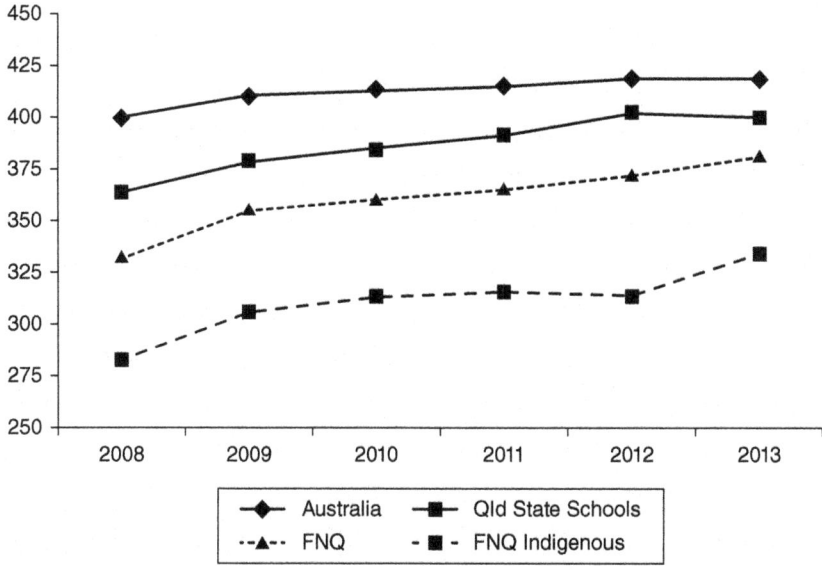

## YEAR 3 NUMERACY 2008–2013 MEAN SCALE SCORE

The initial focus in the region was to improve the performance in reading and literacy more generally. While the improvements in the results for numeracy were not as pronounced, the region continued to improve at a greater rate than Queensland state schools and Australia.

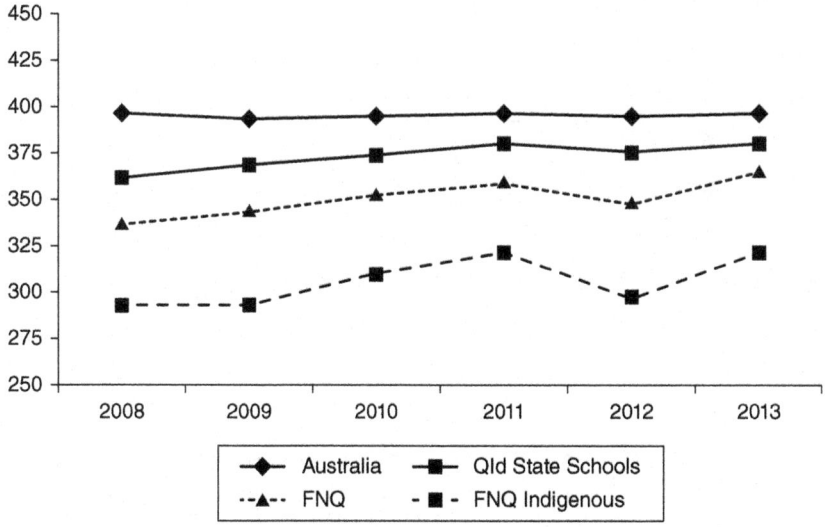

## YEAR 5 READING 2008–2013 MEAN SCALE SCORE

The mean scale score for all students in year 5 reading in Far North Queensland improved from 430.4 in 2008 to 471.3 in 2013. The gap between the performance of students in Far North Queensland and students in state schools in Queensland and Australia was reduced significantly from 2008 to 2013.

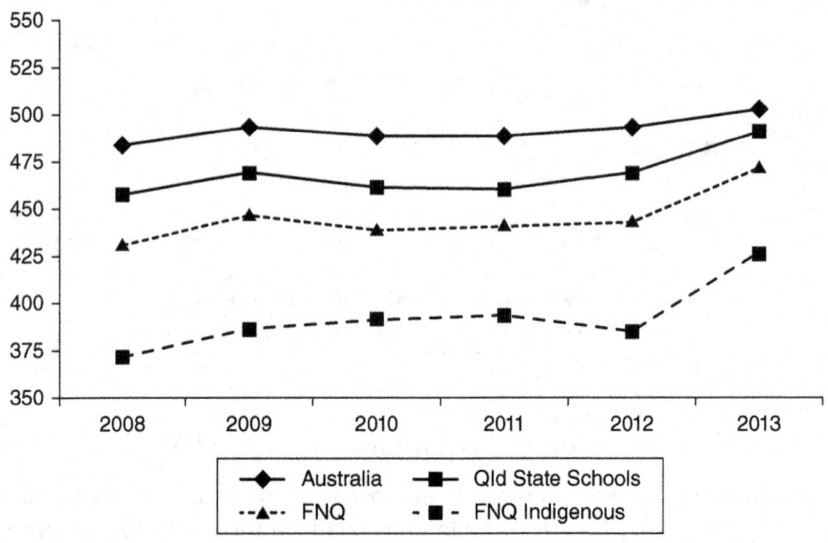

## YEAR 5 NUMERACY 2008–2013 MEAN SCALE SCORE

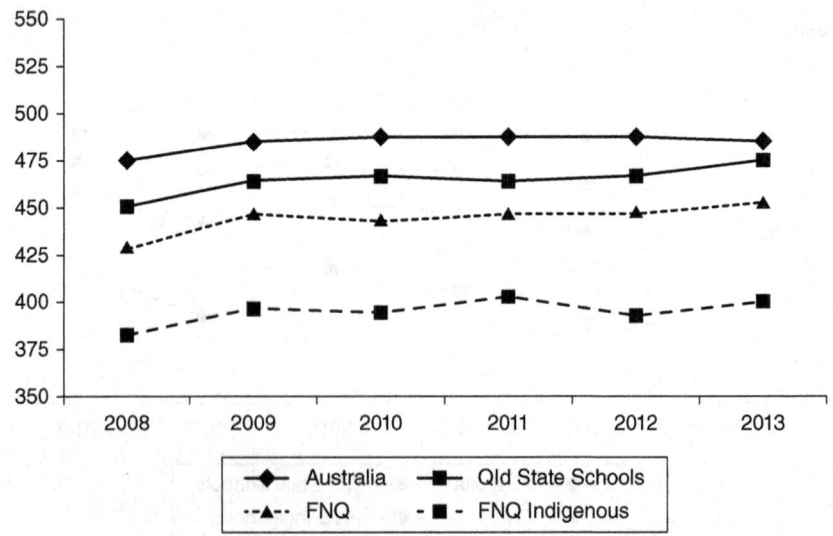

YEAR 7 READING 2008–2013 MEAN SCALE SCORE

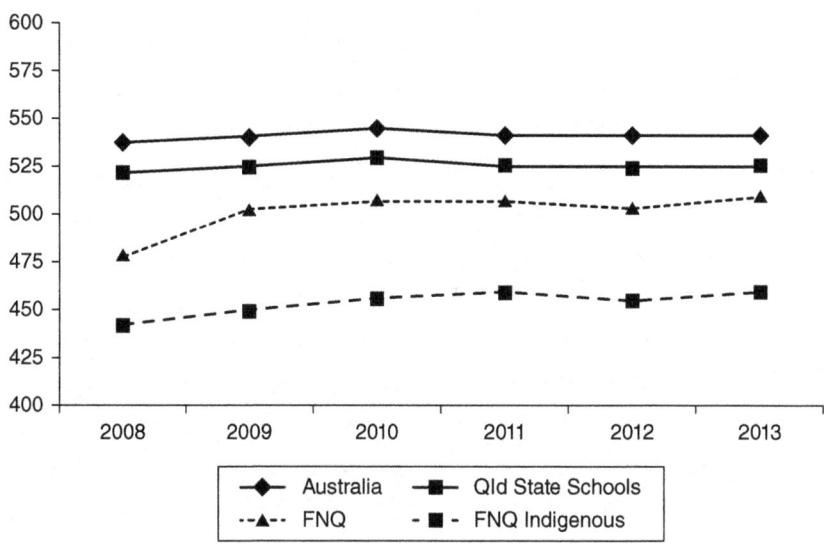

YEAR 7 NUMERACY 2008–2013 MEAN SCALE SCORE

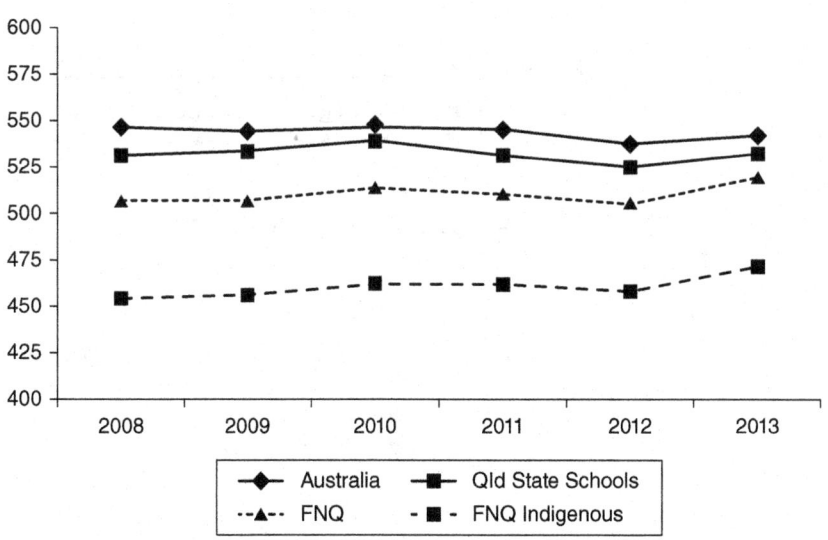

## YEAR 9 READING 2008–2013 MEAN SCALE SCORE

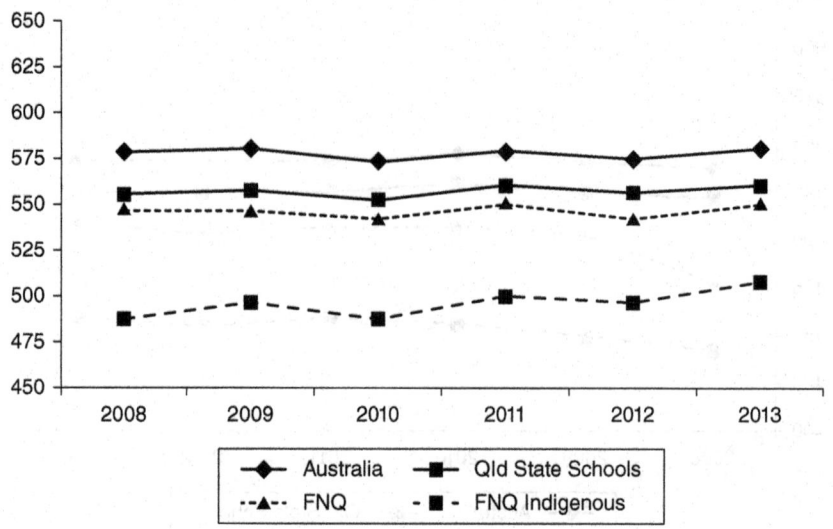

## YEAR 9 NUMERACY 2008–2013 MEAN SCALE SCORE

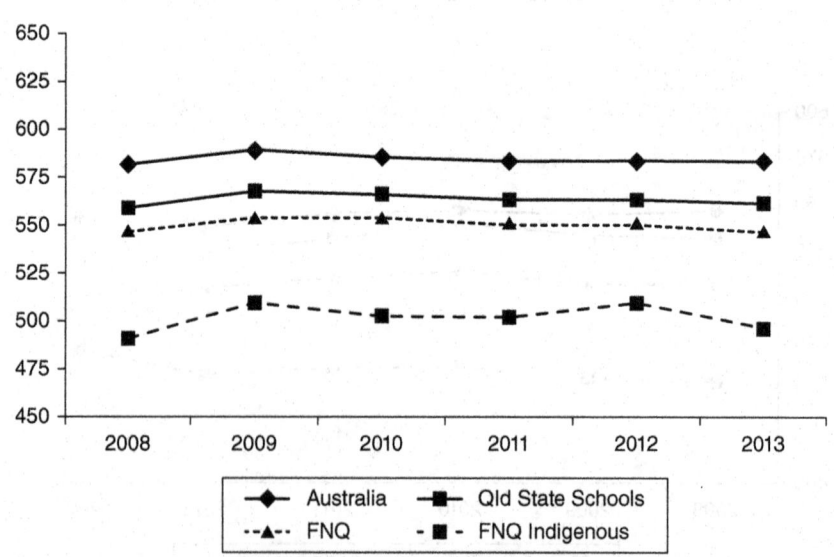

# Conclusion

We present these results because so often programs/initiatives are not connected to outcomes, or outcomes are not clearly related to specific programmes. We simply state that the implementation of Systems Leadership had a significant part to play in achieving these results. We also ask that any other approaches are examined in the same way. Do they actually deliver? What is the evidence? In particular, our approach does show real and significant improvements in "closing the gap". This was done without pumping in expensive or highly specialised resources but by implementing systems that demanded the same expectations from all, and equalisation rather than differentiation. It seems to have worked.

Figures do not tell the whole story but without them a story is just that. We will now go on to look at specific case studies.

# **16** *Case studies*

## Case study 1: Malanda State School

By Mark Allen, Principal

### CONTEXT

Malanda State School (MSS) is set in a rural community with an economy that has been associated with the dairy industry for more than 90 years. It is located 74 km south west of Cairns, in Far North Queensland, Australia, with 335 students from Prep to year 6. MSS' Index of Community Socio-Educational Advantage (ICSEA) is 975. ICSEA values typically range from approximately 500 (representing extremely educationally disadvantaged backgrounds) to about 1,300 (representing schools with students with very educationally advantaged backgrounds). Under 1,000 is considered to be disadvantaged.

The school has had seven principals from 2012 to 2016, due to complexities associated with a previous principal (ongoing). Prior to my appointment, the substantive deputy principal for 12 years did a pleasing job in a difficult situation as acting principal.

I discovered on arrival that the school has an incredibly strong community. The Parents & Citizens' (P&C) Committee is focused and passionate about the school and its connection to the town. The P&C president is the current P&C area coordinator – Peninsula. The P&C president is highly active in the school, and led the community's drive to find a replacement principal with the capability to lead, develop and sustain school improvement.

Forty people, many of who have served twenty-plus years in the setting, staff the school. Of the school's twenty teaching staff, there are four ex-teaching principals who have the knowledge and understanding of the complexity of the work leading a small school and therefore are happy to assist. There are three graduates and the total teaching staff comprises four levels of teacher classification, with an apparent absence of associated accountability. The teaching capability of the teachers was unclear when I arrived.

Like the teachers, I found that the school's teacher aides (TAs) are also dedicated and many have served for more than twenty years. Their work was not clear when I arrived, and a lot of their work was channelled at a minor percentage of the student body/general TA tasks (resourcing and so on).

The business services manager role was left vacant in the final week of 2015 due to ill health, which left the school without a person in the role for much of the first term. When I sourced someone suitable for the role, she was still attached to a previous school, and operated both for many weeks. There were constant issues with her access to the MSS computer network also, as the Education Queensland (EQ) system continually locked her out. She lost at least five days being unable to access the EQ network, the management system Oneschool, MyHR and Outlook.

MSS had very little exposure to Systems Leadership modelling until the commencement of the 2016 school year, when I arrived. I discovered that a benefit to our school was the Malanda State High School's (MSHS) long engagement with modelling, and its application, in all areas of the school's operation. I have no doubt that this long engagement contributed to the successful transition of MSHS in 2016 from the previous principal to the current incumbent, as the school continues to flourish academically and culturally. I identified some of the systems in place in MSHS, which I thought would benefit us at MSS with minor modifications – enrolment, attendance, IT, innovation via Agriculture Science and student transition – and commenced planning their adaption and implementation in MSS.

Systems Leadership modelling's impact on me has been significant since 2010, when I was first exposed to the material. Life before Systems Leadership was hectic and less fulfilling, leaving me feeling overwhelmed regularly and frustrated with the lack of results and slow progress of projects. I felt like I was letting everyone down. My work was not well planned, was reactive and was at times little more than "event management". It affected me personally too, as the stress remained with me outside work. Perhaps the greatest epiphany came in the form of learning how to divide my work into "improving" and "sustaining", and the scheduling of such tasks which followed has left me in a position where I feel highly effective, and running an organisation which benefits from this. I have now applied this knowledge to other areas of my life, which has been highly beneficial, and I am a better person for it.

Needless to say, being a greenfield site provided an excellent opportunity for me to establish a culture where the modelling is not only valued, but is welcomed by staff who have experienced feelings of uncertainty about the work of their roles, and the confusion which spreads to the teams in the absence of consistent high-quality leadership.

## PURPOSE

This case study explains my application of Systems Leadership material at MSS to demonstrate rapid progress in creating our desired culture.

## METHODOLOGY

As principal, I applied Systems Leadership material in the following ways:

- Improving clarity through the accurate identification of "what is the work?" in the social, technical and commercial streams of the organisation with an emphasis on the social and technical components
- Engaging with the Systems Leadership consultant has been of great value re advice about the practical application of the concepts, models and tools to do my work
- Analysing and revising what was in place – for example, the Annual Improvement Plan (AIP) – resulting in a reduction in the improvement focus from seventeen initiatives to five
- Identifying and addressing the critical issues
- Applying the Tools of Leadership model:
  - Identifying the existing culture by:
    - Analysing and or revising teacher expectations, classroom practice and explicit teaching
    - Conducting a detailed analysis of staff mythologies and data to identify an accurate baseline from which we can all move forward.
  - My behaviours have been/are instrumental in the successful culture change at MSS:
    - From the first meeting on the pupil-free days, I introduced the team leadership and team membership steps and traps, the values continua and our own agreed staff meeting protocols (Be Safe, Be Respectful, Be a Learner) – behaving in this manner is not just for students
    - The greetings I use in the mornings and afternoons – scheduled time in my calendar daily
    - I visited/visit the staffroom most days at 11am – as scheduled; this is an accountability of my leadership team members that is also described in their specific role descriptions
    - Modelling the team leader behaviours/steps – and referring team members to behaviours/steps at every meeting/when redirection is required.
  - Implementing key systems – systems drive behaviour
    - Organisation chart – clarifying authorities
    - Accurate specific role descriptions – clarifying authority and accountability
    - Annual action plans – demystifying the work.
  - Symbols – symbols are my favourite tool
    - Assigning tasks using the Task Assignment model
    - Creating new mythologies

- ■ Analysis of the technical component and subsequent clarification of the work to be focused on
- ■ The right people in the right roles doing the right work – reflected in the allocation of resources
- ■ Designing essential systems using the Twenty Questions.
- o Reading system, daily writing system, students educationally at risk system

    - ■ The P&C president and I work continually; we meet in the early hours of the morning, which suits his business operations.

## RESULTS

Some of the results I have seen as principal include:

- An excellent productive working relationship with the P&C president; together we are applying Systems Leadership material to our P&C organisation
- The creation of new mythologies with leadership team members – staff in the leadership team experiencing greater clarity in the work of their roles; weekly reporting indicating significant progress; team leadership and membership steps evident in interactions between the team, and respect for delegated "authority" to complete work; my leadership by attending staffroom at 11am each day to interact with the teaching team
- Delivering on the Systems Leadership principle of the right people in the right roles doing the right work
- More productivity – progress is highly evident in all area of the leadership team's specific roles, evidenced through rapid transformation of areas relating to the AIP
- Productive new systems:
  - o Staff have a universal language to apply when engaging in discourse about the social component of their work
  - o Leadership team members have engaged with the Task Assignment model, and completed some pleasing work as a result.

As a classroom teacher under Mark's leadership, the school is much calmer because we know the support is there. He has worked with us to design and implement whole-school systems like School Wide Positive Behaviour Learning (SWPBL), Sound Waves, Guided Reading and Daily Writing Consolidation systems. With this calmness comes self-assurance for the staff, because we are valued as an individual who is part of a team, creating a network, a community among the school staff. We are comfortable because there is no 'in crowd' and no 'out crowd'. Everyone is different, but in this culture difference is respected and our tasks are done more efficiently and effectively. We are able to put forward ideas from our role and know they are considered.

An MSS teacher

*Writing system*

As head of curriculum, focusing on the development of a writing system, the application of Systems Leadership to my work in 2016 enabled me to operate at a high level of detail effectively for the first time, successfully using social process to have teachers know the key issues and together develop a targeted response, one where they were the key players. From the first time the data yelled at us to do something, it was thoroughly analysed and planned in detail from the start. It meant that I was able to use knowledge I had been storing away to choose the right people for the right work. I was able to use their skills and their standing in the school to influence the staff in a positive way. Building this effective writing system easily provided the methodology to maintain and improve it and when I went on leave it was easily transferrable to my replacement. The Systems Leadership process I had worked through meant that I had made a sustainable system, a system that is powered by the teachers and is supported by the other systems in the school.

This "relative writing plan" of the MSS students from years 3 to 5 is demonstrating performance significantly above the "average gain" of Queensland schools – as a direct result of the Daily Writing Consolidation system, which was implemented in 2015.

*Reading system*

As lead teacher, use of Systems Leadership has facilitated ownership of the reading system by all involved through the effective application of social process. The efficient, successful reading system design has delivered:

- Clear understanding of authority and accountability, scripted well-resourced systems, effective training, clear expectations and timelines with accurate data collection
- A change of the TAs' role from that of simply reading with students to working at a para-professional level with efficient program delivery, improved skill and knowledge capability and involvement in system innovations

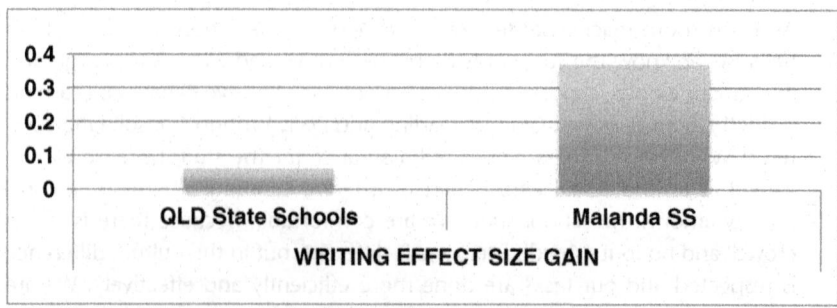

**Figure 16.1**    Writing year 3/2014 to year 5/2016

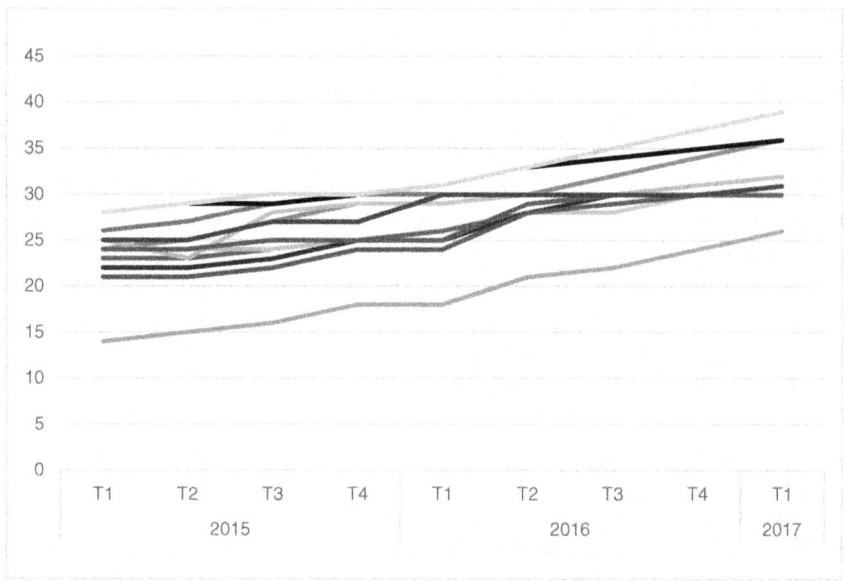

**Figure 16.2**    Reading year 3/2015 to year 5/2017

- Analysis of recordable data allowing individual students' achievements to be monitored and alterations made to the system, if necessary, to ensure continual reading growth
- Creating reading goals with students and informing stakeholders of progress has effectively motivated all involved
- The work of my role as TA team leader and custodian of the reading system, listening to employees' suggestions, ensuring timelines are met, quality-assuring the results, continually identifying and implementing innovations is necessary for success.

In 2018 our year 3 to 5 effect size relative gain in reading (compared to the nation) was 9.6 times higher than the nation.

The student data above demonstrates the reading systems' consistency of purpose and practice, delivering continual, more consistent improvement of reading results in 2016 and 2017 regardless of these students' ethnicity, socioeconomic status and minor intellectual or behaviour disorders.

*Pause system*

In 2018 I employed a teacher to design a system who had developed high capability in mindfulness and neuroscience and their practical application to facilitate emotional self-regulation of students in her classroom over seven years. The purpose of the system is to improve teacher well-being as a result of students being able to emotionally self-regulate their behaviour. The system was conceptualised, designed and trialled in all Prep to year 6 classrooms. This led to further improvements to the design for introduction to another trial school and for these improvements to be implemented in our school in 2019.

I could not imagine a school without Pause now. The emotional self-regulation of students that is evident in my school is translating into a calmer, more settled place. Children are achieving better and we are dealing with less erratic behaviour. As a rural school with socio-economic complexity, Pause has given us – students, staff, parents and caregivers – a universal language to provide our students with the capability to make great choices.

Pause is another exceptional thing that has been delivered through the practical application of Systems Leadership in our school and the benefit to the whole school community is staggering.

## SUMMARY: LESSONS LEARNT

The application of the Systems Leadership material facilitates identification of "what is the work" and how my staff and I can get our work done efficiently, effectively making rapid continual progress as my team becomes more proficient with the material and its application.

# Case study 2: Tagai State College

By Judith Ketchell, Stephanie Savage, Ned David and Steve Foster

## BACKGROUND

The story of Tagai and his twelve crewmen starts when he was out on their canoe. They were out fishing and Tagai left the boat for a short time. When he returned, he found that the crew had greedily consumed all of the food and water. Tagai punished the crew by banishing them from the canoe. Tagai became part of the sky and his position in the southern sky meant that he was never in the sky at the same time as his crew. The full constellation of Tagai includes stars for his canoe, the anchor and a suckerfish. The name "Tagai" comes from the name of a large constellation in the southern sky and the right hand of Tagai is commonly known as the Southern Cross. The knowledge of Tagai's journey across the Torres Strait is known to all Torres Strait Islanders, and he is known as "He who could make the best weather, he who controls the wind, thunder, and the rains".

Tagai is known as the heavenly clock and his position in the sky is central for our seasonal calendar and tells us when the monsoon is near, when to prepare gardens and when to repair fish traps from the beginning of the year to the end of the year.

The Torres Strait Islander people use the stars of Tagai for navigation and each star's position therefore is vital to ensure a safe journey. Like the constellation, each leader at Tagai State College is committed to our vision of providing the highest standards of teaching and learning. Students are considered a star in our constellation reaching their destinations for a successful journey ahead.

Tagai State College's name is anchored on the constellation of Tagai, a symbol that unites the people of the Torres Straits. The position of Tagai across the sky instructs the world order, predicting new seasons and everything has a place.

Tagai State College, like the constellation, is a collection of individual entities that make up the whole. With each campus considered as equally unique and important as the stars of Tagai, together they form a college far stronger than the sum of the parts.

## CONTEXT

Torres Strait Islanders are a distinct race of Melanesian people who are one of the two Indigenous peoples of Australia. We are seafaring people who use the stars to chart our course. Zenadth Kes, commonly referred to as the Torres Strait, is the body of water between two landmasses: Australia and Papua New Guinea. Zenadth Kes is made up of five nations of people geographically located in specific areas of the Torres Strait. There are two ancestral languages with six dialects spoken, as indicated below. Yumplatok, otherwise known as Torres Strait Creole, is also the recognised language spoken throughout the Torres Strait.

1. Kaiwalagal Nation – Inner Islands – Kala Lagaw Ya – Kawrareg dialect
2. Kulkalgal Nation – Central Islands – Kala Lagaw Ya – Kulkalgaw Ya dialect
3. Kemer Kemer Miriam Nation – Eastern Islands – Meriam Mir – Mer and Erub dialects
4. Gudamaluyilgal – Top Western Islands – Kalaw Kawaw Ya dialect
5. Maluyilgal – Near Western Islands – Kala Lagaw Ya – Mabuyag dialect.

**Table 16.1**    Tagai State College campuses

| Badulgaw Ngurpay Lag | Dauan Ngurpay Lag | Iama Ngurpay Lag | Kubin Ngurpay Lag | Erub Eruer |
|---|---|---|---|---|
| Mabuygiw Ngurpay Lag | Kadhego Ngurpay Lag | Masig Muysaw Ngurpay Lag | Ngurpay Mudh | Mer Eruer Uteb |
| St Pauls Ngurpay Lag | Malu Kiyay Ngurpay Lag | Poruma Ngurpay Lag | | Ugar Eruer Uteb |
| | | Warraber Ngurpay Lag | | Waybeni Buway Ngurpay Mudh |
| | | | | Waybeni Koey Ngurpay Mudh |

It has been thirty-one years since the Department of Education took over the responsibility of delivering education services; prior to this the Department of Aboriginal & Torres Strait Islander Affairs had control of all schools.

Tagai State College was established in 2007 and is an amalgamation of seventeen campuses spread across fifteen islands located in the 48,000 sq km of the Torres Strait Region, Queensland. The purpose of the college is to have one single point of accountability responsive to the educational aspirations of the Torres Strait Islander people; Tagai State College is committed to providing education and training services that are holistic and designed to respond to the academic, social, emotional and physical needs of every child.

*Our vision*

Navigating YUMI [see below] to a successful future, by embracing our unique Torres Strait Island identity to achieve a world-class standard of education.

*Our mission*

Tagai State College guarantees the highest standard of teaching and learning to achieve the aspirations of the Torres Strait Nation.

*Our Learner Guarantee*

Tagai State College guarantees that every student upon graduating year 12 will have engaged with the unique language and culture of the Torres Strait and achieve an OP [Overall Position] and university entry or be progressing on a clearly articulated VET [Vocational Education and Training] pathway or be in quality paid employment or have a clearly defined transition plan for identified students.

*College targets 2016*

- Attendance >90%
- Levels of achievement: C or higher 80%; A standard 10%
- NAPLAN: 100% at the national minimum standard (NMS)
- Upper two bands: 7% in all domains except Spelling 10%
- VET completion rate 100%; QCE [Queensland Certificate of Education] completion rate 100%; SOS [Student Opinion Survey] measure >90%.

As Indigenous leaders of the Tagai Executive team, we are proud to serve the Torres Strait Nation and work hand in hand with our school communities to brand the delivery of education to a traditional system within our ways of being, knowing and doing.

When the college commenced operations, the critical issue that emerged was "What if the western education system does not value and respect Torres Strait Islander ways of being, thinking and doing?" Hence, the YUMI way of working was embedded in the design of all systems at the college. The YUMI way is our way of doing business. YUMI (pronounced *You-Me*) is a term from Torres Strait Creole. In this context, the YUMI way demonstrates respect for the peoples, place, languages, cultures and protocols in order to do business the "prapa [proper] way in the Torres Strait Region". The YUMI way refers to a process for ensuring inclusiveness and ownership of a system that has been quality assured by the Indigenous peoples of the Torres Strait since time immemorial. Associate Principal Steve Foster composed this definition so that the college was able to clearly align all college systems to the Torres Strait context and communicate this expectation to every student, staff and community member in everyday operations.

*School profile*

* Coeducational or single sex: coeducational
* Independent public (state) school: yes
* Year levels offered in 2016: Early Childhood to year 12.

The college annual report (covering 2013–2016) outlines the following statistics:

* 1,788 Preprep to year 12 students enrolled; seventeen campuses with seventeen P&C associations; 175 teachers, including thirty-five Indigenous teachers; forty classified officers; ten new leaders each year; fifteen beginning teachers; eight mentors; 268 campus buildings; 156 units of teacher accommodation; services and support is across 48,000 sq km; college attendance has ranged from 85% to 89% over the last four years; reading data has improved over the last four years; the turnover of staff is currently 3.5 years
* The last audit report indicated the college had effective systems in place.

**Table 16.2**    Student enrolments for Tagai State College

|  | **Total** | **Girls** | **Boys** | **Indigenous** | **Enrolment Continuity (Feb–Nov)** |
|---|---|---|---|---|---|
| **2014** | 1,505 | 724 | 781 | 1,439 | 91% |
| **2015** | 1,492 | 718 | 774 | 1,439 | 89% |
| **2016** | 1,544 | 752 | 792 | 1,469 | 90% |

**Table 16.3** 2016 Education for Life Prep to year 3

| | **Danalgaw Ngurpay** Education for Life **Mabuyag** | **Igililmay Ngurpay** Education for Life **Kalaw Kawaw Ya** | **Danalgaw Ngurpay** Education for Life **Mabuyag dialect with Kulkalgaw Ya** | **Danalgaw Ngurpay** Education for Life **Kawrareg** | **Kemer Eruer** Education for Life **Meriam Mer** |
|---|---|---|---|---|---|
| **Campuses** | • Mabuygiw Ngurpay Lag <br>• Badulgaw Ngurpay Lag <br>• St Pauls Ngurpay Lag. | • Malu Kiyay Ngurpay Lag <br>• Kadhego Ngurpay Lag <br>• Dauan Ngurpay Lag. | • Poruma Ngurpay Lag <br>• Iama Ngurpay Lag <br>• Warraber Ngurpay Lag <br>• Masig Muysaw Ngurpay Lag. | • Kubin Ngurpay Lag <br>• Ngurpay Ngurpay Mudh. | • Mer Eruer Uteb <br>• Ugar Eruer Uteb <br>• Erub Eruer <br>• Waybeni Buway Ngurpay Mudh. |
| **Target language/ dialect** | Mabuyag | Kalaw Kawaw Ya | Mabuyag Dialect with Kulkalgaw Ya | Kawrerag | Meriam Mer |
| **Mode** | Immersion | Immersion | Immersion | Immersion | Immersion |
| **Language proficiency** | Beginner | Beginner | Beginner | Beginner | Beginner |

Sixteen primary outer island campuses feed into the secondary campus on Thursday Island together with two boarding colleges that accommodate students that move from their home island to access secondary school. Parent occupations are varied and range from the fishing industry to public service, hospitality, small business, childcare and local councils. There is a very small population of non-Indigenous students who attend school in the Torres Strait.

## EDUCATION FOR LIFE PROGRAM

Igililmay Ngurpay (Top Western Islands), Danalgaw Ngurpay (Near Western, Kaywalagal and Central Islands), or Kemer Eruer (Eastern Islands) is the YUMI way model of delivering the traditional language and cultural content languages from Prep to year 3 across Tagai. Our full immersion model is designed to restore the traditional languages and subsequent dialects of Meriam Mir and Kala Lagaw Ya to build on our children's linguistic and cultural competencies.

The Learner Guarantee is the college platform for the teaching and learning service provided to students. The purpose of this model is to ensure continuity and consistency from Preprep to year 12 services based on the YUMI way of doing business. Tagai State College values all learners and believes all students can learn. We focus on the development of the whole child to be "two-way strong" and meet the Learner Guarantee.

The college structure was designed to provide a range of centralised services to improve the efficiency and effectiveness of the organisation. The college structure includes executive services support, student support services, the Malu Os special education outreach service, an ICT support service, curriculum support teams and a business service unit.

In 2015, the college introduced Systems Leadership as the signature way of working and communicated what this meant in all of the specific role descriptions. The term "signature way of working" was created by a group of leaders at their training program. Our collective belief for change prompted the college to then introduce the Systems Leadership Academy in 2016 to support the ongoing Systems Leadership training, coaching and mentoring provided to all of our school and community leaders.

Our signature way of working together is built on our foundation stone, the YUMI way, and practices drawn from Systems Leadership. Systems Leadership is the college's signature way of working together, where concepts, models and tools are implicitly embedded in everyday practice throughout the college.

## PURPOSE

To work together with our school communities to build a strong and proud nation using Systems Leadership.

## METHODOLOGY

In 2015, a Systems Leadership review was undertaken to determine the impact that using the framework and tools had on improving student outcomes. This internal review was an opportunity to feed forward into planning the 2016 whole-college review undertaken by the School Improvement Unit in 2016.

As the result of the Systems Leadership training review, the Tagai Executive team designed and implemented the following model and tools:

- A college and campus organisational structure to communicate clear lines of accountability to guide weekly progress conversations
- An audit of the existing culture to ensure high expectations inform the desired culture
- Introduction of a yearly theme and symbol at the beginning of each year; the 2017 theme was "Empower YUMI", which translated the key messages shown in Figure 16.3.
- Clarifying common mythologies:

   a.  It was unfair and undignifying to believe that the current Western education system properly values Indigenous history, culture and protocols.
   b.  It is unfair to blame students' and families' language background as a deficit for poor literacy and numeracy standards.
   c.  It is unfair and undignifying to not be accountable for campus decision making.

- Designing college systems that used the Twenty Questions to quality-assure the design process and linkages to other systems

   o  Example 1: College well-being strategy.

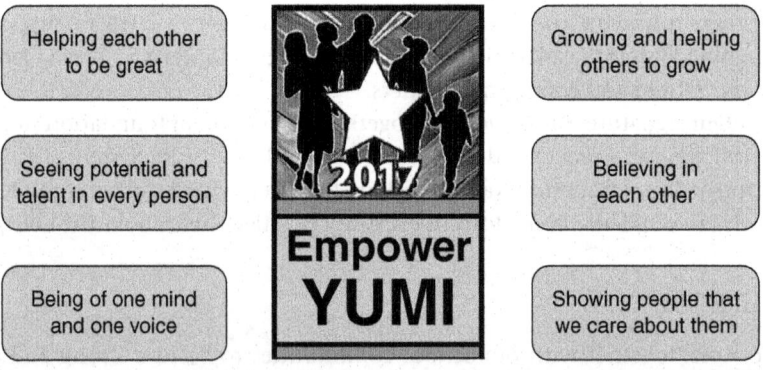

**Figure 16.3**    The 2017 YUMI theme

Purpose: The staff well-being system is to improve staff health and well-being within our workplaces.

Context: Good health, safety and well-being practice means productive behaviour in the workplace. Each team leader is responsible for working with team members to understand the desired culture in their campus. Team leaders are trained in Systems Leadership, HR, WH&S and finance polices to coach staff to be safe, healthy and productive in the workplace. The work ahead is to turn intention into reality.

Quality impact measures: Measures of success and data monitoring for the college well-being system include school opinion survey results, WH&S audit checks, campus run charts, WorkCover claim data, staff absence data, well-being survey data.

o   Example 2: Staff recognition system.

Purpose: To acknowledge and recognise staff contribution that support each other to be great while better understanding our strengths in our campuses.

Context: The YUMI way incorporates the traditional cultural practice of acknowledging and recognising staff for the work they perform in their roles.

Quality: Service recognition awards, beginning-of-the-year acknowledgements, team leadership and team membership acknowledgements.

Resources: Public media recognition, school noticeboard space; Tagai business card template, Tagai appreciation certificates and letters, farewell gift register, staff well-being template.

o   Example 3: Communication system

Purpose: To provide clear lines of communication to and from staff and community.

Context: Tagai has over 400 staff employed in seventeen campuses across 48,000 sq km that have limited connectivity throughout the year.

Quality modes of communication: One Portal announcements, campus staff, events term calendar, staff discussions lists, staff emails, newsletters/*Torres News*, college weekly bulletin, TSIMA – radio educational hour, weekly leader's webinar, Blackboard Resource site, Tagai Ed Studios, Tagai website.

It is very important that Tagai leaders have a good understanding of the following critical issues and ensure that they are fully addressed into the planning and accountability system:

- What if we do not have the right people in the right role doing the right work?
- What if staff do not have clarity of their roles and/or can answer these questions:

  o   What am I expected to do in my role?
  o   Who is going to give me regular feedback about how well I perform my role?
  o   What is my future in this organisation?

**Table 16.4**    Parent opinion survey results

| Performance measure | | | |
|---|---|---|---|
| Percentage of parents/caregivers who agree that | 2014 | 2015 | 2016 |
| Their child is getting a good education at school | 95% | 93% | 93% |
| This is a good school | 97% | 95% | 95% |
| Their child likes being at this school | 96% | 96% | 96% |
| Their child feels safe at this school | 93% | 94% | 93% |
| Their child's learning needs are being met at this school | 94% | 92% | 90% |
| Their child is making good progress at this school | 96% | 95% | 92% |
| Teachers at this school expect their child to do his or her best | 97% | 95% | 97% |
| Teachers at this school provide their child with useful feedback about his or her school work | 90% | 91% | 93% |
| Teachers at this school motivate their child to learn | 97% | 95% | 95% |
| Teachers at this school treat students fairly | 90% | 89% | 91% |
| They can talk to their child's teachers about their concerns | 95% | 95% | 95% |
| This school works with them to support their child's learning | 94% | 93% | 93% |
| This school takes parents' opinions seriously | 93% | 90% | 90% |
| Student behaviour is well managed at this school | 83% | 84% | 88% |
| This school looks for ways to improve | 96% | 93% | 94% |
| This school is well maintained | 94% | 94% | 91% |

In 2016, eighteen external reviewers, who are highly respected principals, reviewed the college's explicit improvement agenda. The level of systems design work introduced in our college that contributed to the success of the whole-college review was acknowledged in the 2016 review as outlined below.

## RESULTS

Systems Leadership has helped the college achieve consistency of practice in a number of important ways. The most successful output has been that all school and community leaders use a common language and have a consistent understanding of Systems Leadership tools. Systems Leadership has improved the organisational effectiveness and led to improved student outcomes in the data demonstrated in Box 16.1 and Box 16.2.

---

**Box 16.1    Parent opinion survey**

- Student, staff and community measures consistently above 90%
- Queensland Headline Indicator is 90% or more
- Family empowerment strategies implemented consistently.

---

**Box 16.2    Student opinion survey**

- School opinion survey student measures consistently above 90%
- Sporting excellence, celebrating primary and secondary students in regional and state sporting achievements
- Indigenous language and culture program implemented in all campuses successfully.

---

**Table 16.5**    Student opinion survey results

| Performance measure | | | |
|---|---|---|---|
| Percentage of students who agree that | 2014 | 2015 | 2016 |
| They are getting a good education at school | 95% | 96% | 92% |
| They like being at their school | 95% | 96% | 94% |
| They feel safe at their school | 90% | 91% | 90% |
| Their teachers motivate them to learn | 97% | 95% | 97% |
| Their teachers expect them to do their best | 96% | 98% | 98% |
| Their teachers provide them with useful feedback about their school work | 91% | 91% | 92% |
| Teachers treat students fairly at their school | 91% | 91% | 89% |
| They can talk to their teachers about their concerns | 84% | 86% | 83% |
| Their school takes students' opinions seriously | 86% | 87% | 84% |
| Student behaviour is well managed at their school | 75% | 79% | 75% |
| Their school looks for ways to improve | 94% | 94% | 955 |
| Their school is well maintained | 89% | 89% | 88% |
| Their school gives them opportunities to do interesting things | 91% | 92% | 91% |

**Table 16.6**    Student attendance 2016

| Description | 2014 | 2015 | 2016 |
|---|---|---|---|
| The overall attendance rate for the students at this school | 88% | 88% | 89% |
| The attendance rate for Indigenous students at this school | 88% | 87% | 89% |

**Box 16.3    Attendance**

- 89% student attendance
- Unexplained absences reduced by 50% in more than ten campuses
- Reduced the number of students who are coming to school less than 85% of the time.

**Box 16.4    Year 12 outcomes**

- 100% QCE completion rates
- Highest Far North Queensland consecutive rates for the last four years
- 100% VET completion rates
- Year 12 students completed their qualification in Coxswain Grade I & II.

**Table 16.7**    Attendance rate range (Semester 1)

| | Attendance | 0% to 85% | 85% to 90% | 90% to 95% | 95% to 100% |
|---|---|---|---|---|---|
| **This school** | 2016 | 25.8 | 13.3 | 20.9 | 40 |
| | 2015 | 30.8 | 14 | 21.4 | 33.9 |
| | 2014 | 30 | 13.8 | 18.2 | 38 |
| | 2013 | 38 | 14.2 | 19.2 | 28.6 |
| | 2012 | 36.7 | 14.8 | 24.4 | 24 |
| **State Prep to year 10/ Prep to year 12 schools** | 2016 | 21 | 12.4 | 24.8 | 41.8 |
| | 2015 | 21.8 | 13.1 | 25.7 | 39.4 |
| | 2014 | 22.8 | 12.8 | 25 | 39.5 |
| | 2013 | 23.3 | 12.7 | 24.6 | 35.7 |
| | 2012 | 22.8 | 14.2 | 27.3 | |

**Table 16.8**  Outcomes for our year 12 cohorts

| Description | 2014 | 2015 | 2016 |
|---|---|---|---|
| Number of students receiving a Senior Statement | 50 | 46 | 39 |
| Number of students awarded a Queensland Certificate of Individual Achievement | 2 | 1 | 1 |
| Number of students receiving an OP | 6 | 12 | 8 |
| Percentage of Indigenous students receiving an OP | 12% | 25% | 19% |
| Number of students who are completing/continuing a School-based Apprenticeship or Traineeship (SAT) | 3 | 1 | 0 |
| Number of students awarded one or more VET qualifications (incl. SAT) | 40 | 39 | 33 |
| Number of students awarded an Australian Qualification Framework Certificate II or above | 34 | 37 | 33 |
| Number of students awarded a QCE at the end of year 12 | 48 | 45 | 38 |
| Percentage of Indigenous students awarded a QCE at the end of year 12 | 98% | 98% | 97% |
| Number of students awarded an International Baccalaureate Diploma (IBD) | 0 | 0 | 0 |
| Percentage of OP/IBD eligible students with OP 1–15 or an IBD | 50% | 25% | 50% |
| Percentage of year 12 students who are completing or completed a SAT or were awarded one or more of the following: QCE, IBD, VET qualification | 96% | 98% | 97% |
| Percentage of Queensland Tertiary Admissions Centre applicants receiving an offer | 83% | 92% | 100% |

**Table 16.9**  VET qualification

| Number of students awarded certificates under the Australian Qualification Framework | | | |
|---|---|---|---|
| Years | Certificate I | Certificate II | Certificate III or above |
| 2014 | 25 | 26 | 9 |
| 2015 | 21 | 37 | 8 |
| 2016 | 15 | 33 | 0 |

**Box 16.5    NAPLAN Improvements**

Year 3 NAPLAN Numeracy NMS from 78% in 2015 to 82% in 2016

Year 3 NAPLAN Reading NMS from 79% in 2015 to 82% in 2016

Year 3 NAPLAN Writing NMS from 91% in 2015 to 98% in 2016

Year 5 NAPLAN Writing NMS from 60% in 2015 to 69% in 2016

Year 7 NAPLAN Reading NMS from 58% in 2015 to 65% in 2016

Year 7 NAPLAN Writing NMS from 41% in 2015 to 58% in 2016

Year 9 NAPLAN Reading NMS from 56% in 2015 to 66% in 2016

---

**Box 16.6    Extract taken from 2016 whole-college review executive summary**

1. Tagai State College has strong systems and protocols in place to support the consistency of practice.
2. Tagai State College leadership team has established and is driving a strong improvement agenda grounded in evidence from research and practice and expressed in terms of improvements in measurable student outcomes.
3. Data is used extensively in college decision making for student outcomes.
4. Tagai State College works to maintain a learning environment that is safe, respectful, tolerant and inclusive.
5. Tagai State College has clear expectations for student behaviour and learning.
6. Tagai State College leadership teams have developed systems to proactively respond to the wide range of challenges in managing financial, human and physical resources across 17 geographically isolated campuses.
7. Workforce planning is a priority and there is a range of proactive strategies to recruit, induct and support staff.
8. Tagai State College has implemented a significant language program that values traditional practices in each community. Professional Learning is classroom based and linked to priorities.
9. The college leaders have a deep awareness and strong commitment to working respectfully with the community. The YUMI way is embedded in all aspects of college life.
10. The college has implemented processes to ensure students make successful transitions across all sectors.

## SUMMARY

In summary, the Systems Leadership model has contributed to the design of customised systems in the college to drive the expected staff and student behaviour that our community deserves and continually strives to refine. The Department of Education develops policies and programs that need to be contextualised for implementation into the college. The Systems Leadership model will support the college in continuing to sustain improvement during times of people and program changes. Its results include:

- There has been a huge positive learning culture shift.
- The school organisation is systematically designing systems to be more efficient and effective.
- The college has become a safe, respectful, tolerant and inclusive learning place.
- Staff show high levels of commitment and believe that our student will succeed with the right conditions.
- Students speak highly of teachers and highly respected role models in our community.
- Parents are treated as partners in student learning partnerships. The college has set clear expectations for behaviour and learning.
- New staff are fully inducted into the college systems over time.
- Teachers are aware of culturally appropriate behaviours for themselves and others in the wider community.
- A college-wide handbook is available to all which covers how we work together using Systems Leadership in the context of YUMI.

Tagai State College will continue to navigate YUMI to a successful future.

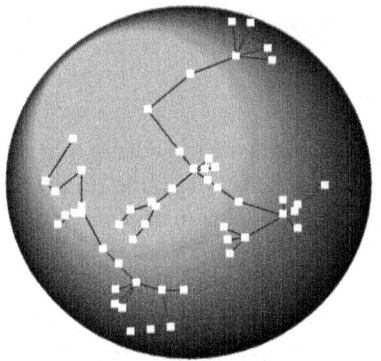

# Case study 3: Whitfield State School

By Ken Maclean

## CONTEXT

Systems Leadership is being applied in many settings and organisations. This case study is based on the work completed at Whitfield State School in Far North Queensland as part of a regional approach that commenced in 2014.

Whitfield State School is a Prep to year 6 school located in the western suburbs of Cairns. The school has an ICSEA score of 970 and has an enrolment of 871 students representing thirty-six different countries. Twenty-two percent of our students identify as Aboriginal or Torres Strait Islanders.

## THE PURPOSE

Across Australia, there is ample evidence that some schools have been able to rapidly move from a context characterized by low achievement to one where the majority of students are achieving at or above national mean standard scores. These schools achieve this transformation in a few years, irrespective of the socio-economic index or cultural backgrounds of their students.

The change agenda in these schools is "all encompassing". Reforms are made to the key systems of curriculum, assessment and pedagogy; staff capability to effectively deliver the programs; data tracking to monitor and inform student learning; and support for students with special needs, learning difficulties and high attendance.

This case study explores the way that the Whitfield leadership team used Systems Leadership to effectively design, implement and refine this broad improvement agenda and to embed the changed practices and behaviour over time. School leaders used the tools and models to implement highly effective systems where productive teams of teachers and TAs consistently adopt new practices at each step in a logical and planned, sequential improvement journey.

## METHODOLOGY

The systems approach was designed to ensure that all improvement elements were implemented in a logical way to build on previous work, so there was a consistent uptake of desired behaviour and processes by all staff.

The main system elements included:

- The recruitment of an executive and middle leadership team with sufficient capability to lead the broad improvement agenda
- Clear roles and authorities for each leader

- Individual leader performance and development plans to support capability development required to enact the work
- An annual school improvement plan with elements distilled from a four-year school improvement plan
- Task assignments to allocate the work to people in the leadership team
- Line management processes and system controls to monitor and continuously refine the implementation of the tasks by each leader
- An annual review to evaluate the impact and outcomes of the year's work and to inform planning for the following year
- A staff capability development system to ensure that all teachers and TAs were continuously improving their practice
- A student learning outcome data tracking system to monitor the learning of each student; this system allowed teacher teams to continuously monitor each student's performance and tailor lessons to ensure that every student was achieving
- A student support system to individually case manage and support students'
  - Learning
  - Behaviour and participation
  - Attendance
  - Family and home environment
  - Parental engagement and communication system.

Systems Leadership provided models and tools to design and implement complex systems. Well-designed systems drive consistency of staff behaviour, a critical factor in whole-school adoption of new practices and processes.

In the human-dense school environment, social processing is very important. Social processing extends from ensuring that every conversation effectively meets the needs of all parties through to reculturing the beliefs and assumptions of all staff to accept that every student can be a successful learner.

## RESULTS

**Table 16.10a**   NAPLAN performance

| Year | Year level | Reading | | | Writing | | | Spelling | | | Grammar and punctuation | | | Numeracy | | |
|---|---|---|---|---|---|---|---|---|---|---|---|---|---|---|---|---|
| | | Mean | U2B | NMS | Mean | U2B | NMS | Mean | U2B | NMS | Mean | U2B | NMS | Mean | U2B | NMS |
| 2008 | 3 | 360.3 | 27 | 88 | 392.2 | 30 | 89 | 353.2 | 17 | 86 | 354.1 | 18 | 84 | 349.4 | 13 | 86 |
| | 5 | 462.6 | 21 | 77 | 466.3 | 14 | 83 | 473.8 | 26 | 85 | 471.2 | 23 | 80 | 456.8 | 7 | 85 |
| 2017 | 3 | 421 | 45 | 92 | 403 | 53 | 93 | 433 | 61 | 94 | 424 | 53 | 91 | 406 | 40 | 95 |
| | 5 | 499 | 35 | 97 | 458 | 8 | 90 | 508 | 33 | 97 | 490 | 26 | 94 | 478 | 19 | 97 |

**Table 16.10b**    Legend

| Black | Performance statistically below Nation |
|---|---|
| White | Performance statistically similar to Nation |
| 61 | Performance statistically above Nation |

| Mean | Mean scale score of student group |
|---|---|
| U2B | % of students in the upper two bands |
| NMS | % of students achieving above national minimum standards |

**Table 16.11a**    Attendance and school disciplinary absences

| Year | 2013 | 2017 |
|---|---|---|
| Average student attendance | 92.4% | 93.5% |
| % of students attending <85% | 15.3% | 10.4% |

**Table 16.11b**    Attendance and school disciplinary absences

| Year | 2013 | 2017 |
|---|---|---|
| Short suspensions | 50 | 36 |
| Long suspensions | 17 | 0 |
| Exclusions | 0 | 0 |

**Table 16.12**    Student achievement

| Percentage of students receiving A, B or C grades in English | |
|---|---|
| 2013 | 2017 |
| 55.2% | 81% |

## THE LESSONS LEARNT

- System Leadership provides a principal with the models and tools to develop a clear purpose for the improvement agenda and to clearly articulate the work that must be completed.
- Principals use the tools to ensure that individual leaders clearly understand what work they are expected to do within the school.
- Good design enables the principal to ensure that each improvement initiative is implemented in an aligned way that complements and amplifies the impact of each part of the improvement cycle.

- Judicious monitoring of control measures ensures that system implementation and maintenance can be consistently fine-tuned to ensure the desired impacts are achieved.
- The implementation of good system design tailored to an improvement agenda will result in a consistent uptake of the desired behaviour and processes by all school staff.
- The impact of positive social processing in a human-dense environment cannot be overstated. The capability of leaders and other staff members to engage effectively in dialogue is critical.
- A win/win outcome from individual, small group and large group conversations contributes to high staff morale and commits all stakeholders to undertaking the heavy workload required. Staff members are committed to continuous improvement through adopting the desired behaviours, processes and practices.
- Effective school systems need to have well-designed feedback triggers which "turn on" or "turn off" behaviours and processes.

## NEXT STEPS

At the time of writing, there are two years remaining in the six-year planned cycle of improvement. While the systems are continuously fine-tuned to enhance performance, the basic elements remain in place. The implementation of new initiatives is logically sequenced to build seamlessly on what is already in place according to the level of staff capability. Student learning outcome data at both the individual and aggregated scale continues to be monitored for improvement to ensure that the new initiatives are having the desired impact.

**Ken Maclean** was the principal of Whitfield State School from 2014 until 2017. He was previously the principal of the Northern Peninsula Area College (NPAC), where under his leadership over a five-year period that school achieved an outstanding improvement in test scores from the NAPLAN.

Ken introduced "explicit teaching" at NPAC and implemented a range of systems, including student data collection and analysis, capability development, learning intervention and school leadership. Much of this work informed the elements of the improvement agenda for the region. In his mission to understand research-based theory and translate it effectively into practice, he willingly shares and truly collaborates with colleagues.

Ken is currently an assistant regional director in the Far North region. In his role, he is leading a project to implement the work described in this case study to improve the performance of a group of schools.

# Case study 4: Woree State High School

By Bruce Houghton, Principal

## CONTEXT

Woree State High School (SHS) is located in the southern corridor of Cairns and has a student population of 930. The school has a diverse student population with approximately 40% being Aborigines and Torres Strait Islanders. Twenty-five percent of students have a language background other than English. The school has a 2017 ICSEA score of 870 and is considered educationally disadvantaged.

Woree SHS operates the award-winning SchoolTech/MarineTech program on behalf of the Far North Queensland region, which focuses on transitioning students to apprenticeships from TAFE [Technical and Further Education] and the International Marine College. The school is a designated school of Vocational Education Excellence. The Cairns Hospital class is staffed by Woree SHS teachers and they cater for just over 1,000 students per year from across Far North Queensland.

The school has a large student support services focus to cater for the social, emotional and behavioural development of students. The Clontarf Academy has been a recent addition with nationally recognised programs to assist and support Indigenous male students.

Every four years Education Queensland schools are required to have a school review conducted by the School Improvement Unit based on the nine domains of the National School Improvement Tool. The tool was developed by the Australian Council of Education Research (ACER) and consists of "nine domains, which combine and overlap to provide a comprehensive framework for school improvement" (ACER n.d.).

Prior to 2015 this process was called the teaching and learning audit. The audit conducted in July 2014 had a series of commendations and recommendations. In 2013 the student outcomes were poor and staff morale was low.

At the time of the audit the school had what would be a traditional secondary school meeting structure. That is an executive team consisting of the principal and deputy principals that met twice a week, and a management meeting (all classified officers) that was held once a week. Staff meetings (whole-school and faculty) were held each week.

## THE PURPOSE

This case study explains the application of Systems Leadership at Woree SHS since July 2014, when significant changes were introduced in response to the findings of the teaching and learning audit. Since 2014 the school executive team and leadership team have worked on two main cultural changes.

The first part of the case study will focus on how the school executive used the Tools of Leadership model to produce highly productive teams to develop effective, authorised systems with full documentation to drive a strong learning culture within the school and create positive mythologies within the school community.

The second part of the case study will follow the development of a strong learning culture within the overall student body using Systems Leadership modelling.

## METHODOLOGY

*Phase one: highly effective teams*

The first thing that the executive team (principal and two deputy principals) did was to establish an organisational chart in order to provide better clarity of work required for what lay ahead. Key to the organisational change was the establishment of an educational services branch headed by one deputy principal, and a student services branch headed by the second deputy principal. This organisational chart allowed each deputy principal to have clarity of role descriptions, allowing them to really focus on their work. Educational services commanded the human resources, facilities and timetabling required to drive the implementation of the curriculum, while student services brought all internal and external student-focused agencies into line. Having the best people in the right role certainly made the difference.

The 2014 audit highlighted a large number of areas for improvement. Due to the need to develop systems across a broad range of key school areas, the school executive team made significant changes to the way designated leaders across the school worked together. The executive team identified what systems were required to drive the desired behaviour to create a great school culture. Once systems were identified, task teams were created to complete the work or key components of the system. Task teams consist of a team leader (an executive member or head of department) and team members identified by the executive. Much time is spent on identifying the best leaders and members to work on particular tasks.

Each task team has work assigned to them by the executive team. This is in the form of a task assignment written by the executive team. These task teams operate along the lines of team leadership and team membership behaviour. Task teams meet every two weeks to work on the tasks assigned to them.

The significance of the use of the task assignment and the careful selection of team leaders and members is that teams have not been told how to develop the system or work required, just the quantity and quality of the system required. This has led to the development of highly effective systems, processes and work that in most cases far exceeded the expectations of the executive (task designers) as the creative forces of the teams were unleashed. Key to this was the technical leadership of the faculty and sector heads of departments who brought their expertise to the table. Often the recruitment of classroom teachers to develop systems led to highly productive and authorised systems as they easily identified counter-productive process and applied their knowledge and skills, honed from many years' practice, to refine processes that were highly productive.

All work done in the school is designated by the executive in consultation with the leadership team (curriculum heads of department, HOSES [Head of Special Education Services], GO [Guidance Officer] and program managers) and a task assignment is created. No work is done without a task assignment.

During the leadership team meetings (principal, deputy principals, curriculum heads of department, HOSES, GO and program managers) every fortnight, the work from the task teams is presented for feedback or clarifying questions. This process has enabled teams to gather further information to continue their task until completion. Major systems are presented to the leadership team first in the implementation phase.

As the system development gathered momentum, and a notable shift in culture was evident, the school executive authorised a deputy principal to work solely on system development across every facet of the school. This decision was a game changer for the school as system development went from fortnightly meetings, weekends or whenever it could be slotted in to front and centre of school operations. Having the space to work one on one with key staff members, teachers and heads of department to go through the fine details of every system over a fifteen-month period took system development to a completely new level of quality in the school. There is no doubt that the recruitment of the right person for the task resulted in the successful completion of twenty-seven effective and documented systems strongly aligned to the nine domains of the National School Improvement Tool. All of these systems are housed in the school's strategic framework drive. Systems are periodically reviewed and refined to ensure that they are authorised and effective. They are:

1.  An explicit improvement agenda

    • Planning and accountability system
    • Review of school systems.

2.  Analysis and discussion of data

    • Data system.

3. A culture that promotes learning

- Junior secondary system
- Senior secondary system
- Student leadership system
- Student support services system
- Student-led conference system.

4. Targeted use of school resources

- Facilities system
- Financial system
- HR and timetabling system
- Woree operational resource management system
- School information communication technology system
- Work health and safety system.

5. An expert teaching team

- Teacher capability and development system
- Teacher services system
- Coaching system
- Professional development system.

6. Systematic curriculum delivery

- School curriculum system
- Sports system
- VET system.

7. Differentiated teaching and learning

- Response to intervention system
- Special education program system
- Differentiation system.

8. Effective pedagogical practices

- Teaching and learning system.

9. School–community partnerships

- Enrolment system
- Parent and community engagement system.

*Phase two: highly effective students*

Phase two of the cultural change in the school has focused on the development of highly effective and productive students, and the systems, symbols and behaviour required to produce this culture. This work is ongoing and is based on the academic work of Fullan and Sharratt and the practical application of this by William Ross High School in Townsville.

The core of this work is in the feedback culture that has gained traction in the school. Teachers are required to conference with students their individual data and what is required to improve at various junctures during the year. The students are required to track their individual data, personally account for their actions and identify the required behaviour to enable improvement. The student-led conference process ties this all together. Students conference their results with their parents/carers, the principal and head of junior or senior secondary. This process allows students to account for their results, reflect on their academic behaviour and set goals for the future. This highly symbolic process is developing a strong academic culture in the school.

Key players in this cultural change are the head of junior secondary (years 7 to 9) and head of senior secondary (years 10 to 12), who focus on individual students and work closely with the faculty heads of departments and teachers to ensure student success. The introduction of the school-based Junior Certificate of Education, which is based on the QCE, is building a strong academic culture for most students.

The senior secondary academic improvement process that sits within the senior secondary system has developed a vastly improved academic culture within the student body. Students have an understanding of what is required to successfully complete school and have risen to the challenge. This individualised approach to students has been highly successful and has in many cases re-engaged severely disengaged students in educational pathways. No students fall through the gaps, and as a result academic performance has improved dramatically.

The process described above has required extensive system development by teams to collect, analyse and distribute student academic results.

## RESULTS

The implementation of Systems Leadership models has seen a significant shift in the culture of the executive team, leadership team and school in general. Highly productive teams are successfully progressing the systems work across the school. Effective systems are being developed and this is very much evident in the positive mythologies about the school from the whole school community. With the development of systems has come the desired student outcomes and an extremely positive report from the School Improvement Unit in 2016.

The practical implementation of Systems Leadership has been presented at various educational forums in Far North Queensland and many primary and secondary schools have visited Woree SHS to hear of the journey and gather information. All system documentation is provided to schools if asked for.

Woree SHS is currently the subject of two research projects based on student outcomes:

- University of Queensland, Griffith University and University of Southern Queensland – Engaging Schools: What works to keep young people engaged in meaningful learning in low-SES [socio-economic status] schools. The Engaging Schools project aims to explore the positive strategies implemented by schools that have been identified by Queensland DET [Department of Education and Training] as having improved student attendance and academic/vocational outcomes.
- Deloitte Access Economics – Youth Engagement Practices in Schools: Your school has been selected on the basis of its high or improving performance with respect to both student engagement and student achievement. This performance is indicated by retention and attendance rates, and student learning gain and achievement level measured by NAPLAN results. Your Regional Director has supported your nomination as an invitee school to participate in critical research regarding Youth Engagement practices in schools. Deloitte Access Economics has been engaged by the Department of Education to undertake research to identify how principals can best utilise resources to achieve optimal engagement and re-engagement in schools, while sustaining strong academic results.

*School opinion survey*

In the staff school report, among all staff items, of the forty-two areas thirty-eight have improved.

The three key areas for the creation of positive mythologies among the staff are:

1. Student behaviour is well managed at this school.
2. I feel that staff morale is positive in this school.
3. The school is well organised.

*NAPLAN data*

Regarding the year 7 NAPLAN NMS, Woree SHS showed:

- A decline in the percentage of year 7 students at or above the NMS for reading, from 93.2% in 2015 to 89.1% in 2017
- An improvement in the percentage of year 7 students at or above the NMS for writing, from 73.9% in 2015 to 78.9% in 2017
- An improvement in the percentage of year 7 students at or above the NMS for spelling, from 85.1% in 2015 to 94.3% in 2017
- An improvement in the percentage of year 7 students at or above the NMS for grammar and punctuation, from 74.6% in 2015 to 85.1% in 2017

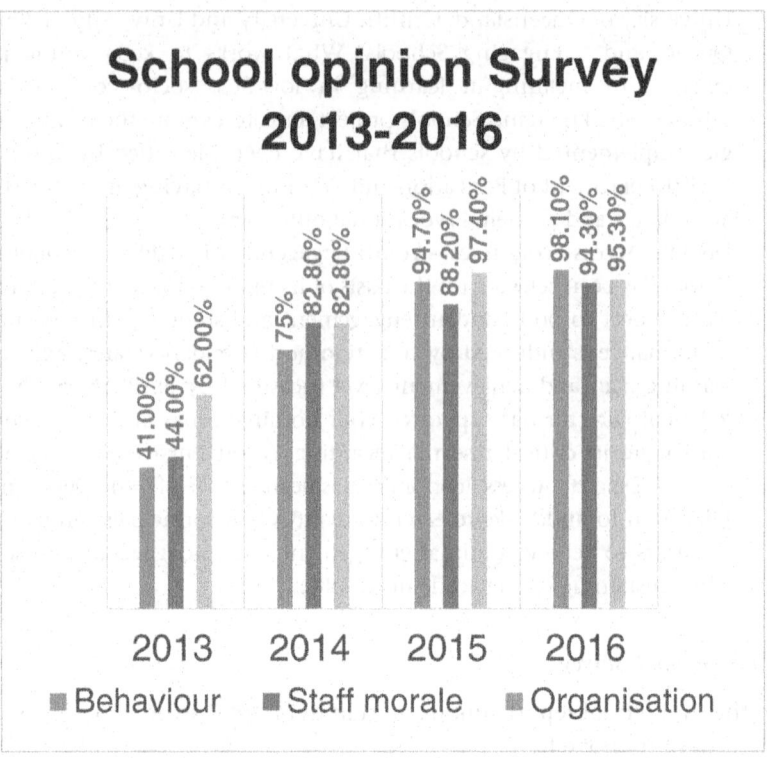

**Figure 16.5**    School opinion survey results

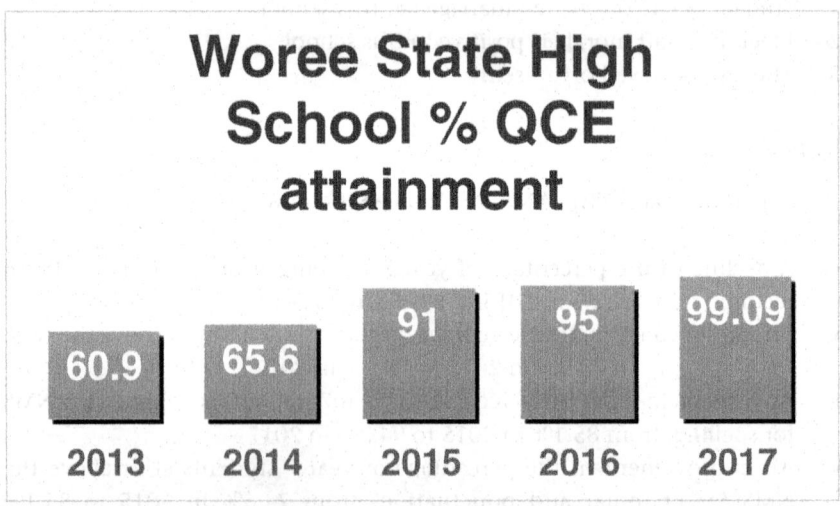

**Figure 16.6**    Woree SHS percentage of QCE attainment

- A decline in the percentage of year 7 students at or above the NMS for numeracy, from 94.1% in 2015 to 89.6% in 2017.

Regarding the year 9 NAPLAN NMS, Woree SHS achieved:

- An improvement in the percentage of year 9 students at or above the NMS for reading, from 77.4% in 2015 to 84.0% in 2017
- An improvement in the percentage of year 9 students at or above the NMS for writing, from 58.4% in 2015 to 59.8% in 2017
- An improvement in the percentage of year 9 students at or above the NMS for spelling, from 79.4% in 2015 to 88.5% in 2017
- An improvement in the percentage of year 9 students at or above the NMS for grammar and punctuation, from 68.4% in 2015 to 78.8% in 2017
- An improvement in the percentage of year 9 students at or above the NMS for numeracy, from 92.5% in 2015 to 96.2% in 2017.

There is an improvement trend in the percentage of year 9 students at or above the NMS at Woree SHS in all five elements from 2015 to 2017. Significant improvements have been achieved in spelling in both year 7 and year 9 in the percentage of students at or above the NMS and in the percentage of students in the upper two bands. The percentage of students in year 7 and year 9 in the upper two bands for spelling in 2017 is greater than the average percentage for all Queensland state schools. (Year seven was introduced to secondary school in 2015.)

## SUMMARY

The practical application of Systems Leadership modelling at Woree SHS has, to quote a staff member, "created sense from the chaos". That is, work has been clearly identified by the findings and recommendations from the 2014 teaching and learning audit and processes have been put in place for multiple systems and processes to be developed simultaneously. The key to this massive amount of work being done at once is having strong systems at the executive level to monitor progress and gauge any workload issues that might arise with task team members. In order to do this a master project board of all systems has been developed to track progress. Templates have been developed for project boards, task assignments, flowcharts and style guides for system documentation. The school strategic framework based on the nine domains has been situated on its own drive in the school network for ease of access.

We have found that when short cuts are taken (for example, task assignments not properly designed, or systems poorly designed) then mistakes occur, leading to work being of poor quality, and frustration from the staff involved in the system. As the work has progressed over the last four to five years the notion of the systems driving behaviour is clear for all to see.

An important aspect of the cultural change was the extensive support from the school's assistant regional director, who clearly understood the work required and backed the implementation of the modelling and the development of the systems. This support helped legitimise the innovative cultural change work in the eyes of the school staff, resulting in high levels of engagement.

## NEXT STEPS

As with a lot of change processes there is a slight dip in enthusiasm four or five years into the process, and this is evident in the staff responses to the 2017 school opinion survey. The next crucial phase is to continue to build in a cycle of system reviews to ensure that they remain highly effective and responsive to the changing educational environment. A key finding by the members of the executive is that authorised unproductive systems are easily identified by the staff that are actually at the coal face implementing the system. This has led to some very creative work by teaching staff and heads of department to improve the system. The challenge of the executive is to be in tune with these developments and establish review process to enhance systems within the school.

# 17 *The benefit of foresight*

This book is about turning intention into reality. It is no accident that this is our definition of "work" and the subtitle of this book. This is not a book about quick fixes or the "several magical steps" that guarantee success. This book has not identified issues that have never been thought of before. What we have tried to do is to give a practical account as to how those issues might be better addressed. The reason that school leaders in the region achieved what they did was because we had a coherent and integrated approach based on sound theory but with clear guidance as to how the concepts can be practically implemented. The tools of Systems Leadership are based on established principles underpinning human behaviour. We do not assume that people are mad, bad or stupid; rather, we all have a rationalisation for our behaviour that makes sense to us even if it does not make obvious sense to others. Understanding why people behave as they do and what is driving that behaviour is essential work for leaders if they are to build, with their teams, productive and cohesive organisations that achieve their purpose. It is not easy.

At the heart of this book is a desire to see improved educational opportunities for all young people. If this is to happen then schools and colleges must be designed in a way that enables learning. Schools must be safe places with a clear purpose and where the structure and systems are such that they encourage the appropriate behaviour and that the purpose can be achieved and sustained over time.

We are not arguing that we are the first people to think about organisation, but we are arguing that the impact of the way that an organisation is set up and run is often underestimated in terms of well-being and the achievement of purpose. Teachers are more likely to leave the profession because of the way that work is organised or the way that they are led than because they do not like children. It is difficult to know what makes for a good organisation because in this area, unlike other disciplines, there is not a set of shared definitions or agreed meanings of terms. This makes conversation and action around organisation more difficult, especially when we do not realise that the same terms may mean different things to different people. In this book we have offered clear and behavioural definitions of such widely used (and abused) terms as "culture", "leadership", "systems", "authority", "complexity", "structure", "teamwork", "capability", "social process" and others that form the basic building blocks for a good organisation. Unless there are shared understandings of what these terms mean then as we said earlier in the book we are simply lost with Alice in Wonderland, where words can mean whatever anyone wants them to mean.

Stressing the importance of clarity, which we have done throughout this book, does not restrict creativity or imagination or innovation. Indeed, we would argue it is a necessary condition for innovation to occur.

Of course, we recognise that there is both complexity and ambiguity around us and in our work. All we are saying is that there is no need to add to complexity or ambiguity and thus cause stress and anxiety for those in the organisation. In our experience people can use a lack of clarity and ambiguity to exercise power.

We have tried to be disciplined rather than dogmatic in our approach. We are not saying these are the only concepts or models that are relevant. However, we are arguing that Systems Leadership gives a coherent and integrated approach that connects concepts that are often seen as separate, including the basic terms of systems and leadership. The book has demonstrated that when a coherent approach is applied with persistence and consistency over time it can deliver results. All we are asking is that if this approach is compared to others then those other approaches should be examined in terms of:

1.   Their theoretical foundation
2.   The practicality of their approach
3.   Actual evidence that this approach has resulted in positive change.

We have presented material in this book that addresses and connects all of those three points.

Turning intention into reality is hard work. It is not good enough to have ideas or visions; we need people who have the courage and determination to test those ideas in practice. We have described case studies where people have had such courage and determination. However, there were many others in the region, too numerous to mention here, who also applied these ideas in their schools and colleges. We thank them for giving Systems Leadership a "fair go". The purpose of course has never been to implement Systems Leadership; that has always been a means to an end. The end being improvement in student outcomes. We hope that we have demonstrated through the work of others that this has been possible in a context where many have struggled and continue to struggle to improve.

Schools are unique places. We know of no sector other than education where work is organised into chunks with long gaps in-between. Why have we got such organisational arrangements that place unique stress on both staff and students? Organisation in academic terms may date back to origins where young people were needed to bring in harvests or go to work. However, we still seem to accept this arrangement along with many other strange organisational practices as just "part of the way things are". Paradoxically it is often easier to try and work with the system, however poor, rather than to change it. We have had the privilege of working with people who have dared to change things. They have met resistance, cynicism or bewilderment, which given the history of initiatives and change is not surprising. However, using Systems Leadership along with other established professional practices, they have persevered and achieved great outcomes not just for themselves but for the young people in their care. We thank them.

Using Systems Leadership does not solve all the problems in education or a school. However, it does provide an opportunity to better understand what is happening and what might be done about it. It concentrates very much on the "how". Much is written about what needs to be done, but far less is written specifically about how this work can be done. Just because Systems Leadership is based on sound psychological theory does not make it simply an academic process. The tools are very practical; we subscribe to the notion that "there is nothing so practical as good theory". When the things go wrong in organisations, particularly when there are catastrophes, enquiries are discounted because "life is so much easier with the benefit of hindsight".

Systems Leadership may not guarantee success, but it does give "the benefit of foresight".

We hope that the book has provided not just an account of what happened in a particular region in Australia, but ideas and concepts that can be applied anywhere in education throughout the world to improve the quality of working life for those in education and the improvement of educational opportunities for all students wherever they may be.

# *Glossary*

**Accountability:**   A component of a work relationship between two people wherein one accepts the requirement to provide an account to the other of the following three questions relating to work:

- What did you do?
- How did you do it?
- Why did you do it that way?

The most common application of the concept of accountability is that which applies as a function of a contract of employment within an organisation, and though in our experience this requirement to accept accountability is rarely articulated clearly in the contract, it should be. An effective accountability discussion includes a discussion of the three questions above, including how and why the person used particular processes to turn inputs into required outputs.

*Accountability* is not a collective noun for tasks, the use to which it is now applied in contracts and in role descriptions, as in "Your accountabilities are . . . " This confuses *work* and *accountability*. A role may describe work, but we are still to discover if the person is actually held to account for that work.

Accountability as a concept applying within coherent social groups is brought to the fore for society in general by the process of the courts wherein people in the witness box are required to answer in public questions as to what, how and why something was, or was not, done and judgement is passed as an outcome of this process.

**Authority:**   The right, given by constitution, law, role description or mutual agreement for one person to require another person to act in a prescribed way (specified in the document or agreement). The likelihood of exercising authority effectively will usually depend upon good **social process skills**.

The acceptance of the exercise of authority within a work organisation is a function of the contract of employment.

Is it essential that there is a clear understanding of the difference between *authority* and *power* (see below) and that authority is not a one-way process. In a correctly functioning organisation, for example, a manager has the authority to assign tasks to a direct report and the direct report has the authority to require a task performance review by the manager.

**Authority and power:**    Person A has authority or power in relation to person B when person A is able to have person B behave as A directs. If person B does not so behave neither authority nor power applies.

Authority applies within the boundary and constraints of the law, policy and rules of the organisation and those of accepted social custom and practice.

Power breaches one or more of these constraints to authority.

Clarity of understanding of the constraints to authority and its correct distribution to the roles within an organisation is essential for speed of reaction to the unexpected.

Within society at large an acceptance of the exercise of authority is essential to maintain social cohesion. However, there is a sharply attuned recognition within societies of the constraints that apply to that authority, and an exercise of power by "appointed authority" is strongly resented.

**Authority (resource):**    The ability of a role incumbent to apply resources to a task without reference to another person.

**Application:**    The effort, attention and energy that a person puts into applying the other elements of capability to their work.

**Association:**    People coming together for a purpose. The purpose is either agreed tacitly or expressed in a written document (Brown 1971: 48).

**Capability – elements of individual capacity:**

- Knowledge
- Technical skills
- Social process skills
- Mental processing ability
- Application – desire energy and drive applied to work.

**Coaching:**    Using a process of observation and feedback to help a person to improve in their role.

**Constraints (for a task):**    Limitations within which a task must be completed. It is the work of the task assigner to articulate these constraints to the task doer and confirm they are understood.

**Context (of a task):**    The situation in which the task assigner predicts the task will be performed, including the background conditions, the relationship of this task to other tasks and any unusual factors to be taken into account.

When the task performance is being reviewed the actual context needs to be considered in the review.

**Critical issue:** Something that if not satisfactorily resolved threatens the achievement of the purpose of the work of an individual, team or organisation. "What if this happens? How will we address it?"

**Culture:**    A culture is a group of people who share a common set of mythologies.

The group may be very large or relatively small and the strength of the culture will be determined by the number of mythologies that are common to the group.

It is normal for there to be smaller common-interest groups within a large cultural group and these are often referred to as sub-cultures.

The commonality of the mythologies causes all the members of a culture to ascribe the same value assessment to a system, symbol or behaviour that they experience, be that assessment positive or negative.

The process of changing or creating a culture requires the generation of new mythologies that are common to the group.

**Curriculum:**    What is to be taught in a course or program of study.

**Disciplinary absence:**    A student is suspended from attending school for a period of time or excluded from a school because he or she has breached the school's code of behaviour.

**Dissonance:**    A state of mind generated by the clear failure of a prediction that has been based upon a strongly held belief.

Dissonance can be generated by the behaviour of another person or group, the activity of a system or the appearance of a symbol.

Because we need to be able to predict with reasonable accuracy to be and feel safe, dissonance generates anxiety and the need to formulate an explanation. The generation of dissonance is the first step in the process of formation of new mythologies.

**Far North region:**    One of seven administrative regions of the Queensland Department of Education. The Far North region extends from Cardwell in the south to the Torres Strait in the north and west to the town of Croydon. The regional office is based in the eastern coastal city of Cairns.

**Hierarchy:**    An organisation structure wherein the authority available to a role increases upwards through the structure, increasing as work complexity increases.

The authority structure of the organisation is made extant by means of role titles. In a correctly structured organisation each role has the authority that is necessary to perform the work assigned to the role and this provides the connection between role authority and work.

**Indigenous:**    Australia's Indigenous peoples are two distinct cultural groups made up of Aboriginal and Torres Strait Islander peoples. But there is great diversity within these two broadly described groups, exemplified by the 250-plus different language groups spread across the nation. An accepted definition of an Indigenous Australian proposed by the Commonwealth Department of Aboriginal Affairs in the 1980s and still used by some Australian Government departments today is "a person of Aboriginal or Torres Strait Islander descent who identifies as Aboriginal or Torres Strait Islander and is accepted as such by the community in which he or she lives" (Australian Institute of Aboriginal and Torres Strait Islander Studies 2018).

**Influence:**    Activity that attempts to have an effect on the behaviour or beliefs of another individual or group.

**Instructional leadership:**    Principals' and other school leaders' active engagement in the leadership of the Technical Domain of the school; that is, teaching and learning.

**International Baccalaureate Diploma (IBD):**    An internationally recognised course that operates in schools across the world, offering four programs that cover all stages of education for students aged from 3 to 19.

**Knowledge:**    That array of facts and relationships that an individual has available to him or her for the performance of work. It may be part or all of an accepted body of knowledge, or knowledge that has been produced as largely self-generated content by the individual.

**Knowledge field:**    The knowledge held by an individual about a specific subject. The knowledge will be gained from a range of sources, from personal experience to formal study.

This is the knowledge which a person brings to their work in an endeavour to solve problems that seem to relate to that particular field. Should they appreciate the need to do so, additional knowledge may be sought to resolve a work problem and any knowledge gained then becomes part of that field.

Each person has unique knowledge fields as they are what he or she has built up through life to date about a particular subject. There will be a core of knowledge in each field that is common to most people in a cultural group with similar educational experiences.

**Language – social and scientific meanings:**

- Social meaning: A term which is assumed to provide a similarity of understanding for the purpose of social interaction – "You know what I mean?"

In our everyday lives we approximate and assume an understanding without concern as to whether we mean precisely the same thing.

- Scientific meaning: A precisely defined term with deliberately clear boundaries for the purpose of explaining relationships and testing hypotheses – "This is what I mean." An entity or term has a clearly defined meaning by which we can determine whether an entity is "one of those" or not.

**Leader:**   A leader is a person who is able to demonstrate the exercise of power or authority, or both, and cause a group of people to act in consort to achieve a purpose.

The objective of a correctly functioning organisation is to have all its leaders clearly identified and exercising authority for the effective and efficient achievement of the purpose of the organisation, where that authority is willingly accepted.

Within an employment hierarchy, all managers are leaders, but not all leaders are managers.

**Leader, work of:**   The work of a leader is to create, maintain and improve the culture of a group of people so they achieve objectives and continue to do so over time. In short, it is to change behaviour.

**Levels of work:**   The sequence of qualitatively different complexity pathways that need to be created to achieve goals when performing work. Depending upon the inherent complexity of a particular task it will only be completed successfully if that complexity is resolved; hence, it will fall into a specific level of work.

**Management:**   The work of ordering and sequencing the application of resources to achieve a predetermined purpose. Good management does this effectively and efficiently.

Human capability, in all its aspects, is one of the resources available to a manager that needs to be applied through a person-to-person interaction, whereas other resources involve person-to-object interactions.

**Manager:**   A person who is accountable for his or her own work and the work performance of people reporting to him or her over time. All managers are leaders of people; they have no choice. Their only choice is to be a good or bad leader.

**Mental processing ability:**   The ability to make order out of the chaotic environment in which humans live out their lives and in which they work. It is the ability to pattern and construe the world in terms of scale and time. The level of our mental processing ability will determine the amount and complexity of information that we can process in doing so.

**Meritocracy:**   An organisation wherein people are assigned work, rewarded, promoted and titled based upon their capability to do the work of a role.

**Mythology:**   From *mythos* – a story with emotional content – and *logos* – the explanatory rationale or meaning of the story.

Mythologies are the stories that inform us about what constitutes good and poor behaviour.

We look at systems, symbols and people's behaviour through the lens of our mythologies and assign what we see to a place on one or more of the scales of human values.

Our mythologies are our beliefs about whether what we see strengthens social cohesion in our group or whether it weakens it.

Mythologies are not changed; new ones need to be constructed. Mythologies may lie dormant for years and can be enlivened by an event in the future.

**National Assessment Program of Literacy and Numeracy (NAPLAN):**
"NAPLAN is an annual assessment for all students in Years 3, 5, 7 and 9. It tests the types of skills that are essential for every child to progress through school and life. The tests cover skills in reading, writing, spelling, grammar and punctuation, and numeracy. The assessments are undertaken every year in the second full week in May" (Australian Curriculum, Assessment and Reporting Authority n.d.).

**Network:**   People working towards a common purpose or with common interests where there is no requirement for members of the network to have a work relationship with others, and there is no requirement for mutuality as there is with a team.

**Operation work:**   Work that is directly connected to the output that an organisation has been established to produce.

Operation work will be directed to developing a product to satisfy the perceived needs of customers, producing a product to satisfy the current needs of customers or directed to the selling of those products to customers.

All three aspects of Operation work are essential if a business or service organisation is to remain viable over time (see also **Service work** and **support work**).

**Organisational level:**   A band across an organisation in which all the roles have a similar distribution of work complexity (level of work).

**Organisational structure:**   The arrangement of the roles in an organisation that, when correctly done, identifies and matches work complexity and the authority necessary to perform that work so the purpose of the organisation is achieved efficiently and effectively over time.

The structure is the equivalent of the bone structure of the organisation; its form is made extant by way of its titling system.

**Output:**   The observable result of work having been done. It is assessed in terms of quality and quantity.

**Overall Position Score (OP):**   An OP is a student's position in a state-wide rank order based on their overall achievement in authority subjects. It indicates how well a student has done in comparison to all other OP-eligible students in Queensland and is used for tertiary entrance purposes only. Students are placed in one of 25 OP bands, from OP1 (highest) to OP25 (lowest).

**Pedagogy:**   The methods and practices of teaching children.

**Power:** See **Authority**.

**Process:**   The mechanism by which inputs are converted into the specified outputs.

**Purpose (of a task assignment):**   What is to be achieved by accomplishing a task. Of an organisation, policy or system, the objective intended by its action in practice.

**Quantity/quality (of a task assignment):**   The expected output of the task and the standard expected. These are treated as a single dimension as one cannot have quantity without quality, nor quality without quantity.

**Queensland Certificate of Education (QCE):**   The QCE is Queensland's senior school qualification, which is awarded to eligible students usually at the end of year 12. The QCE recognises broad learning options and offers flexibility in what, where and when learning occurs.

**Responsibility:**   Synonymous with *accountability* but long use in organisations that failed to hold people responsible for their work has led to its general use as a collective noun for tasks, as in "Your responsibilities are as follows . . . " and "The general responsibilities of the role are . . . "

**Resources (necessary to complete a task assignment):**   Authority, facilities, equipment, money, people, access to information, access to assets, time.

**School-based Apprenticeship/Traineeship (SAT):**   An apprenticeship or traineeship undertaken by a secondary school student, usually in combination with other school subjects.

**Service work:**   Service work is directed towards the efficient and effective performance of those functions that are essential for the continuing activity of the operations functions; for example, in accounting and finance: statutory reporting, regulatory compliance, audit of personnel and payroll.

**Social process:**   Person-to-person interaction wherein the behaviour of each has a bearing upon the thoughts, emotions and behaviour of the other.

**Social process skills:**   Social process skills are those skills that give the ability to observe social behaviour, comprehend the embedded social information and respond in a way that influences subsequent behaviour in a predictable way. In an organisation this results in behaviour that contributes to the purpose of the organisation.

**Staff relationship:**   A work relationship wherein a person accepts freely that his or her work performance will be judged on the basis of his or her personal work contribution and recompensed accordingly, as opposed to a third-party-determined requirement such as seniority, union-nominated classification or externally determined qualification.

**Strategy:**   A military term related to the disposition and deployment of large military units, such as entire armies, so that the enemy's forces may be defeated.

In business, when correctly applied it is a plan for the achievement of the organisation's purpose, developed and implemented by the upper levels of the organisation.

**Structure:**   The nature of working relationships that formally exist in an organisation.

Work complexity is a fundamental basis of the organisation structure from which authority flows.

When correctly designed it generates working relationships that are consistent with the differing capabilities of people to generate order from the chaos and so perform productive work that is required to achieve the purpose of the organisation.

It makes good sense to structure an organisation in a way that is in accord with the thinking patterns of people.

**Supervisor:**   A leadership role. A supervisory role does not have the full range of authority that defines a managerial role but is one of the most important leadership roles in an organisation.

**Support work:**   Sometimes referred to as *Improvement work* is that work which is directed towards the improvement of the systems and processes the organisation employs to perform its operations and service activity.

It is a part of the work of each role incumbent to think of ways to improve upon his or her current work. The support roles develop and test these ideas as well taking a wider perspective and seeking to improve the systems and processes that span numerous roles and activities.

**Symbol:**   The outward manifestation of a cultural group; for example, flags, rituals, medals, posters and slogans.

Symbols are interpreted as representing a position that is strongly positive on the values continua by the culture that employs the symbol, and strongly negative by members of counter-cultures.

**System:**   A system is a framework that orders and sequences activity within the organisation to achieve a purpose within a band of variance that is acceptable to the owner of the system.

Systems are the organisational equivalent of behaviour in human interaction.

Systems are the means by which organisations put policies into action.

It is the owner of a system that has the authority to change it, hence his or her clear acceptance of the degree of variation generated by the existing system.

**System audit:**   A periodic review of a system by an external party that examines the system in use to determine whether or not it is being used as designed and intended; whether the control data is valid; whether it is being reported, reviewed and acted upon; and whether or not the system is achieving the purpose for which it was designed. A system audit is performed on behalf of the system owner.

**System control:**   A statistically valid sample of data from the system that allows the system custodian to confirm that the system is operating as it was designed to operate, or to institute corrective action should it be required to have the system function as designed.

Note the difference between system control and controls as applied in safety systems. In safe work systems controls are activities that form part of the system itself.

**System custodian:**   The role within the organisation that does the work required to review the control data from a system and to advise the system owner of the state of use of the system and indicators of a system functioning drawn from the control data.

The system custodian many be the system owner.

**System owner:**   The role within the organisation that authorizes the purpose of the system and its design and implementation to achieve that purpose.

Only the system owner has the authority to change the system.

**Systems Leadership:** An internally coherent and integrated theory of organisational behaviour. It is a body of knowledge that helps not only to understand why people behave the way they do, but also and perhaps more importantly to predict the way that people are likely to behave in organisations.

Systems Leadership is essentially about how to create, improve and sustain successful organisations.

**Systems of differentiation:** Systems that treat people differently; for example, remuneration systems based on work performance.

All systems of differentiation should be based on the work (to be) done.

**Systems of equalisation:** Systems that treat people the same way irrespective of any organisational criteria; for example, safety systems.

**Task:** A statement of intention articulated as an assignment to carry out work within limits that include the context, purpose, quantity and quality of output expected; the resources available; and the time by which the objective is to be reached.

**Task assignment process:** The clear articulation to the task doer of context, purpose, quantity/quality of output, resources and time to completion (CPQQRT).

**Task feedback:** Information the task doer receives regarding how well he or she carried out the task. This can come from nature, customers, peers or the person's leader.

**Task review:** An assessment by the task doer's leader of how well the task was performed. Task review provides information that is given to the task doer and comes from the task doer on a regular but random basis, the purpose of which is for the task doer and the leader to learn from both success and failure so performance may be improved. Note: in a correctly organised work hierarchy a task doer (direct report) has the authority to require a task review and report from his or her leader. Task review includes all the components of the task: CPQQRT.

**Team:** A team is a group of people, including a leader, with a common purpose who must interact with each other in order to perform their individual tasks and thus achieve that common purpose.

**Teamwork:** You are part of the whole. It is only by active cooperation, however, that the whole will be greater than the sum of the parts. The work of interaction that needs to be done by each team member to promote efficient and effective team functioning.

**Technical skills:**   Proficiency in the use of knowledge. This includes learned routines that improve the efficiency and effectiveness of work required to complete a task.

**Time (in a task assignment):**   The targeted completion time is a boundary condition – a deadline indicating by when the task is to be completed.

**Time (as a resource):**   The amount of time available prior to the deadline. This may be expressed as people's work hours available or the sum of hours prior to the deadline.

**Universal values**:   A typology of six universal human experiences that rate or judge all behaviours, systems and symbols heuristically. Behaviour, systems and symbols that are demonstrated and rated positively create social cohesion. Those that are demonstrated and rated negatively destroy it.

There are six values, which are, expressed positively: love, trust, fairness, respect for human dignity, honesty and courage.

As a set they are mutually exclusive and comprehensively exhaustive and apply universally in all human societies.

The mythological lens that is used to position a system, symbol or behaviour on the values continua, either positive or negative, is unique to each person, having been developed by their experience of life.

**Vocational education and training (VET):**   Qualifications including Certificate I, II, III, IV, Diploma or Advanced Diploma.

**Work:**   Turning intention into reality.

**Work performance:**   An assessment made by a leader about how effectively and efficiently a direct report has worked in performing an assigned task, taking into consideration the actual context in which the task was done.

# Bibliography

Archer, A.L., and Hughes, C.A. (2010) *Explicit Instruction: Effective and Efficient Teaching*. New York, NY: Guildford Publications.

Australian Council of Education Research (n.d.). 'National School Improvement Tool'. Retrieved from www.acer.org/gb/school-improvement/improvement-tools/national-school-improvement-tool.

Australian Curriculum, Assessment and Reporting Authority (n.d.). Home page. Retrieved from www.acara.edu.au/.

Australian Institute of Aboriginal and Torres Strait Islander Studies (2018). 'Indigenous Australians: Aboriginal and Torres Strait Islander People'. Retrieved from https://aiatsis.gov.au/explore/articles/indigenous-australians-aboriginal-and-torres-strait-islander-people.

Baddeley, A.D. (2000) 'The Episodic Buffer: A New Component of Working Memory?' *Trends in Cognitive Sciences*, 4(11): 417–423.

Baddeley, A.D., and Hitch, G. (1974). 'Working Memory'. In G.H. Bower (Ed.), *The Psychology of Learning and Motivation: Advances in Research and Theory* (Vol. 8, pp. 47–89). New York, NY: Academic Press.

Bennett, J. (1956–1966) *The Dramatic Universe*. London: Hodder & Stoughton.

Blakey, J., and Day, I. (2012) *Challenging Coaching: Going Beyond Traditional Coaching*. Boston, MA: Nicholas Brealey Publishing.

Blau, P.M., and Scott, W.R. (1962) *Formal Organizations*. San Francisco, CA: Chandler.

Bloom, B.S., and Krathwohl, D.R. (1956) *Taxonomy of Educational Objectives: The Classification of Educational Goals Handbook I: Cognitive Domain*. New York, NY: Longmans, Green.

Brown. W. (1971) *Organisation*. London: Heinemann.

Burns, T., and Stalker, G.M. (1966) *The Management of Innovation* (2nd ed.). London: Tavistock Publications.

Council of Australian Governments (2008) 'National Indigenous Reform Agreement (Closing the Gap)'. Retrieved from www.federalfinancialrelations.gov.au/content/npa/health/_archive/indigenous-reform/national-agreement_sept_12.pdf.

Cross, R., Rebele, R., and Grant, A. (2016) 'Collaborative Overload'. *Harvard Business Review*, January–February: 74–79.

Csikszentmihalyi, M. (1997) *Finding Flow*. New York, NY: Basic Books.

Dawkins, R. (1976) *Hierarchical Organization: A Candidate Principle for Ethology*. Cambridge: Cambridge University Press.

Education Queensland (n.d.) 'Principal Capability and Leadership Framework (PCLF)'.

Education Queensland (n.d.) 'Principal Performance and Development Plan (PPDP)'.

Education Queensland (2018) 'Developing Performance Framework (DPF)'.

Eikon (n.d.). Home page. Retrieved from www.eikon.org.uk.

Goleman, D. (1996) *Emotional Intelligence: And Why It Can Matter More Than IQ*. London: Bloomsbury.

Hattie, J. (2009) *Visible Learning: A Synthesis of Over 800 Meta-Analyses Relating to Achievement*. Abingdon and New York, NY: Routledge.

Hopkins, D. (2013) 'Exploding the Myths of School Reform'. Centre for Strategic Education Seminar Series Paper No. 224.

Jaques, E. (1976) *A General Theory of Bureaucracy*. London: Heinemann.

Jaques, E. (1989) *Requisite Organization*. Falls Church, VA: Cason Hall and Co.

Jaques, E. (1990) 'In Praise of Hierarchy'. *Harvard Business Review*, January–February.

Jaques, E., Gibson, R.O., and Isaac, D.J. (1978) *Levels of Abstraction in Logic and Human Action: A Theory of Discontinuity in the Structure of Mathematical Logic, Psychological Behaviour, and Social Organization*. Portsmouth, NH: Heinemann Educational Books.

Janis, I.L. (1971) 'Groupthink'. *Psychology Today*, 5: 43–46, 74–76.

Kern, M.L., Waters, L.E., Adler, A., and White, M.A. (2015) 'A Multidimensional Approach to Measuring Well-being'. *Journal of Positive Psychology*, 10(3): 262–271.

Kohlberg, L. (1971) *Cognitive Development and Epistemology*. New York, NY: Academic Press.

Kolbe, K. (1991) *Conative Connection: Acting on Intent*. Boston, MA: Addison Wesley.

Lane, T.S., and Tripe, P.D. (2006) *Relationships: A Mess Worth Making*. Greensboro, NC: New Growth Press.

Macdonald, I. (1984) 'Stratified Systems Theory: An Outline'. Individual and Organisational Capability Unit, BIOSS, Brunel University.

Macdonald, I. (1990) 'Identity Development of People with Learning Difficulties through the Recognition of Work'. PhD Dissertation, Brunel University.

Macdonald, I., Burke, C., and Stewart, K. (2018) *Systems Leadership: Creating Positive Organisations* (2nd ed.). Abingdon and New York, NY: Routledge.

Macdonald, I., and Couchman, T. (1980) *Chart of Initiative and Independence*. Slough: NFER.

McKinsey & Company (2007) 'How the World's Best-performing School Systems Come Out on Top'. Retrieved from http://mckinseyonsociety.com/how-the-worlds-best-performing-schools-come-out-on-top/.

McLeod, S.A. (2012) 'Working Memory'. Retrieved from www.simplypsychology.org/working%20memory.html

Mintzberg, H. (1979) *The Structuring of Organizations*. Englewood Cliffs, NJ: Prentice-Hall.

Morgan, G. (1986) *Images of Organization*. Beverly Hills, CA: Sage.

Murphy, J., Elliott, S.N., Goldring, E., and Porter, A.C. (2007) 'Leadership for Learning: A Research-based Model and Taxonomy of Behaviors'. *School Leadership & Management*, 27(2): 179–201.

Nye, J.S., Jr. (2004) *Soft Power: The Means To Success In World Politics*. New York, NY: Public Affairs.

Piaget, J. (1971) 'The Theory of Stages in Cognitive Development'. In D.R. Green, M.P. Ford and G.B. Flamer (Eds.), *Measurement and Piaget*. Columbus, OH: McGraw-Hill.

Riley, P. (2017) 'The Australian Principal Occupational Health, Safety and Wellbeing Survey'. Institute for Positive Psychology and Faculty of Education and Arts. Australian Catholic University Fitzroy, Victoria.

Royal Society for the Encouragement of Arts, Manufactures and Commerce (RSA) (n.d.) Home page. Retrieved from www.thersa.org.

Siegrist, G., Green, R.B., Brockmeier, L., Tsemunhu, R., and Pate, J. (2013) 'A Brief History: The Impact of Systems Thinking on the Organization of Schools'. *National Forum of Educational Administration and Supervision Journal*, 31(4): 1–9.

Simon, H. (1962) 'The Architecture of Complexity'. *Proceedings of the American Philosophical Society*, 106(6): 467–482.

Stamp, G. (1978) 'Assessment of Individual Capacity'. In E. Jaques (Ed.), with R.O. Gibson and D.J. Isaac, *Levels of Abstraction in Logic and Human Action*. London: Heinemann.

State of Queensland (2002) 'Queensland the Smart State: Education and Training Reforms for the Future'. Retrieved from http://scpp.esrc.unimelb.edu.au/objects/reports/Qld-2005-SmartState2002.pdf.

UK Department of Education (2015) 'Promoting Children and Young People's Emotional Health and Wellbeing: A Whole School and College Approach'. PHE Publications. Gateway No. 2014825.

Waters, L., and White, M. (2015) 'Case Study of a School Wellbeing Initiative: Using Appreciative Inquiry to Support Positive Change'. *International Journal of Wellbeing*, 5(1): n.p.

Watson, J. (2006) '*Every Child Matters* and Children's Spiritual Rights: Does the New Holistic Approach to Children's Care Address Children's Spiritual Well-Being?' *International Journal of Children's Spirituality*, 11(2): 251–263.

Weber, M. (1922) 'Bureaucracy'. In J. Shafritz, S. Ott and Y.S. Jang (Eds.) (2016) *Classics of Organisational Theory* (8th ed.). Boston, MA: Cengage Learning.

Weber, M. (1922) *Economy and Society: An Outline of Interpretive Sociology* (2 vols). University of California Press, new ed., 1978. See also Gerth, H.H., and Mills, C.W., 1946, when Weber was first translated into English.

Weinberg, A., and Doyle, N. (2017) 'Psychology at Work: Improving Wellbeing and Productivity in the Workplace'. British Psychological Society. Retrieved from www.bps.org.uk/news-and-policy/psychology-work-improving-wellbeing-and-productivity-workplace.

Whitmore, J. (2009) *Coaching for Performance: The Principles and Practices of Coaching and Leadership*. London: Hodder & Stoughton.

Whyte, L.L., Wilson, A.G., and Wilson, D. (1969) *Hierarchical Structures*. New York, NY: American Elsevier.

# Index

Page numbers in *italics* indicate information in figures; those in **bold** refer to tables. Glossary terms are shown by 'g' after the page number e.g. 234g.

Taylor & Francis Group
an **informa** business

# Taylor & Francis eBooks

www.taylorfrancis.com

A single destination for eBooks from Taylor & Francis
with increased functionality and an improved user
experience to meet the needs of our customers.

90,000+ eBooks of award-winning academic content in
Humanities, Social Science, Science, Technology, Engineering,
and Medical written by a global network of editors and authors.

## TAYLOR & FRANCIS EBOOKS OFFERS:

A streamlined
experience for
our library
customers

A single point
of discovery
for all of our
eBook content

Improved
search and
discovery of
content at both
book and
chapter level

## REQUEST A FREE TRIAL
**support@taylorfrancis.com**

 Routledge
Taylor & Francis Group

 CRC Press
Taylor & Francis Group